Electric Vehicles

Electric Vehicles

Technology, Policy and Commercial Development

João Vitor Fernandes Serra

publishing for a sustainable future

London • New York

First published 2012
by Earthscan
2 Park Square, Milton Park, Abingdon, Oxon OX14 4RN

Simultaneously published in the USA and Canada
by Earthscan
711 Third Avenue, New York, NY 10017

Earthscan is an imprint of the Taylor & Francis Group, an informa business

British Library Cataloguing in Publication Data
A catalogue record for this book is available from the British Library

Library of Congress Cataloging in Publication Data
Serra, João Vitor Fernandes.
  Electric vehicles : technology, policy, and commercial development / João Vitor Fernandes Serra.
     p. cm.
  Includes bibliographical references and index.
1. Electric vehicles. I. Title.
  TL220.S465 2011
  629.22'93--dc22

                                                                      2011003940

ISBN: 9781849714150 (hbk)

Typeset in Sabon
by MapSet Ltd, Gateshead, UK

Printed and bound in Great Britain by the MPG Books Group

Contents

Foreword   *vii*

Introduction: A Contemporary Crisis   *ix*

PART I — PRIVATE TRANSPORT: SEIZING THE OPPORTUNITY

1   How Combustion Beat Electric   3

     The rise of the automobile   4

     A century of automobile industry   13

     Looking ahead   19

     Where to now?   25

2   Global Sustainability in Check   29

     Energy consumption and resource constraints   29

     Impacts on the environment   35

     The alternatives   43

     Seizing the opportunity   47

PART II — TECHNOLOGICAL FEASIBILITY

3   Vehicle Propulsion   53

     A few basic concepts   53

     The internal combustion engine vehicle   56

     The electric vehicle   61

     Hybrids: The electrification spectrum   66

     Approaching a verdict 1: Better at the core   72

     Appendix: Vehicle classifications   73

4   Energy Storage   77

     Energy storage performance parameters   78

     Combustion-based energy storage systems   80

     Electrochemical battery energy storage systems   81

     Fuel cell energy storage systems   92

Ultracapacitor energy storage systems   95
Approaching a verdict 2: Closing the gap   100

5   **The Electric Vehicle Recharging Infrastructure**   103
Energy services   104
Impact on the power grid   118
Approaching a verdict 3: A ripe whole-product solution   125

PART III — ELECTRIC VEHICLE ROADMAP

6   **Electric Vehicle Cost-Effectiveness**   **131**
Capital costs   132
Operating costs   135
Social costs   139
Cost-effectiveness of electric mobility   144
A convenient truth   151

7   **Electric Vehicle Adoption Trajectory**   **155**
Market forecast review   156
The nascent market (2010–2020)   164
Crossing the chasm (2015–2025)   173
A silver bullet?   179

8   **Electric Vehicle Policy Support**   **183**
Rationale for government action   183
The road ahead   189
In conclusion   196

Index   *201*

Foreword

The world is searching for alternatives to the internal combustion engine, and the electric vehicle option is gathering momentum as we move into the early decades of this century. If electric vehicles do in fact achieve a perch in the commercial market, the story will be one of the most interesting written in the post-industrial revolution. This book is a unique contribution to that unfolding narrative.

Aimed at a broad, educated and increasingly eco-friendly audience—students, academics, business analysts, and investors, not to mention specialists in the EV industry—Electric Vehicles offers unusually comprehensive and readable coverage of issues surrounding the shift in transportation technology towards a more sustainable solution. The book is especially effective in covering technical areas—vehicle design, battery requirements, and support infrastructure, to name the most important. However, the book stands out from the growing body of literature on the topic in its review of commercialization and related policy measures—including those in the developing world, such as retrofits—that could either threaten to block or promise to facilitate the technological transition to a more environmentally friendly future.

To those probably already suspicious or anxious about oil dependence, like members of Gen X and Millennials, ready as consumers to enter the car market and voting booths with energy on their mind, the author offers a comprehensive and up-to-date perspective on important global and local issues such as climate change and energy efficiency. The book tackles these issues with creativity and analytical rigor in a manner that is accessible to those without a technical background.

While industry leaders like General Motors, Ford, and Toyota are probing the market with new ideas about fleets and automated guidance and safety electronics inside electric cars, this book sticks to the fundamental questions surrounding the personal transportation transition.

We are a turning point in history marked by several distinctly urban features. For one, as we have been reminded many times, the urban transition has been completed. For the first time in history, more people are now living in cities than in the countryside. Not so frequently mentioned is that nearly a thousand cities around the globe are deeply dependent on transportation and increasingly engaged in a search for new ideas and new solutions to transport. Adoption of electric vehicles could dramatically shift the stakes in the coming decades for nations struggling to supply fossil fuels for automobiles, for cities grappling with congestion and pollution, and for billions of people looking for a better way to get around town. *Electric Vehicles* is a timely, balanced, and effective guide to help readers understand the place and prospects of a coming new wave.

Dr Tim Campbell

Introduction

A Contemporary Crisis

It always seems impossible, until it is done.

Nelson Mandela

At the start of the new millennium, society is faced with one of the most pressing crises in human history. As though the 2008 financial crisis were not enough to dampen growth prospects around most of the globe, the combination of energy security and environmental concern have cast a shadow on the way we live our lives. Since the 1990s, the world has gradually become increasingly aware of these challenges to sustainable growth. The 1992 Rio Earth Summit and the 1997 Kyoto Protocol took important first steps towards holding industries accountable for their carbon dioxide emissions. And while coal may still dominate global power markets, renewable sources – such as wind and solar technologies – have finally achieved a competitive position in some market segments. Not that any single solution will ever become a silver bullet, but together they will contribute to diversify power generation and reduce dependence on dirty hydrocarbons.

The shift towards a sustainable lifestyle has hardly managed to scratch one of society's core addictions: personal mobility and its dependence on gas-guzzling automobiles. While coal may be the world's dominant electrical energy source, petroleum is, hands down, the world's dominant primary energy source due to its prevalence in transportation. What is more, a full 67 per cent of petroleum consumption in the transportation sector results from private road transport, or so-called light duty vehicles (LDVs). We might say that petroleum dependence and carbon emissions lie right at our front doors – if not in our back yards – whether we like it or not.

While wind farm and solar panel projects might now be called commonplace, sustainable transport remains an alien concept. However, contrary to common perception, LDV technology is a prime candidate for a shift towards sustainability. This book makes the case for an energy-efficient and low-carbon transportation future based on electric propulsion. Granted, many aspects of an electric vehicle (EV) solution still require fine-tuning, but this is to be expected in the initial stage of any major technological innovation. No matter, the EV is the most cost-effective, and perhaps the only, acceptable technological solution to sustainable transportation in sight.

The book hopes to appeal to a wide range of readers – from a technologically inclined audience new to the subject, to those interested in the broader policy aspects of clean transportation, to the petrol-heads afraid that EVs will put an end to their fun. Its goal is to provide an introduction to the complex array of issues surrounding EVs – a coherent foundation for what has tended to be an overwhelmingly confusing discussion.

The book cannot forgo some technical discussions. However, because the intended audience is assumed to be of varied background and interest, the book adopts a fluid conversational tone and provides abundant illustrations to support technical discussions. Wherever technical details are not absolutely crucial to the core discussion, complementary boxes have been included for the slightly more curious. This should help readers to keep track of the basic storyline even if they make brief detours into more detailed specific areas along the way. The reader should also be warned that, although predominantly based on scientific evidence and scholarly material, the discussion must at time draw on current news and material published on the internet as this is a fast-paced topic.

Part I of the book provides a contextual background for the discussion. Chapter 1 offers a historical overview of the development of the automobile – from the first steam-powered vehicle to the 2008 meltdown of what became a mammoth enterprise over little more than one hundred years. This is meant to help the reader understand what has led us to our current technological scenario. Chapter 2 turns the spotlight on some of the historical and still powerful influences on the industry today, but is concerned in this discussion with identifying what is different from the context that prevailed up to the end of the millennium. It highlights factors that are likely to transform the automotive industry in the decades to come.

Throughout Part I, the reader will perhaps be reminded of the Chinese word for crisis – *weiji* – which emphasizes both a sense of imminent threat and a call for change or transformation. By the end of Part I, the reader should have a sense of the urgent need to shift away from internal combustion engine vehicle (ICV) technology, but also an initial understanding of why present conditions finally favour the EV.

Part II of the book dives into an evaluation of the EV solution. Chapters 3 and 4 provide an overview and comparative analysis of the technology behind the ICV and EV – notably their vehicle propulsion and energy storage systems. Chapter 5 shifts attention to one of the most pressing issues in EV development – the recharge infrastructure and associated energy services.

Indeed, this is the heart of the book. By the end of Part II, the reader should have a well-rounded understanding of the EV solution – from its internal workings and performance, to its interface and impact on the electrical grid, to the business challenges and opportunities that can make or break this solution. This discussion assesses how well the EV solution works, according to the criteria that a prospective consumer/driver or vehicle/service provider would take into account: What are the key emerging vehicle options? What mileage can the consumer get from each? How far can the consumer go before 'recharging'? How is the recharge infrastructure likely to evolve? What are the risks that the consumer or the producer will get stranded with a rapidly obsolete option?

The third and final part of the book shifts the focus back to the initial concern and aims to assess, in Chapter 6, whether, all things considered, the EV is indeed a cost-efficient low-carbon transportation solution. Chapter 7 discusses what an EV implementation strategy might look like by, initially, examining various recently published market forecasts and, ultimately, developing an independent market penetration outlook. It is worth noting that technological transformations are neither linear nor continuous. Rather, historical evidence suggests sudden irreversible bursts. Finally, Chapter 8 evaluates the scope for policy intervention as a way to accelerate and smooth the transition away from ICVs – particularly motivated by potential economic and environmental benefits.

Before diving into the main discussion, it is worth making two points that might be seen as the underlying assumptions for the analysis developed in this book.

As indicated at the start, society is faced with a crisis of paramount proportions for which conventional solutions are inadequate. While the book presents seemingly insurmountable obstacles – most of all, perhaps, when evaluating EV infrastructure deployment – the reader should realize that our situation today is in many ways not unprecedented. Throughout history, society has overcome far more complex problems with only a fraction of the resources that may be needed to shift away from petroleum-dependent private transportation.

In 1858, after the better half of a century living with open sewage and cholera epidemics, the British Parliament commissioned the development of what was to be the first modern sewer system in London. The 22,000km of underground sewer channels, which eliminated London's cholera epidemics, were built in merely two decades and established the basic parameters by which every sewer system would be designed to this day.

London's sewer system is by no means a unique case of large-scale infrastructural or technological development in a short period of time or of one that transformed the lives of its customers. The industrialized world has many other such examples – Germany's Autobahn highway network development during the 1930s; the reconstruction of Europe following the Second World War through the Marshall Plan; NASA's Apollo programme which landed the first man on the moon; the development of the mobile phone industry and infrastructure, to name but a few. Furthermore, emerging markets have proven equally capable of such achievements. Beyond the obvious present-day case of Chinese development, Brazil's 1956 Plano de Metas aimed to promote '50 years-worth of growth in five years', having established a nationwide highway network, thriving automotive and oil industries, and various other manufacturing and basic industries.

The first point is that society has repeatedly demonstrated its capacity to overcome major technological and infrastructural obstacles in very short periods of time. Indeed, the current EV recharging infrastructure and energy technology obstacles, which will be discussed at length throughout the book, seem to be dwarfed next to previous accomplishments.

This introduction has emphasized the concern over sustainability – on energy security and environmental grounds – as one of the guiding principles to future transportation solutions. Granted, any book on EVs will be motivated to some extent by contemporary concerns over sustainability and how such concerns provide the conditions for an emerging EV market. However, constraining the scope of the discussion to sustainability would be ignoring an important if, for many, superfluous aspect of what drives the automotive market.

For a machine whose sole purpose is transport, the automobile has a mystique like no other product. How cool would James Bond or even Danny Zucco (remember John Travolta in *Grease*?) be if it were not for their rides. Indeed, the automobile is, to a large extent, as much a medium for expressing one's identity as it is a mode of transportation. Or yet, for expressing social status and economic achievement on an individual or family basis.

As such, the second point is that this story is often as much a tale of passion or image as it is a discussion of a sustainability crisis and the potential for transformation. Indeed, the book will pay particular attention to how the driving experience may be affected and how different consumers may react as a result. The author believes the EV provides a solution to modern sustainability concerns in the realm of personal mobility which will not come at the expense of the driving experience. Rather, while they may not know it yet, the EV will soon become a dream come true for current petrol-heads.

Part I

Private Transport: Seizing the Initiative

1

How Combustion Beat Electric

Many of life's failures are people who did not realize how close they were to success when they gave up.

Thomas Edison

Why is it that internal combustion engine vehicles (ICVs) became such a dominant technology while battery electric vehicles (BEVs), which were invented half a century before, failed to enjoy similar market success? Some of the most valuable lessons that history has to offer may often go unnoticed for some time due to the narrow interpretation of the constraints and opportunities we face at any given point. Perhaps our evaluation of ICVs and BEVs over the past half-century has been skewed, for instance, by a lack of understanding of the impact – on energy resources and the environment – that the 'Western' way of life and patterns of consumption have led to, as well as by an inability to imagine (and pursue) a future outside of prevailing standards.

Despite being an engineer, the author has a soft spot for history and believes that understanding why and how we arrived where we are provides an important basis to understanding what lies ahead. In this context, this book begins with a historical look at personal mobility, exploring how and why the ICV became the cornerstone of a mammoth automobile[1] industry and for the last century has held an impermeable position as the dominant technology in that market. What dimensions were missed and left by the roadside during its impressive expansion? This chapter hopes to show that the changes that started to manifest themselves, in some cases, nearly 50 years ago have gradually accelerated and gained public visibility over recent decades, creating the conditions at the start of the new millennium for a paradigm shift – towards the era of the electric vehicle[2] (EV).

The Rise of the Automobile

Urbanization, economic growth and the automobile

Since the Industrial Revolution, the world has experienced a dramatic change in the way human beings go about their daily lives. From jet planes and subways, to personal computers, cell phones and the internet, to refrigerators and espresso machines, mankind has witnessed a massive wave of technological advance and a corresponding increase in the rate of energy consumption over this period. In particular, the increased level of mobility offered by motorized transportation has revolutionized the spatial demographics of the industrialized world.

Prior to the Industrial Revolution, the size of human settlements was largely restricted to walking and horse-driven distances. However, with the introduction of motorized transport – in particular steam and electric trains and trams – urban boundaries expanded far afield along the corridors formed by public transportation links. The subsequent development of private transportation went a step further, allowing greater flexibility, beyond public transport corridors, for individuals. Urban areas began to expand in all directions, creating urban sprawl – of which the Randstad, the Eastern Corridor linking Boston and Washington, DC, and the São Paulo Metropolitan Area are just three examples (Figure 1.1).

Throughout the 20th century, economic growth in industrialized nations led to an accentuation in private transportation and automobile ownership, greatly accelerating urban sprawl. In turn, sprawl created a demand for access to ever more distant locations, which, as will be discussed, favoured the range advantages of ICVs for private transport. The growth of cities benefited from the mass-market version of the automobile while the automobile industry boomed with the growth of urban peripheries.

In fact, industrial society has become so dependent on the automobile that public transportation, while critically important to the functioning of cities, could be seen perhaps as a niche transportation market. Even in the case of Europe, public transit deteriorated at alarming rates in the closing decades of the 20th century. In England and Wales, for instance, the share of public transit trips dropped from 33 per cent in 1971 to 14 per cent in 1991 (Cervero, 1998). A similar trend can also be observed in the megacities of developing countries such as Buenos Aires (Argentina), Bangkok (Thailand) and Manila (Philippines).

Private transportation, the automobile industry and urbanization became mutually reinforcing symbols of modernity and progress in the 20th century. Indeed, one can hardly imagine a world without ICVs and the gas stations which service them. So how did this particular technology become such an intrinsic component of the modern way of life? Let's look back at the origins of the automobile.

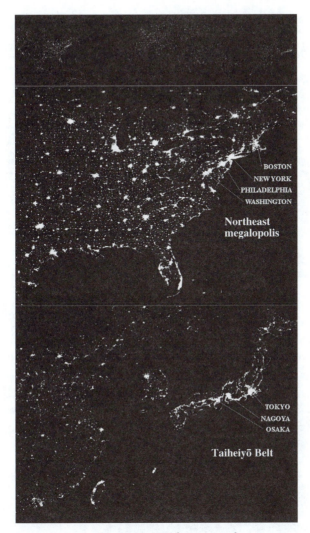

Figure 1.1 *Urban sprawl*

Source: Bill Rankin (2009)

Innovators and early vehicle development

In 1801, Richard Trevithick, a Cornish mine manager, built the first steam-powered carriage (Figure 1.2) – also considered to be the first automobile or motor vehicle – giving way to the era of horseless transport. However, automobiles were not an immediate success. The steam engines that powered them were noisy and dirty and did not offer a significant improvement in performance relative to horse-driven transport.

The next major breakthrough in motor vehicle technology came in 1834, when Thomas Davenport, an American blacksmith and inventor, developed the first direct-current electric motor and used it to power model locomo-

(a)   (b)

Figure 1.2 *(a) Richard Trevithick and (b) his Steam Vehicle (1801)*

Source: portrait by John Linnell (1792–1882)

tives. In subsequent years, inventors developed an array of non-rechargeable battery-powered electric vehicles, including Robert Anderson's BEV, which gave origin to the Detroit Electric (Figure 1.3). While such BEVs provided a more efficient, quieter, cleaner, and thus more desirable, method of transport than

Figure 1.3 *Anderson's Detroit Electric*

Source: Asterion (Wikimedia Commons)

Figure 1.4 *Gaston Planté*

Source: Wikimedia Commons

their steam-powered rival, they were significantly limited by dependence on non-rechargeable batteries.

Four decades later, in 1865, Frenchman Gaston Planté (Figure 1.4) developed the first rechargeable lead-acid battery, causing a landslide of development. By 1884, the Electric Carriage & Wagon Company, founded by Morris and Salom, was producing the Electrobat, which was used as a delivery vehicle in Philadelphia and as a taxi in New York City. By 1886, Frank Sprague had developed the first electric trolley system (Figure 1.5) in Richmond, Virginia.

Figure 1.5 *Sprague's Electric Trolley*

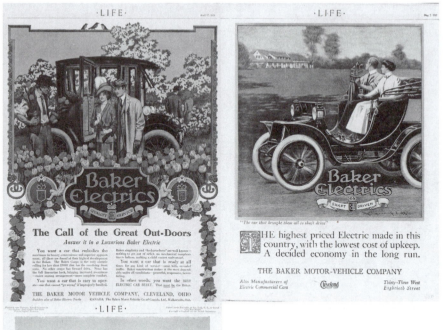

Figure 1.6 *Three advertisements for Baker Electrics vehicles*

Source: Aldeń Jewell (www.flickr.com/photos/autohistorian)

Founded in 1899, Baker Electric (Figure 1.6) became one of the leading automobile manufacturers in America, producing only BEVs for nearly two decades. And – guess what? – the classic American manufacturing icons, Oldsmobile and Studebaker, were formed in 1897 and 1902, respectively, to produce BEVs!

In Europe, the London Electric Cab Company was launched in 1897, operating 15 electric taxis in the British capital (Figure 1.7). That same year, regenerative braking (Chapter 4) was developed by M. A. Darracq, greatly improving the energy efficiency and range of BEVs. Bouquet, Garcin & Schivre,

Figure 1.7 *London Electric Cab Company vehicle*

Figure 1.8 *La Jamais Contente*

Source: Wikimedia Commons

a French BEV and battery manufacturer founded in 1899, soon achieved a record range of 290 kilometres per charge. And – hold on to your seat! – on 1 May 1899, Camille Jenatzy drove his bullet-shaped creation (Figure 1.8) La Jamais Contente ('The Never Satisfied'), to a world speed record of 110km/hr in Achères, France. Yes, the BEV was the first vehicle to break triple digit speeds.

The BEV success was far from limited to the Northern Hemisphere. In 1918, The Rio de Janeiro Tramway, Light and Power Company Ltd, commonly known as 'Light' by its customers, inaugurated a battery-powered electric bus service which operated in the capital's downtown area. Local newspapers praised the clean and silent nature of the electric buses next to its ICV rivals.[3] In fact, the public transportation system in Rio de Janeiro came to be dominated by electricity, both battery-powered buses and grid-connected trams, throughout the first half of the 20th century. Alas, the last electric buses dropped out of service in 1948, though a few tramlines remain in operation to this day. In 2007, the last electric truck from Light's original fleet was restored and now stands proudly in the atrium of the company's headquarters in downtown Rio de Janeiro (Figure 1.9).

(a)

(b)

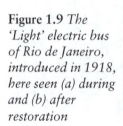

Figure 1.9 *The 'Light' electric bus of Rio de Janeiro, introduced in 1918, here seen (a) during and (b) after restoration*

Source: LIGHT SA Photography Archive

Figure 1.10 *Benz's Patent Motorwagen*

Source: Wikimedia Commons

So where was the ICV while all of this was happening? Well, to the surprise of most people, it was not until 1885, more than half a century after Davenport's original BEV, that Karl Benz conceived the first ICV (Figure 1.10)! Interestingly, its success was not immediate – at least not among the well-to-do who could afford the early-era automobiles. Its noisy and polluting propulsion system was considered a major public disturbance. And, while modern vehicles start without hesitation, the early ICVs required the driver to put some muscle behind the vehicle's crankshaft to get it started, thus excluding most women and the elderly as potential drivers. These consumers were drawn to the ease and safety of the early BEV.

However, the luxury of silent and clean transport came at a hefty price – BEVs were equivalent in price to a modern-day Rolls-Royce. No wonder they were the preferred method of transport amongst the wealthy elite but were shunned by the lower and middle classes. The automobile – of whatever type – had yet to penetrate the mass market.

Out of the 4200 vehicles sold in the US in 1900, 38 per cent were BEVs, only 22 per cent were ICVs, with the steam-powered carriage making up the rest. Steady sales brought BEV registrations in the country up to 34,000 units by 1912. However, three critical factors came together in the opening decades of the 20th century to put an end to the success the BEV had enjoyed up to then.

Figure 1.11 *Ford Model T*

Source: Wikimedia Commons

The first blow to the BEV was its limited range capabilities. Despite the 290km mark referred to above, battery technology remained underdeveloped. Many sources highlight how weak market penetration in Europe compared to the US should have provided the BEV industry with the first signs of the trouble ahead (Ehsani et al, 2004, p13). Indeed, the BEV enjoyed much of its early success in America, where paved roads were limited mostly to major urban areas, so an automobile's range was not a significant constraint. The process of paving European roads was years ahead of the American context, thus accentuating the BEV's range constraints as drivers covered greater intercity distances.

However, it was the introduction of Henry Ford's Model T (Figure 1.11) that revolutionized the private transportation market, transforming the automobile from an elite product to a product for the masses. The Model T was first introduced to the market in 1909 at the 'low' price of US$850 (equivalent to US$20,120 in 2008 prices). In principle, Ford's accomplishment was process-focused, as any vehicle could be mass-produced to reduce costs. However, the BEV's battery, as will be discussed in Chapter 4, could not benefit from a similar reduction in costs, thus making it an excessive burden on the vehicle's price tag. By recognizing this and betting on the as-yet unproven ICV, Ford successfully

Figure 1.12 *Charles Kettering*

managed to cross the so-called 'market penetration chasm' into the mass market soon after. All of a sudden, BEVs and their elite consumers became a minority.

Ironically, it was the electric motor itself that provided the fatal blow to the EV market. In 1911, Charles Kettering invented the ICV starter motor, an electric motor that eliminated the need for a manual crank-start (Figure 1.12), redefining the potential consumer base for ICVs. By the 1930s, BEVs had all but vanished from the market and ICVs had become the sole dominant technology.

A Century of Automobile Industry

As various technology innovation case studies show, dominance is neither achieved by first-comers nor by technological superiority. Rather, it is they who can successfully break into the mass market who achieve dominance. Although the period running into the first decade of the 20th century was marked by a flourish of technological inventions in the car market, it is unquestionable that, by the middle of the second decade, the ICV had overtaken the BEV on the road to automobile market dominance.

Indeed, the ICV is one of mankind's most successful modern creations and its major global manufacturers (henceforth referred to as Big Auto) form one of the most powerful industries in history. The 30 largest global players in the automobile industry brought in a total revenue of US$2 trillion in 2007 – equivalent to 3.8 per cent of global gross domestic product. Such a mammoth makes modern-day giants, such as the multi-billion dollar internet industry, look like butterflies. So, to what do they owe this success?

Fordism: The birth of Big Auto

In developing the Model T, Henry Ford (Figure 1.13) did not merely create the first mass-market automobile – he defined the rules of the industry for what would be the better part of the century. Ford's business model of spewing out cars at the fastest possible rate and lowest cost proved monumentally successful and set the standard for nearly every manufacturer around, in the auto and other industries.

Figure 1.13 *Henry Ford in 1934*

Source: United States Library of Congress's Prints and Photographs Division, 78374

Ford believed that, given the right price, the automobile was a desirable product for all consumer groups – even his mechanics should be able to afford the company's cars. However, the production of automobiles suffered from inherently high capital costs. Ford sought to reduce these by applying mass-production principles to produce automobiles in the most efficient manner possible.

Meanwhile, the sequential production system adopted by the company meant that workers focused on specific tasks, allowing for optimal equipment layout. This not only reduced training requirements but reduced overall tooling costs and labour time normally wasted on finding and waiting for tools. Model T production aimed to eliminate time and resources wasted on unproductive activities. This eventually led Ford towards vertical integration of the entire production process under one roof. At the core of Ford's philosophy lay a belief in standardization, which later became one of the guiding principles in the automobile industry. Referring to his vision for the Model T, Ford stated, 'Any customer can have a car painted any colour that he wants, so long as it is black.'

Though Ford is often credited as being the founder of mass production, in fact, the concept was already being applied to shipbuilding in the 14th century by the Venetian Arsenal, arguably the largest industrial complex in the world prior to the Industrial Revolution. However, Ford was the first to implement the principles of mass production in the automobile industry, taking the processes and the industry to new heights. The Ford Motor Company achieved unprecedented throughput, producing a car from scratch in just 98 minutes, and allowing production to expand at exponential rates (Figure 1.14). By 1916, the company was selling more than half a million units annually and, just four years later, it hit the million-unit mark. Indeed, Ford's high-volume production, reduced waste and standardized design permitted the company to slash the price of its vehicle from the original US$850 in 1909 (US$20,120 in 2008 terms), down to US$260 by 1925 (US$3170 in 2008 terms) – without harming profits.

However, despite innovative vision in the early days, Ford later proved inflexible in his ideas. By the mid-1920s, competitors had adopted Ford's manufacturing philosophy while providing a higher degree of product differentiation. After years of resistance, in 1926, as Model T sales began to wither, Ford finally accepted his son's advice to develop a new car. The Model A (Figure 1.15) was brought to market in 1927 and sold four million units by the time it was discontinued in 1931. The company, like its competitors, then adopted a system of annual remodelling of its vehicles.

Now fast-forward half a century and we find a largely unchanged industry. Of course, consumers gained a range of colours and accessories from which to choose, vehicle performance and durability increased, and, more importantly, safety and comfort improved enormously. But vehicles remain largely standardized in design, features and manufacturing processes.

Just consider Volkswagen (VW). The company uses the same VW Group's A platform[4] to produce the Audi A3, Audi TT, VW Golf, VW Caddy, VW

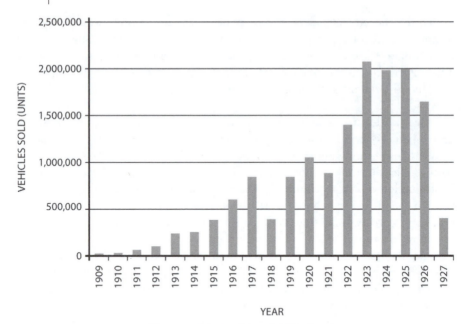

Figure 1.14 *Ford Model T sales*

Touran, SEAT Léon, SEAT Toledo and Skoda Octavia. It also built the first generation Audi A4 using the B5/PL5 platform from the fourth generation VW Passat. Even the Audi R8 sports car is a redressed Lamborghini Gallardo. Not satisfied with the VW group's uniformity? Well then consider the Chevy/Geo

Figure 1.15 *The Ford Model A*

Figure 1.16 *Two cars from one assembly line:*
(a) The Geo Prizm and (b) the Toyota Corolla

Source: Wikimedia Commons

Prizm and the Toyota Corolla (Figure 1.16) that were not just based on the same platform, but were built in exactly the same assembly lines at NUMMI in Fremont, California!

Indeed, the automobile industry, led by the American 'Big Three' (GM, Ford and Chrysler), was founded on mass-produced, low-cost, standardized products aimed at the middle class. Not much has changed since then and for good reasons. By 1950, Detroit, aptly named Motor City or Motown, had become the gem of the American economic success story, attracting over a million workers while maintaining the highest wages in the country.

Interdependent industries: The internal combustion vehicle and petroleum

With the growing scarcity of suitable whale oil and a subsequent rise in costs, businesses were encouraged to explore new fuel sources. In the middle of the century, coal-based alternatives, such as kerosene and 'town gas', rapidly gained market share. Whale-oil consumption peaked in 1847 and by the 1860s the industry had all but disappeared, despite a still-abundant supply at the time.

By 1859, the American oil driller Colonel Edwin Drake had discovered petroleum in Pennsylvania, marking the beginning of the modern-day petroleum industry. The coal-based oil dominance of the late 1840s and 1850s was rapidly complemented by petroleum in the early 1860s. At a third or quarter of the price per equivalent level of energy density, petroleum helped coal-based oils eradicate whale-oil markets.

In the early 1900s, oilfields being explored around the world produced petroleum on a large scale. But while the petroleum industry replaced most of the coal-based fuel markets, it was not until the rise of the ICV and the automobile industry that the petroleum industry became the large player in the market that we know today.

The first ever commercial gasoline filling station, located at the city pharmacy in Wiesloch, Germany, was inaugurated in 1888, providing fuel for Bertha Benz's round-trip voyage between Mannheim and Pforzheim. In these early days, filling services were typically provided as a side business. Though unintuitive to the modern consumer, pharmacies were perhaps natural suppliers of petroleum due to their experience with supplying controlled substances. Indeed, it was not until 1905 that the first purpose-built filling station was put in place in St Louis, Missouri, with others slowly springing up across America in subsequent years.

The introduction of Ford's Model T and the subsequent surge in ICV ownership drove the development of filling stations over the following decades. California-based Standard Oil Co. alone operated 218 stations (55 per cent market share) in the Western US by 1919, more than tripling that to 735 stations (though dropping to a 28 per cent market share) by 1926. The growth continued throughout the century, such that, according to the American Census, the number of filling stations in the country exceeded 120,000 in 2002.

Unsurprisingly, by mid-century, petroleum had replaced coal altogether as the world's primary energy source – driven predominantly by ICV fuel consumption. Looking back at the history of early vehicle development, one can see that the relatively late emergence of cheap petroleum coincides with the ICV's late blossoming. However, by the time both markets had been established, their combined strengths proved unrivalled.

The rising sun: Lean manufacturing

In an attempt to revive national industry following post-war decadence, Japanese automobile manufacturers turned to their Western counterparts to learn about the latest industry practices. Toyota engineers, led by Taiichi Ohno, spent 12 weeks visiting factories in North America and Europe in the mid-1950s. To their disappointment, the team observed vital inefficiencies in the mass-production processes that were being used in the West. Prevalent in the Ohno team's observations were the high levels of inventory and material wastage driven by Big Auto's focus on pushing supplies into the market without due consideration of demand conditions.

Toyota set out to redefine the production process, leading to what came to be known as the 'lean manufacturing' era in the automobile industry. In contrast to Ford's low unitary production cost philosophy, Toyota proposed to reduce costs on a system-wide and product life-cycle basis. What does this mean?

Toyota strategically selected high-quality suppliers, while imposing strict in-house quality controls and only producing vehicles to order. Ohno believed that they could offset the additional unitary production cost with long-term savings. How? First, Toyota ensured a better quality product. In turn, this reduced costs for both manufacturer and consumer over the life of the car by minimizing recalls[5] and maintenance. The increase in customer satisfaction, due to improved product quality, ensured a higher level of buyer retention in the future, thus reducing the manufacturer's need to spend on marketing. Second, by producing vehicles to order, the company limited their exposure to unexpected variations in demand conditions. This simultaneously ensured that Toyota was able to adapt its product offering based on shifting consumer needs and constraints.

Today the American Big Three are a rather pale image of what they were in the boom decades and are decreasingly expressive in terms of defining the future of automobile technology. Even before the 2008 economic crisis, American manufacturers had fallen deep into the red, unable to push merchandise off the lots at acceptable prices, while Toyota and Honda were seeing growing profits. According to *The Harbour Report* (Oliver Wyman, 2005), American manufacturers incurred US$350 to US$500 in additional labour costs per vehicle due to lower labour productivity compared to Toyota. The Big Three suffered catastrophic losses because of huge inventories, while the Japanese were able to adjust production with greater flexibility and thus limit the impact of the downturn in demand on their business.

No wonder manufacturers now look East in search of the best practice in automobile production. Indeed, the global automobile industry is beginning to look leaner and more flexible than in the last century and thus should be better prepared to address the necessary technological shifts of the future.

Looking Ahead

The world has changed dramatically since the beginning of the automobile industry. Important events have come about since the 1970s that have had a strong influence on global economies and the world of transportation. As noted,

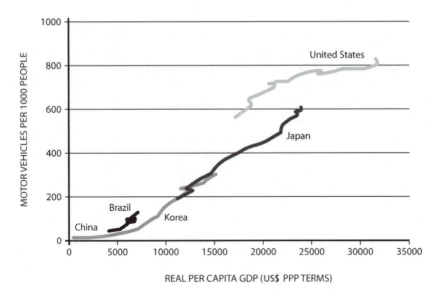

Figure 1.17 *Vehicle ownership by income per capita*

Source: IMF (2005)

lean manufacturing emerged half a globe away from Motown and, in 2008, a financial crisis rocked the foundations of developed-country markets. In addition, over recent decades, oil prices have taken a rollercoaster ride, women have significantly increased their presence in the workforce and environmental awareness has made the front page of newspapers.

Eastern promises

The 20th-century boom in the automotive industry was driven predominantly by the urbanization and economic growth in industrialized nations. However, today urbanization has largely stabilized and GDP growth rates are 'modest', around 2–3 per cent per year, in industrialized nations (IMF, 2010, p155). In contrast, 84 per cent of the world's population lives in developing countries (World Bank Institute, 2011), where many of the trends seen in the industrialized world over the last century are only now beginning to take hold. Countries like China and India have enjoyed extraordinary GDP growth over the last decade, expanding at average annual growth rates of 10.3 per cent and 7.6 per cent respectively between 2002 and 2009 (IMF, 2010, p160).

Indeed, CSM Worldwide, an international automotive market analysis firm, estimates that the Indian, Chinese and Brazilian markets will have surged by 45 per cent, 39 per cent and 26 per cent respectively between 2007 and 2011 (Timmons, 2009). It is not surprising that automobile sales volumes in China surpassed those of the US in December 2008. While many thought this was a blip caused by the 2008 financial crisis, it is increasingly clear that China is the new global automobile market leader. According to data from the International Organization of Motor Vehicle Manufacturers, production in China rose by 48

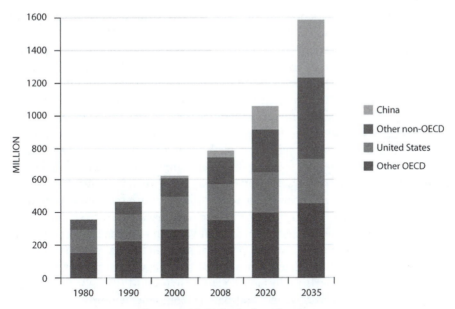

Figure 1.18 *Vehicle fleet forecasts*

Source: World Energy Outlook 2010 (Presentation to the Press, 9 Nov 2010) © OECD/IEA, Slide 7

per cent to 13,790,994 vehicles in 2009, and provisional figures for 2010 report a further 32 per cent rise to 18,264,667 (OICA, 2011). Note that this makes China the largest global automobile producer ever, even compared to the 2007 peak production in the US and Japan.

As the income per capita and average family wealth in developing economies increase, so will the density of private transportation, as shown in Figure 1.17, in the same way that occurred with industrialized nations throughout the 20th century. Obviously, the relationship between vehicle ownership and income per capita is not linear; however, the IMF estimates fleet penetration, using regression analysis[6] and data from 48 countries.

Chinese fleet penetration rates are expected to expand from 5.9 per cent to 26.7 per cent between 2010 and 2030. As shown in Figure 1.18, China is expected to surpass the US as the country with the largest national vehicle fleet, while non-OECD countries increase their share of the global fleet from 23.3 per cent to 44.6 per cent over the same period.

Moreover, the rate of expansion in vehicle ownership actually might outpace what is suggested by the above historical relationship with wealth levels. This is largely because vehicles are no longer the expensive item that they once were. Today, the Ford Focus, a popular American vehicle, costs US$16,000, compared to US$20,120 (inflation adjusted) for the original Ford Model T. In comparison, in January 2008, Indian car manufacturer Tata Motors launched its version of a 'people's car', the Nano, with a whopping US$2000 price tag, making vehicles more accessible to the common person in the developing world.

Furthermore, social conventions have evolved. Consider Los Angeles over the 20th century as discussed by Wachs (1993). During the 1920s, Los Angeles witnessed a vehicle ownership boom driven by the initial emergence of private transportation – think of this as the urbanization and Model T phenomena. Following the Great Depression and World War II, rapid economic and population growth, particularly in suburban areas, led to a further boom in vehicle ownership. More recently, the growth in average household incomes and the increased proportion of women in the workforce have taken vehicle ownership per household to new heights. Indeed, many of these factors are likely to converge over a shorter timespan in the case of emerging markets, leading to a more accentuated car ownership growth path than shown in Figure 1.18.

The vast majority of emerging-market consumers are truly new to modern markets, particularly 'luxury' segments such as private vehicles. Thus their preferences are not constrained by traditional Western parameters. This presents an interesting opportunity for new products such as the EV since consumers may lack an inherent prejudice or a resistance to change that operates in favour of the ICV in other markets. In fact, BYD Company Ltd ('BYD') (Box 1.1), a Hong Kong-listed electric vehicle and battery company, has proved to be the single strongest performing stock among those that make up the NEX index, rising more than 400 per cent in the first ten months of 2009 (New Energy Finance, 2009).

If Big Auto does not provide emerging market-friendly solutions, new companies, particularly from emerging markets, will. Indeed, these new companies (and their governments) have the most to gain and the least to lose

---

Box 1.1 *BYD*

In October of 2008, Warren Buffett stunned the business world when he invested US$230 million for 10 per cent of BYD Company Ltd, an until then largely unknown Chinese manufacturing group. There is no doubt that when Mr Buffett revealed the company's plan to launch the world's first mass-produced BEV by 2010 and put it in North American showrooms soon after, most people looked around in confusion: Is Warren Buffett kidding?! A Chinese battery company, which has never sold a car outside of China, intends to guide the Western World into the future?!

Slowly it became apparent that the BYD just might have the right tools. BYD was founded in 1995 by a Chinese chemist and government researcher, Wang Chuan-Fu, to provide low-cost batteries for the Chinese domestic market. By 2002, BYD was among the four largest battery manufacturers worldwide and was the largest manufacturer in China. While BYD offers low-cost batteries, it does not compromise on quality. On the contrary, BYD's batteries are found in today's most advanced microelectronic appliances, including Apple's iPhones and iPods. What is more, while today's high-end battery manufacturers – such as Sony and Sanyo – have invariably faced recalls, BYD holds a flawless track record.

Meanwhile, BYD Auto was launched in 2003, when BYD acquired a state-owned car company, and by October of the same year, the BYD F3 became the bestselling car in China. Wang's next plan was to expand his automobile business abroad. Aware of its comparative advantage against other automobile manufacturers – its being both a leading battery and automobile manufacturer – BYD is en route to making history.

from an automobile industry mutation since they stand to capture a share of the market from traditional players. As such, they demonstrate no cognitive lock-in – indeed, on the contrary, seek new 'disruptive' business models. Their performance to date suggests that they are aware of the BEV's merits and are focusing on exploiting exactly these elements to address consumer concerns and penetrate profitable market segments, such as 'no frills' and low cost.

Note that governments in emerging economies face huge infrastructure gaps. As they develop their transportation infrastructure, this gap may represent an opportunity for leapfrogging to more sustainable solutions, if the potential to reduce air and noise pollution in fast-growing, densely populated cities is recognized. While industrialized nations drove the development of the 20th century automobile industry, it is the emerging markets that can be expected to dominate in the 21st century. Consequently, it is imperative that developing countries play a central role in the political and business decisions regarding future vehicle technology.

Diversifying transportation options

It was seen that the introduction of the automobile has made the urban/suburban lifestyle a reality for a good part of the world's population. After a century of evolution, the luxury of mobility is no longer a luxury, but rather a necessity and a core element of modern life. However, as Figure 1.19 illustrates, road systems built to service the personal automobile have reached saturation points again and again, generating negative value to consumers – hours spent in congestion, the hassle of finding a parking spot, urban air pollution, nervous drivers and so on – and requiring new investment in expansion again and again. So much for the convenience of mobility!

Public transport would be the logical alternative to automobile-based mobility. In a recent blog, Judt (2011) argues in favour of a revival of the rail system which fell from grace between the 1950s and 1990s. Notably, 'for any trip under ten miles or between 150 and 500 miles in any country with a functioning railway network, the train is the quickest way to travel as well as, taking all costs into account, the cheapest and least destructive'. As will become clear, this proves to be extraordinarily significant to the case of EVs.

The literature on public transportation solutions and how these successfully address modern transportation dilemmas is ample, and a review would be beyond the scope of this book. Perhaps the most comprehensive evaluation of such solutions is presented by Robert Cervero's *The Transit Metropolis: A Global Inquiry*, which reviews the cases of cities which have successfully implemented public transportation solutions to improve overall transportation quality.

Paradoxically, even in these cases, attachment to the automobile remains strong, with no signs of easing up. Sir Mark Moody-Stuart, former Chairman of Royal Dutch/Shell Group, illustrates the essence of this relationship:

Figure 1.19 *Congestion both sides of the Equator*

Note: Locations shown are (a–b) São Paulo's Rodovia Dutra and (c–e) Los Angeles freeways.

A European environment minister once asked me how to get people off their love affair with the motor car. I believe we should not even try and interfere with that love. It is deeply imbedded, and interfering in other people's love affairs is seldom productive. But the love is with personal movement and space and the freedom that it brings. [What we need is] to make great strides in transport efficiency ... to engage the consumer, not force him or her into public transport.

Indeed, there are signs that market conditions and public policy are beginning to motivate consumers to diversify the transportation options they use, ranging from subway and bus rapid transit to cycling and walking. The notable trend in recent decades has been the rise of vehicle sharing services – particularly, though not exclusively, in EU markets. In 2007, the University of California found 400,000 drivers participating in 18 car-sharing programmes across the US. While this might not seem particularly impressive, what is phenomenal is that the 18 programmes combined operated a mere 7000 vehicles – which means 57 drivers per vehicle. Granted, not all drivers would necessarily have bought a car if the programme did not exist.

Beyond directly reducing wasteful resource consumption associated with the production of surplus vehicles, this approach encourages drivers to rationalize their driving habits. Consumers will avoid driving short distances just to post a letter or buy milk, which reduces both unnecessary congestion and fuel consumption. Indeed, according to Zipcar, the largest car-sharing service in the world, each of their vehicles replaces 15 private vehicles and, on average, each member reduces their annual driving habits by 6400km, which translates to average monthly savings of US$435 for the driver.

It is becoming clear that such pursuit of more efficient ways of meeting the demand for mobility relies on the availability of multiple transportation solutions which work together to enhance the flexibility and quality of transport systems. Such a scenario, with efficient public transportation and more rational solutions to personal mobility, represents a dramatic transformation in the business environment for Big Auto.

Where To Now?

Contrary to popular belief, the BEV is not a recent invention, having been around for over 150 years, longer than the ICV itself. What is more, the ICV's stranglehold on the automobile industry was not always uncontested. Indeed, ICVs were not actually regarded as an all-out superior technology until the second decade of the 20th century, when Ford's Model T breached the mass-market penetration chasm. However, in an increasingly urbanized world, where individual consumers' preferences are paramount, the early BEV's merits could not match the ICV's long-range and low-cost merits. As a result, BEVs fell decidedly out of fashion and, as is abundantly clear, ICVs have become the centrepiece of our modern lifestyle.

It was also seen that since the 1970s critical changes have set in. Not only has a new production paradigm made its appearance in the automobile industry, but both demand and supply are moving away from the OECD countries, driven by population, economic growth and urbanization in emerging markets. To borrow from Bob Dylan, the times they are a-changing.

As in the emergence of every radical technological innovation, there will be many losers, but those that survive will become the Henry Fords – the giants that redefine the industry. Throughout the book, the reader may become aware of certain solutions to which the author is especially partial, but there is no intention of picking winners. What the book aims to highlight is the fundamental change in the way the automobile market is being reconfigured. Indeed, this feels like a new industry altogether. Thus Chapter 2 looks at a set of current global constraints and concerns which put the sustainability of the ICV model in check – and are likely to drive the next automobile growth wave.

Notes

1 This book focuses on the 'automobile', or the class of vehicles that comprises family cars and light trucks, essentially addressing the needs of urban households and firms. These are also commonly referred to as 'light duty vehicles' (LDVs). While the discussion is often relevant to a broader range of vehicle categories, it does not propose to be comprehensive in covering issues that relate to freight and public road transport, or even rail and air modalities.

2 The book focuses primarily on the BEV resurgence, but recognizes that other forms of EV technologies may play an important role in the solution to transportation challenges over the coming decades. Consequently, the discussion will address these broader technological opportunities explicitly.

3 Based on conversations with Professor Luiz Artur Pecorelli Peres, a leading electric vehicle expert at UERJ (Rio de Janeiro State University).

4 A vehicle platform is its basic skeleton, which includes key mechanical components such as floorpan, wheelbase, steering mechanism and suspension. While variations in this basic skeleton are rarely noticed by consumers, they represent a significant proportion of a vehicle's development costs.

5 Ironically, Toyota was at the centre of a costly and politically embarrassing safety recall in the opening months of 2010. Notice that while such incidents are probably inevitable at some point in the lifetime of a major manufacturer, the company's aim has been to minimize their frequency and extent.

6 Fleet size per capita in a future year is a complicated function of the original fleet size and the future income per capita.

References

Cervero, R. (1998) *The Transit Metropolis: A Global Inquiry*, Island Press, Washington, DC

Ehsani, M. Gao, Y., Gay, S. E. and Emadi, A. (2004) *Modern Electric, Hybrid Electric, and Fuel Cell Vehicles: Fundamentals, Theory, and Design*, CRC Press, Boca Raton, FL

IMF (International Monetary Fund) (2005) *World Economic Outlook*, IMF, Washington, DC

IMF (2010) *World Economic Outlook*, IMF, Washington, DC

Judt, T. (2011) 'Bring back the rails', *New York Review of Books Online*, www.nybooks.com/articles/archives/2011/jan/13/bring-back-rails/, accessed 10 January 2011

New Energy Finance (2009) 'Huge variety in performance as clean energy shares rise in third quarter of 2009', press release, 1 October 2009

OICA (2011) 'Production statistics', International Organization of Motor Vehicle Manufacturers (Organisation Internationale des Constructeurs d'Automobiles), http://oica.net/category/production-statistics, accessed 10 June 2011

Oliver Wyman (2005) *The Harbour Report*, Oliver Wyman, New York

Timmons, H. (2009) 'Ford hopes new Figo will help it win Asian buyers', *New York Times Online*, www.nytimes.com/2009/09/24/business/global/24ford.html?_r=2&adxnnl=1&adxnnlx=1253808332-dCvKo8TUm0ucB9b/iXBLsQ, accessed 10 January 2011

Wachs, M (1993) 'Learning from Los Angeles: Transport, urban form, and air quality', *Transportation*, vol 20, pp329–354

World Bank Institute (2011) Global Statistics Data Catalog, http://data.worldbank.org/data-catalog/global-statistics, accessed 10 January 2011

2

Global Sustainability in Check

The time is always right to do what is right.

Martin Luther King, Jr.

Most people have probably come across conflicting views on the problems surrounding the continued use of the internal combustion engine vehicle (ICV) and are not really sure what to make of what they hear. Sure, oil will run out one day, but won't we have discovered or created a substitute, or something even better by that time? And the climate will probably change but, given the wide range of outcomes emerging from the scenarios that scientists have come up with, should we really be worrying about the more catastrophic ones? Plus, is the aftermath of the deepest recession since the Great Depression really the right time to spend billions on expensive high-tech novelties? And, after all, how do we know that the alternatives to the ICV will even work, let alone work better, in satisfying current concerns in our quest for personal mobility?

This chapter takes a first look at how resource constraints and environmental concerns are changing the transport industry at the global scale. In so doing, it tries to highlight the extent to which these factors are prevalent in the current political and economic context. These factors will be revisited in greater detail or from different angles in other parts of the book.

Energy Consumption and Resource Constraints

The automobile is undoubtedly among the key technological advancements separating today's world from the pre-industrialized world. It introduced a degree of mobility which redefined the way people live and do business, reshaping our economy. As discussed in Chapter 1, much of this is owed to a solid partnership between ICVs and their petroleum fuel source. However, the continued growth of the global economy over the last century has gradually exposed the risks posed by dependence on petroleum. While petroleum remains a cost-effective transportation fuel for consumers today, both resource depletion and supply insecurity are now clear warnings that the petroleum-based ICV solution is unsustainable in the near future.

Total energy consumption

Over the course of the last half-century, the world became accustomed to consuming vast quantities of energy resources. As can be seen in Figure 2.1, economic growth and energy consumption have been closely linked over this period, so, in the absence of a radical change in societal patterns of behaviour and production, increasing amounts of energy resources will need to be made available in order to sustain future growth.[1]

Even in the unlikely event that economic growth slowed down permanently in industrialized nations, developing countries can be expected to demand increasing levels of energy to drive their economies over the coming decades, as they strive to reduce poverty and improve living conditions for their populations. Note especially that two particularly high performers, China and India, have the largest populations in the world but per capita incomes and per capita levels of energy consumption that remain significantly below those of the EU and the US.

Economic growth and energy consumption will thus continue to be a high priority for lower- and middle-income countries. According to the International Energy Agency's World Energy Outlook 2009 (IEA, 2009a), in a business-as-usual scenario, global primary energy consumption is estimated to expand by 40 per cent from 2007 to 2030. Non-OECD countries are expected to account for 90 per cent of this increase, with China and India alone accounting for 53 per cent of the global total![2]

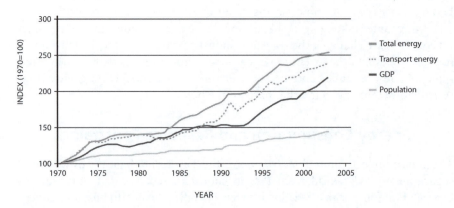

Figure 2.1 *Energy consumption (by end use), global GDP and population*
Source: OECD (2006)

Also of special concern is the fact that fossil-based resources are expected to represent 77 per cent of the additional energy consumption. While coal is set to see the largest increase in demand of any primary fuel, oil will continue to hold the largest share of the primary fuel mix. The *World Energy Outlook* highlights that crude oil consumption in OECD countries is expected to drop during the period. Unfortunately, this is offset by strong growth from non-OECD countries that will drive up consumption by 24 per cent.

The transportation sector and the petroleum industry, as discussed in the previous chapter, have a long history of interdependence, with the sector accounting for 61 per cent of all petroleum consumption, and petroleum-derived fuels accounting for 94 per cent of all transportation energy requirements in 2007 (IEA, 2009b). This degree of interdependence is particularly disconcerting given the growing relative scarcity of petroleum resources, the geopolitical risk associated with supplies and the lack of any immediate widespread alternative.

Resource depletion

Fossil fuels are a scarce resource which society has been consuming at dangerously accelerated rates despite warnings dating back nearly half a century.[3] Indeed, if the reader is concerned with the rate of petroleum depletion now, imagine the scale of the problem by 2030. To illustrate this, if society were to freeze energy consumption at 2008 levels, the world's oil reserves would be depleted within 44 years and coal reserves within 147 years, as shown in Table 2.1.

Granted, oil reserves refer merely to the oil resources that have already been identified and which experts consider recoverable, given the latest technologies and economic conditions. It is reasonable to assume that, as resources dwindle further and demand continues to expand, prices will rise, justifying the use of more advanced and currently uneconomic exploration technology, leading to an increase in proven reserves.

While experts often measure petroleum depletion with reference to estimates of future annual peak rates of petroleum production ('peak oil'), it is perhaps more significant to refer to the evolution of petroleum resource discoveries. In doing so, it can be seen that 75 per cent of current petroleum production origi-nates from oil fields discovered before 1970. Furthermore, as shown in Figure 2.2, global annual petroleum production has exceeded annual discoveries since 1983, such that society now discovers only one barrel (bbl) for every three being consumed.

Table 2.1 *Oil and coal reserves and depletion rates*

	Coal	Petroleum (2000)
Proven reserves	910 billion tonnes	1.136 trillion barrels
Consumption rate	6.2 billion tonnes/year (2006)	31.2 billion bbl/yr (85.5 million bbl/day)
Years to reserves depletion	147 years	44 years

Source: Ehsani et al (2004)

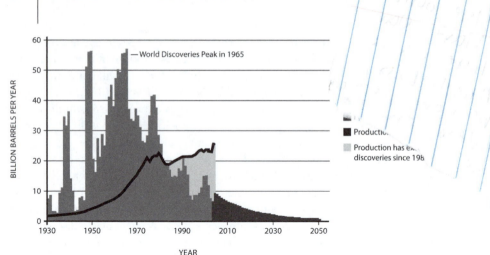

Figure 2.2 *Global oil discoveries and production*

Source: Hughes (2004)

Of course, on the demand (or consumption) side, progress can also be expected. Over time, technological development has improved energy efficiency in industrial and other production processes, and there is still potential for society to control consumption in the transport sector by changing behaviour patterns – for instance, by car-pooling and walking whenever possible. However, these savings, if achieved, can quickly be eroded by further population and economic growth. Indeed, IEA (2009c) projections indicate that transportation energy consumption will grow by 50 per cent by 2020 and by 80 per cent by 2030, increases that, as will be seen in Chapter 3, cannot be compensated for even by the most optimistic ICV energy efficiency improvement possible. So where will combustion fuel supplies come from?

Supply security

For more than half a century, countries where the automobile was prevalent consumed oil like an addict consumes drugs – avidly and unreflectively. However, when the oil crises of the 1970s took hold, the potential dangers of severe dependence hit home and drew attention to the fact that not only are petroleum resources scarce, they are also geographically concentrated, as shown in Figure 2.3, making for a politically unstable world.

Since the 1970s, this imbalance in the geographical distribution of oil resources – and, crucially, its disconnect with respect to the main sources of demand – has led to unrelenting geopolitical tensions.[4] The Organization of the Petroleum Exporting Countries (OPEC)[5] control over global petroleum resources is uncontested, with its 12 constituent countries accounting for 40 per cent of daily production and 76 per cent of conventional reserves. It has consistently manipulated petroleum supplies, leading, notably, to both oil crises of the 1970s. What is more, between 78 and 90 per cent of all reserves are in some

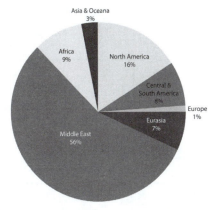

Figure 2.3 *Oil and gas reserves by region*

Source: data from US Energy Information Administration

way controlled by national oil companies (NOCs), as shown in Figure 2.4. This greatly limits the possibility of international oil companies seeking to expand their exploration activities.

If this were a description of luxury footwear or indigenous jewellery markets, then the consequences of a monopolistic/cartel operation might be nothing more than a nuisance to consumers. However, oil consumption represents one of the largest consumer expense bills on the planet. Road transportation alone consumes around 21 million bbl/day globally, which, in periods when prices are low, costs consumers a total of US$570 billion/year excluding taxes. However, during economic booms, such as the summer of 2008, this bill doubled.

Figure 2.5 shows how crude oil price variation since the 1970s has been increasingly erratic in both the short and long term, having a harsh impact on

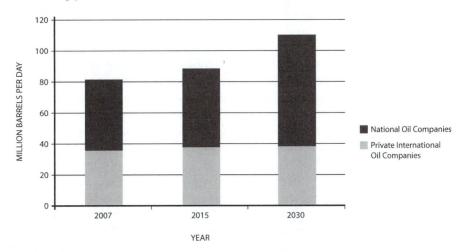

Figure 2.4 *World oil production by company type*

Source: Electrification Coalition (2009)

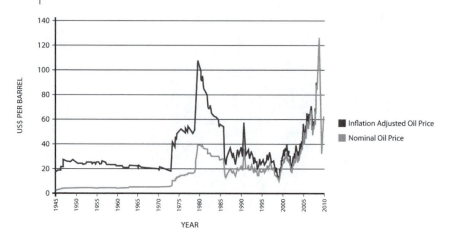

Figure 2.5 *Historical oil prices, 1946–2009*

Source: Timothy McMahon, www.inflationdata.com/inflation/sharedcontent/InsertableContent.htm#Usage

individual consumers and economies as a whole. In contrast to the oil price spikes of 1973 and 1979, the 2008 spike did not result from an OPEC-managed supply shortage. Rather, oil producers were simply not prepared to increase production in line with expanding demand. This supply shortage was caused by two major factors.

First, the prolonged low oil prices over the 1990s set the brakes on exploration investment during the same period. When demand picked up, suppliers simply had no spare capacity. This is a clear sign that drastic price variations, even over longer periods of time, can be damaging to the industry. Second, 'cheap' oil is now considered something of the past, as new oil fields are smaller and technically more challenging and risky to develop, as exemplified by the 2010 BP Macondo Prospect oil disaster described in Box 2.1. The increased cost of exploration and extraction of available resources is a clear sign that reliable oil supplies are diminishing.

It is no secret that the oil price crash during the summer of 2008, which brought prices down to US$33/bbl (January 2009) from their US$147/bbl (July 2008) peak, was a direct response to decreasing demand due to the global economic crisis. However, experts believe the fundamental price drivers remain a problem in the sector. Francisco Blanch, head of global commodities research at the Bank of America-Merrill Lynch, argued in the *Financial Times* (2009) that:

> *demand in emerging markets is coming back with a vengeance, led by China, and will lend tremendous support to the global oil market in 2010. ... Crude oil prices could push above $100 a barrel heading into 2011 due to a combination of a cyclical improvement in demand, the rapid weakening in the US dollar and strong global liquidity growth.*

Box 2.1 The 2010 BP Macondo Prospect oil disaster

On 20 April 2010, Transocean's Deepwater Horizon rig exploded due to a methane gas blowout while drilling at BP's Macondo Prospect oil fields. The explosion initiated the largest accidental marine oil spill in history, gradually releasing 4.9 million bbl (barrels of crude oil) into the Gulf of Mexico over the course of three months. To put this into perspective, the 1989 Exxon Valdez oil spill, which had previously ranked as the largest oil spill in US controlled waters, is estimated to have released between 260,000 and 750,000 bbl.

While the total cost of the disaster remains unclear, and may never be fully known, certain expenditure figures released by BP along with specific damages estimated by the American government and the states of Louisiana and Florida are indicative. As of July, BP reported US$3.12 billion cumulative expenditures relating to the oil spill – ranging from control and clean-up costs to claims paid. By October, the figure had reached US$11.2 billion.

Some of this expenditure has gone towards supporting key industries which have been particularly impacted. For instance, BP has designated a total US$70 million to promote tourism in Florida, Alabama, Louisiana and Mississippi. However, this figure is dwarfed by the US$23 billion which the US Travel Association estimates will be the economic impact on tourism across the Gulf Coast over the next three years. This equates to a 23 per cent dip in annual revenues from the travel industry in the region.

A similar scenario is found in the fishing industry, which saw one-third of the Gulf's fishing zone temporarily shut down. The Louisiana fishing market, for instance, represents 32.5 per cent of oyster landings, 37.7 per cent of blue crab landings, 38.0 per cent of shrimp landings and 76.5 per cent of Menhaden (forage fish) landings for the US market. As a result of the oil spill, the Louisiana Department of Wildlife and Fisheries expects a US$2.3 billion economic impact in the industry.

In response to the expected flood of liability suits against the company, BP has created a US$20 billion spill response fund to compensate all legitimate claims for damages. Nevertheless, the American Federal Government remains unsatisfied with the compensation package proposed by BP and aims to prosecute the company for as much as an additional US$21 billion.

While the above figures may be indicative of the direct financial costs to be incurred by BP as a result of the Macondo oil spill, the consequences suffered by the oil and gas industry are expected to escalate further. Perhaps the first concrete impact is that insurance premiums for oil rigs are set to increase by 40–50 per cent. Furthermore, regulation is likely to tighten, requiring more detailed and costly environmental impact studies.

Indeed, it looks like the days of cheap oil are indeed gone. And despite recent discoveries, supply remains highly concentrated.

Impacts on the Environment

It is hard to imagine that we reverse hundreds of millions of years of evolution every second. Or that we are unleashing toxins into the atmosphere – into the air we breathe – at accelerating rates. The fact that we even need scientists to tell us that this is a dangerous aberration is ludicrous. After all, when was the last time you needed a doctor to warn you that eating fast food for breakfast, lunch and dinner was unhealthy? The planet's consumption of petroleum is not too different.

It is encouraging that concern over the human impact on the environment – and how this, in turn, affects our immediate health and, ultimately, the longer-term resilience and growth prospects of our economies – has proved an important driver of technological change over the years. The Great Smog of 1952 drove the British Parliament to introduce the Clean Air Act of 1956, greatly limiting the use of polluting coal power plants near urban areas. The US Congress followed suit with legislation to control smog and other forms of air pollution through the Air Pollution Control Act of 1955 and a series of Clean Air Acts since 1963, affecting everything from coal power plants to ICVs on a national level. In 1967, motivated by local air pollution concerns in Los Angeles, the California state government established the Clean Air Resources Board (CARB) to regulate air pollution and air quality within the state. And since then, most developing countries have put in place, with greater or lesser success, similar legislation.

Looking beyond local air pollution, during the 1980s, depletion of the Earth's ozone layer brought about international political action, culminating in the Montreal Protocol in 1987, to reduce production and use of chlorofluorocarbons (CFCs). Since the 1990s, global warming, resulting from the accumulation of greenhouse gases in the atmosphere, has been the subject of prolonged scientific debate and international diplomacy. Indeed, climate change and air pollution have now become environmental hot topics for much of the urbanized world.

Climate change

Since the start of the Industrial Revolution, the world has emitted growing volumes of carbon dioxide (CO_2) and other greenhouse gases (GHGs).[6] The vast majority of this pollution is derived from the combustion of fossil fuels – hydrocarbon substances formed from fossilized remains of biomass that have been exposed to heat and pressure over hundreds of millennia. These substances have been chemically and physically separated from the Earth's atmosphere for all of human history – up to the past 200 years, that is. The result of their release has been an increase in the Earth's temperature, setting in course a number of changes to the global climate. A brief summary of these phenomena is given in Box 2.2.

Atmospheric GHG levels, which stood at 280ppm (parts per million) before the Industrial Revolution, have increased by 54 per cent and are now above 430ppm. What is especially worrying is that, while the first 50ppm increase in concentration took place over two centuries, the later 100ppm surge occurred over a mere three decades. As Figure 2.7 demonstrates, average atmospheric temperatures have followed this increase in GHG concentrations and by 2000 were 0.5°C higher than in the pre-industrial era.

Based on studies from the Intergovernmental Panel on Climate Change[7] (IPCC, 2007), if society stabilized global GHG emissions at 2005 rates, GHG concentrations would rise to 550ppm by 2050. However, at current emissions growth rates, the 550ppm level could be reached by 2035. According to Stern (2006), there is a 99 per cent chance that such an increase in GHG concentrations would lead to an atmospheric temperature increase greater than 2°C over

Box 2.2 Global Warming 101

Think of GHGs in the atmosphere acting as a semipermeable skin surrounding the Earth. Every time the sun's rays try to pass this skin, some are reflected back into space while others reach the Earth's surface and remain 'trapped' between the Earth's surface and the skin. Over time, atmospheric GHG concentrations have reached an equilibrium that ensures the relatively stable weather conditions we enjoy on Earth. Indeed, if it were not for GHGs, the average temperature on the planet would drop by 32°C to −18°C (Figure 2.6).

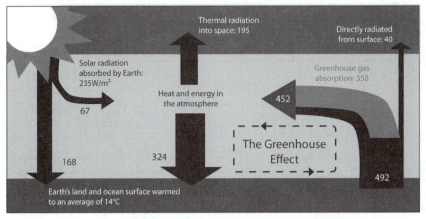

Figure 2.6 *Classic greenhouse effect illustration*

This 'ideal' level of atmospheric GHG is achieved through a delicate balance in the Earth's capacity to absorb GHGs – through trees, oceans, micro-organisms and so on – and the rate at which it produces such gases. However, since the end of the 18th century, with the growth of industry, rapid urbanization and increased use of motorized transport, the rate of growth of GHG emissions has accelerated far beyond the Earth's ability to reabsorb these gases. What is more, having cut down forests, we have destroyed important GHG 'sinks'. As a result, every year the concentration of GHGs in the atmosphere has gradually increased, thus also increasing the Earth's temperature. To reverse the warming process, we now need to reduce our emissions to a level far below the Earth's natural absorption rate.

the next half century. Furthermore, at current rates, GHG concentrations would triple by the end of the century, exposing the world to a 50 per cent risk of an atmospheric temperature increase greater than 5°C. While the thought of a 5°C temperature increase might sound pleasant during harsh winter months, it is important to keep in mind that 5°C is all that separates us from the last Ice Age. Do we really want to experience a Fire Age?

While sceptics have claimed that many of these risks are low-probability events, there is now evidence that even the most dire forecasts are proving too conservative. Greenland's glaciers, for example, were expected to melt within a 50-year timespan, but actually seem to be retreating at an exponential rate. In contrast with melting polar ice caps, Greenland's glaciers sit on the Earth's surface, as opposed to being submerged in the ocean. Imagine the titanic impact that the melting of such a large volume of ice could have on sea levels

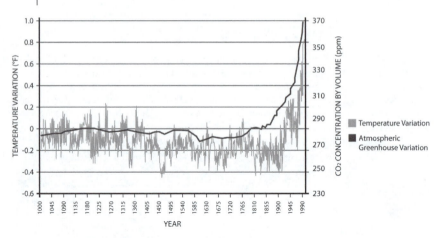

Figure 2.7 *'Hockey stick' diagram of atmospheric CO_2 concentrations and temperature*

and coastal areas. Indeed, melting glaciers is just one of the manifestations of climate change emerging 'prematurely'.

The latest forecasts by the IPCC show that much deeper cuts than those agreed upon in the Kyoto Protocol will be needed to prevent temperature increases greater than 2°C by mid-century – overall GHG emissions will need to be reduced by at least 25 per cent with respect to 2005 levels. Political consensus on the importance of curbing the growth in GHG emissions seems to be strong (Box 2.3), though as the COP16,[8] held in Cancun, showed, this has yet to result in an internationally accepted set of principles and tools for mitigation action.

As shown in Figure 2.8, 13 per cent of total global emissions come from the transportation sector. As discussed in the previous chapter, the growth in global vehicle fleet numbers is set to double, driven by increased penetration of vehicle ownership in emerging markets. As a result, an increase in GHG emissions from the transport sector is expected.

Until recently, transportation technology was seen to have limited GHG mitigation potential, and progress towards new industry standards was largely sidelined. However, the automobile poses both unique challenges and opportunities compared to the other major pollution sources.

In contrast with large stationary pollution sources, such as thermoelectric power plants, each individual ICV is a micro-scale, mobile emissions source. Consequently, it is not economically viable to capture the internal combustion engine's (ICE's) emissions for future storage as is being contemplated for power plants (see Chapter 6). However, it is also important to note that road vehicles have a very short lifespan (on average under 10 years) relative to other major polluters, such as large industrial or power generation projects (30 to 50 years). Consequently, if all new vehicles were carbon-neutral, the existing road vehicle fleet could be effectively decarbonized long before a recently contracted power plant is decommissioned.

Box 2.3 THE CLIMATE CHANGE POLICY DEBATE

Twenty years after the first 'Earth Summit' in Stockholm, the United Nations Conference on Environment and Development, held in Rio de Janeiro in 1992, was an unprecedented global initiative during which a number of agreements were signed calling for immediate collective action to protect the environment. Among these agreements was the United Nations Framework Convention on Climate Change (UNFCCC), which proposed 'stabilization of GHG concentrations in the atmosphere at a level that would prevent dangerous anthropogenic interference with the climate system'.

Despite entering the global agenda and persistent warning from the scientific community, climate change failed to secure a place in the political spotlight of individual countries for many years. This is understandable. While previous environmental issues – for example poor air quality – manifested themselves locally and were readily apparent to the public eye, climate change is an intangible threat, perceived by many to be uncertain and, even if real, affecting only future generations. Curbing it entails costs today to countries that face an array of other priorities, and in a context of constrained resources. The politics are further complicated by the fact that GHG accumulation has largely been the product of industrialized countries over the past 200 years, although emissions by the larger emerging economies (for example Brazil, China, India and Russia) are expected to surpass the former in the very near future. In the parlance of economists, climate change is a global externality that entails both efficiency and equity challenges given the principle, established in the UNFCCC, of 'common but differentiated responsibilities and respective capabilities' of countries.

Media coverage throughout the 1990s proved to be key to bringing the issues to public attention. The British newspaper *The Guardian* politicized the scientific debate during the late 1980s with a series of feature articles. Their coverage 'showed that many of the climate change claims were being eroded by lobbying pressures, mainly associated with the fossil-fuel industry' (Maslin, 2005). By the turn of the century, despite much criticism from rival publications, notably *The Times* in the UK and most of the American media, global warming and climate change were no longer seen as a sensationalist news story but had become a part of the set of major challenges faced by society.

And, indeed, the challenge seems truly immense. Consider, for instance, the Kyoto Protocol. Adopted in 1997, this was the first international agreement focused on climate change to receive ample public attention. The protocol established specific GHG reduction targets for each industrialized country – an average reduction of 5.2 per cent relative to 1990 levels by 2012. It also proposed a number of mechanisms through which industrialized, traditionally polluting countries, could meet their reduction targets while simultaneously benefiting developing countries, through the sale of carbon emissions reductions credits by the latter.

Despite noble promises made during international meetings, the United Nations failed to secure the necessary backing from industrialized countries when the treaty was opened for signatures in 1998. Indeed, it was not until 2002 that even the European Union, Japan and Canada ratified their commitments. The protocol only entered into force in February 2005, following Russia's ratification of the agreement, and even then, major polluting economies such as the US (the world's largest polluter in absolute terms until very recently) and Australia (the largest polluter in per capita terms) continued to avoid emissions reductions commitments.

Local air pollution

Aside from Hollywood, Los Angeles (LA) is best known to the outside world for endless stretches of congested freeways. Not surprisingly, it has also earned the dubious reputation of being the American city with the worst level of air quality for over half a century. The situation reached catastrophic levels in the late 1950s and 1960s. During this period, the city faced between 30 and 40 days

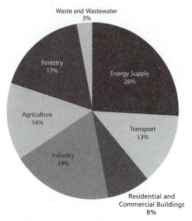

Figure 2.8 *Emissions by sector*

Source: IPCC (2007)

annually with Stage 2 smog alerts, calling for children and the elderly to stay indoors. In addition, the city faced the less critical Stage 1 smog alerts for some two-thirds of the remaining days of the year (Wachs, 1993).

However, LA is only one of many examples of a problem that is becoming increasingly prevalent in other fast-growing cities, such as Shanghai, Bangkok, Mumbai and Dhaka in Asia and Mexico City, São Paulo and Santiago in Latin America, to name but a few. Perhaps the strongest argument against the ICV is that it is one of the most significant sources of urban air pollution worldwide, notably in the fast-growing cities of developing countries, where vehicle owner-ship rates are soaring.

Local air pollution concerns focus on those toxins that have an impact on human health and the local environment.[9] Ideally, engines provide the complete combustion of a pure fuel and pure oxygen, thus resulting only in CO_2 and H_2O exhaust gases. The reality, however, is that neither the fuel nor the oxygen are pure and the combustion is incomplete, which leads to the emission of pollut-ants, as described in Box 2.4.

While the general public is widely aware of the problems of air pollution, its cost to society has been largely understated. Air pollution costs governments billions of dollars each year in healthcare alone. Add to this the cost to society of absence from work and premature death. Impacts on the environment – on buildings, forests and agriculture – also represent a cost to society. Thus it is not surprising that, depending on what is counted and on how, where and when it is counted, estimates of local air pollution costs associated with private transpor-tation will offer widely varying results. For instance, how does one quantify the cost of forest degradation caused by acid rain?

Due to disparate methodological approaches to vehicle air pollution studies, it is difficult to establish a definitive quantitative result on how much air pollu-tion actually costs society. As can be seen in Murphy and Delucchi (1998), however, while a few studies from the 1970s and early 1980s present estimates

---

BOX 2.4 POLLUTION FROM INCOMPLETE COMBUSTION

The (incomplete) combustion process is associated with three big environmental problems. First, it results in both carbon monoxide (CO) and unburned hydrocarbons (H_xC_y). If inhaled, CO is poisonous to humans and other animals as it bonds with haemoglobin in the blood, reducing the body's ability to take in oxygen and provoking suffocation. Meanwhile, unburned hydrocarbons have an array of adverse health effects depending on their nature. Though this is not an exhaustive list, some of these effects include cancer and heart and respiratory disease (such as asthma and bronchitis). Furthermore, combustion occurs in the 'natural' air, as opposed to pure oxygen, which results in the production of nitrogen oxides (NO_x). These substances in turn cause a festival of environmental destruction – from visibility-reducing smog to acid rain that damages property, water resources, forests and agriculture. To complete the trio, most fuels carry impurities such as sulphur. The subsequent combustion of sulphur results in the production of sulphur dioxide (SO_2), contributing to acid rain.

---

below US$10 billion per year, since the late 1980s estimates have only increased, reaching as high as US$220 billion in 1990 (Miller and Moffet, 1993), which, assuming that the air pollution problem has not deteriorated, represents around 1.5 per cent of GDP in 2005. If these estimates are roughly right, the use of government revenues directed towards the development and implementation of clean transportation solutions clearly would not only help compensate for the initial investment required but be well justified in terms of offsetting future public sector costs.

The local or global trade-off

In the past few decades, government regulation has effectively resulted in a reduction in the emissions factor of toxic local air pollutants, through the introduction of catalytic converters and the improved efficiency of combustion processes. By providing a more complete combustion of the fuel, these improvements ensure that carbon monoxide and unburned hydrocarbon residues react fully (Pecorelli et al, 2010). Given the fact that ICE technology has achieved what seems to be an optimal combustion process (Chapter 3), today only an improvement in vehicle fuel efficiency – for instance through reduced engine power or vehicle weight – can further reduce emissions factors from ICVs.

Furthermore, improvements in combustion in the past were achieved at the cost of creating more CO_2 emissions. Thus, until recently, environmental policies implicitly faced a trade-off between the control of toxic pollutants and CO_2. However, the concern with global warming and climate change has introduced gCO_2/km as a key emission factor to be regulated in the transportation sector. Notice that this in no way diminishes the relevance of local air pollution concerns and policy. This book makes use of gCO_2/km as a catch-all pollution indicator, recognizing the potential local air pollution co-benefits to be derived from addressing the now critical CO_2 problem in the transportation sector.[10]

Big Auto and petroleum industry lobbyists have two weak yet unrelenting arguments against future commitments to cleaning up vehicle technology. First, they claim that EU vehicle manufacturers voluntarily meet tight emissions standards (compared, for instance, to those in the US market), such that further tightening would not be achievable. Second, they accuse politicians of creating an unfavourable business environment and threaten to redirect their business somewhere more welcoming.

The reality does not bear out their claims. The EU currently imposes no legally binding emissions standards. The European Commission has repeatedly proposed obligatory targets, but these have consistently been blocked as a result of strong opposition from the European Automobile Manufacturers Association (ACEA). In 1998, a voluntary agreement between the European Commission and the ACEA established voluntary targets of $140gCO_2/km$ and $130gCO_2/km$ for new vehicles, to be reached by 2008 and 2015 respectively. However, only two companies, Fiat and Peugeot, reached the 2008 target in time, while the market average remained $153gCO_2/km$.

Across the Atlantic, the story is much the same. The US Federal Government has historically rejected mandatory CO_2 emissions standards, opting rather to work with fuel economy standards – notably during the aftermath of the 1970s oil crises. More recently, California made attempts to establish state-level CO_2 emissions standards, but these were successfully blocked from taking effect by the last Bush Administration. In contrast, President Obama has promised to establish mandatory federal CO_2 standards, though the details are still being negotiated. It should be noted that the US average fuel economy is nearly half – and consequently CO_2 emissions nearly double – that of the EU. Consequently, the US Federal Government will have to require substantial improvements to new vehicles if it is just to catch up with Europe.

Nevertheless, on an individual basis, there are some manufacturers producing specific vehicles which greatly exceed these standards. For example, according to the UK Department of Transport, the Toyota Prius and the SMART fortwo cabriolet (yes, its name is spelled in modest, small case all the way through), shown in Figure 2.9, offer up to 29 per cent emissions reduction compared to the EU's 2015 target.

(a)   *(b)*

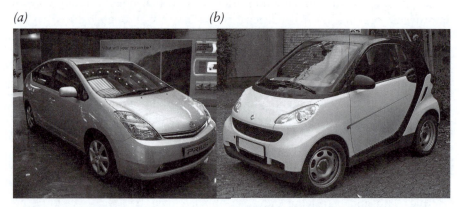

Figure 2.9 *Low emissions vehicles: (a) Toyota Prius and (b) Smart fortwo*

Sources: (a) Pawel Golsztajn (from Wikimedia Commons); (b) Matthias93 (from Wikimedia Commons)

As far as unfavourable business conditions are concerned, it is fair to say that the Japanese manufacturers have repeatedly demonstrated that such claims are unfounded. Indeed, even without significant government support, the early development of hybrid electric vehicles (HEVs) has given them a position of dominance in a market undergoing important changes.

Fortunately, the most recent government initiatives, following the 2008 financial collapse, have been largely welcomed by the automobile industry. Rather than focusing on the supply side and establishing standards, governments have provided consumers with financial incentives to purchase clean vehicles, making them competitive against gas-guzzlers without directly impacting manufacturers' balance sheets. These initiatives have indirectly helped to fuel a rebound in demand in the automobile industry and point to policy options that should be considered in any proposed shift to more sustainable automobile solutions.

However, while financial incentives provide an excellent mechanism for introducing new technologies, unless the next generation of ICVs comes with an emissions collector in place of the exhaust pipe, urban areas will continue to suffer from ever-worsening air quality. Unfortunately, as will be discussed in Chapters 3 and 4, ICV engine technology has reached a technological ceiling whereby efficiency gains and emissions reductions are both marginal or will soon become prohibitively expensive. So before getting to that discussion, let's again briefly consider the alternatives for reducing the ICV's dependence on petroleum.

The Alternatives

The factors discussed in the previous sections of this chapter suggest that moving to alternative energy sources is inevitable. The future will require a personal mobility solution which addresses both energy security and environmental concerns at global and local levels. The options being considered today involve predominantly replacing petroleum with biofuels and the electrification of vehicles.

Biofuels

Many argue that the rational carbon-neutral alternative to petroleum would be the use of biofuels in existing ICVs. Biomass-derived fuels ('biofuels'), such as ethanol and biodiesel, offer many benefits as a petroleum replacement. To begin with, they can be used in conventional ICVs and within the context of the existing refuelling infrastructure with minor or no adjustments – as has been demonstrated for over three decades now in Brazil (Box 2.5).

Biofuels are derived from purpose-grown energy crops, such as elephant grass or sugarcane. As they grow, they absorb CO_2 from the air and convert it into carbohydrate matter through photosynthesis. With time, these plants would naturally die and decompose, releasing their carbon content back into

---

BOX 2.5 THE BRAZILIAN PROÁLCOOL PROGRAMME

The Brazilian Proálcool Programme is the most successful alternative energy initiative resulting from the oil crises of the 1970s. Initially supported by government incentives and subsidies, the country's sugarcane-ethanol producers have become a major independent industrial power-house.

The Proálcool Programme was seen as key to the government's goal to reduce the Brazilian economy's oil dependence from around 40 per cent to 20 per cent over the following decade. In 1975, all unused sugarcane production was channelled to ethanol production. The government required that all petrol be mixed with a minimum of 20 per cent anhydrous ethanol for use in unmodified petrol ICVs. Sugarcane producers benefited from these plans because the government guaranteed ethanol purchases at an equivalent international sugar price.

The second oil shock (1979) increased already elevated oil prices from US$18/bbl (US$54/bbl in 2008 prices) to US$31/bbl (US$90/bbl in 2008 prices). The oil shock also increased popular support for the government's initiative. Refuelling stations were required to supply pure (hydrous) ethanol for the new fleet of ICVs operating solely on this fuel. Ethanol prices were fixed at 60 per cent of petrol prices between 1979 and 1990 (taking into account the relative efficiency of the fuels) and lower sales taxes were charged (and still are) for ethanol ICVs.

With significant oil price drops in the late 1980s, ethanol subsidies became too great a burden for the government to bear and were abandoned during what came to be known as 'the lost decade' of economic growth for Brazil and most other Latin American countries. Without the government's guaranteed purchases of the fuel and with a simultaneous increase in the international price of sugar, Brazilian sugarcane producers halted most ethanol production, substituting it with increased sugar production. In 1990, the Proálcool Programme seemed to have disappeared, along with public faith in the ethanol industry.

However, by the end of the 1990s, sugarcane producers, seeking to expand their business, managed a turnaround. By 2003, they had raised sugarcane productivity by 50 per cent relative to 1980 and were able to supply ethanol at a competitive, unsubsidized price against petrol. The industry has continued to improve production and ethanol has remained competitive even in periods of low oil prices, such as during the aftermath of the 2008 financial crisis. In January 2010, ethanol was being sold at R$1.99/litre (US$1.18/L) while petrol was at R$2.89/litre (US$1.72/L).

It is important to understand that a straight volumetric price comparison, as above, is not enough to demonstrate competitive pricing. Rather, one must account for the fact that ethanol has a lower energy density, which, on average, results in a 40 per cent increase in volumetric fuel consumption.[11] Thus the volumetric petrol price must be at least 40 per cent higher for ethanol to be competitive, which it does based on January 2010 prices. Not bad for an industry that, only a decade earlier, was said to be highly dependent on government support.

---

the air. In turn, new vegetation would grow in their place, restarting the cycle, as shown in Figure 2.10. While ICVs running on biofuels do emit CO_2, they are considered to be carbon-neutral – in other words they do not increase GHG concentrations, because emissions from the use of biofuels and those that would occur from plant decomposition are thought to be roughly the same.

However, although biofuels may be considered carbon-neutral, from a local air pollution perspective this is irrelevant since biofuels will continue to emit exhaust gases. In fact, biofuels result in a significant increase in toxic and carcinogenic gases, notably carbon monoxide, unburned hydrocarbons and aldehydes. Table 2.2 compares average emissions factors for new vehicles using Brazilian gasoline[12] and ethanol.

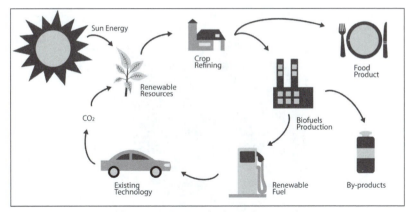

Figure 2.10 *Biofuels carbon cycle*

Source: FAOSTAT, IIASA

Furthermore, widespread global use of biofuels has certain key limitations, notably land availability (Figure 2.11) and the associated trade-offs with respect to food production.[13] According to the IEA, global biofuel production in 2007 reached 1EJ (exajoule), which is equivalent to 1 per cent of global road transportation fuel demand. This level of production required the cultivation of 1 per cent of the world's arable land (IEA, 2007). At this rate, it is not difficult to see how increasing arable land use for biofuel production would soon conflict with the arable land needed for food production.

Crop yields and fuel production efficiencies are expected to increase significantly, particularly if lignocellulose matter becomes a viable biofuel feedstock. Lignocellulose matter, which is a largely wasted by-product of existing crops, could represent 25 to 50 per cent of global bioenergy production by 2050, thus helping to reduce the burden on the food/fuel trade-off. However, the potential for crop yield improvement is limited, particularly if high-yield crops such as Brazilian sugarcane, which cannot be suitably grown in temperate climates, are used as the benchmark for future crop yields.

The world's population is still growing in absolute numbers and much of it is malnourished. With increased income per capita, both food and fuel requirements can be expected to increase. Thus both food and fuel security are and will continue to be major challenges in the decades ahead, albeit for distinct regions of the world.

Table 2.2 *Emissions from gasoline and ethanol vehicles*

Fuel	Pollutants			
	CO	HC	CHO	CO_2
Brazilian gasoline	3.73g/L	0.90g/L	0.023g/L	2167g/L
	0.33g/km	0.079g/km	0.00204g/km	191.77g/km
Pure ethanol	3.67g/L	0.86g/L	0.109g/L	1382g/L
	0.47g/km	0.11g/km	0.014g/km	176.95g/km

Source: Pecorelli et al (2010)

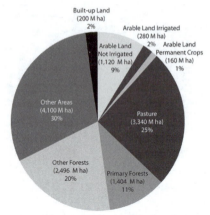

Figure 2.11 *Arable land*

Despite the potential of biofuels as a carbon-neutral substitute for the fossil option, they would fail to be environmentally friendly at the local level and would present a threat to food crop resources if cultivated on a global scale. Indeed, it is fair to say that neither petroleum-derived nor biomass-derived fuels can provide sustainable long-term energy for private transportation.[14]

Electrification

Without a suitable combustion fuel, vehicle technology is set for a technological paradigm shift – away from the ICV and towards electric propulsion. Given that society will continue using automobiles for transportation, then battery electric vehicles (BEVs)[15] provide the only technological platform that can fully address both energy and environmental concerns at global and local levels.

First, national power grids are, at least in theory, inherently independent of any single energy source. Thus BEVs can eliminate the transportation sector's direct petroleum dependence altogether, providing a giant step towards avoiding oil depletion and reducing exposure to supply constraints. Second, BEVs are more efficient than ICVs on a 'well-to-wheel' basis (Chapter 6). Thus, even where the grid is powered predominately by polluting coal, the BEV ensures a reduction in emissions on a per kilometre basis.

However, in the short run, BEVs are unlikely to prove competitive in many market segments. While the book argues that the BEV will prove to be the ultimately long-run solution to private transportation, it will recognize and discuss the role of various types of hybrid EV solutions as an intermediate step. Indeed, hybrid technologies, which combine combustion- and electric-based propulsion systems, offer substantial efficiency gains against ICVs, particularly if the hybrid's ICE is only used as a back-up for extending range in long trips. In fact, recent fuel economy gains in 'conventional' vehicles are largely the result of the ICV's hybridization with electric motors (for example the Toyota Prius in Figure 2.9). However, in the longer term, assuming engineers are able to develop batteries that provide a suitable range at a competitive price, why make the BEV dirtier by adding an ICE?

Up to this point, the discussion has focused on the market forces and environmental constraints that are acting against the future of petroleum-based transportation as a whole. However, this neglects perhaps the strongest driving factor towards sustainable transportation: EVs are a better product. The remainder of the book will detail and elaborate on this point. The following chapters will provide an in-depth evaluation of the ICV and several types of EVs from the technological, economic and environmental perspectives.

Seizing the Opportunity

In June 2008, *The Economist* published a special report on future energy (*The Economist*, 2008) that, among other things, forecast the next economic boom based on the rise of clean energy technology. In September, however, Lehman Bros collapsed, bringing down much of the financial sector and the global economy. By January 2009, oil prices – which had peaked at US$147/bbl six months earlier, acting as a key driving factor towards the development of alternative energy and transport technologies – had tumbled to US$33/bbl. Meanwhile, clean energy investments during the first quarter of 2009 collapsed by 53 per cent year-on-year to US$13.3 billion (New Energy Finance, 2009a).

Against all odds, however, clean energy development has rebounded from the initial impact of the 2008 economic downturn and actually accelerated its advance during the aftermath of the crisis. During the second quarter of 2009, investments in this sector went up to US$28.6 billion, while stock prices surged 36 per cent based on the NEX clean energy index, compared to a 15 per cent rise in the S&P 500 index.

Politicians in the US, Europe and Asia see the 2008 crisis and the economic stimulus packages that have emerged as an important opportunity to move away from the dirty technologies of yesteryear and towards the clean technologies that will ensure future energy and economic sustainability. Furthermore, an August 2009 Gallup opinion poll, which asked consumers for their perception of 19 key industries, ranked oil and gas joint last, just ahead of automotive. Even banking did better, coming in 15th place! For a society that was on the verge of 'going green', recent events appear to have provided a shove towards this goal.

According to Michael Liebreich, CEO of New Energy Finance (2009b), a leading clean energy consulting firm:

> *Energy conversion, power storage and efficiency stocks were previously regarded as unglamorous, but are now liked because of two new influences. One is the increased likelihood that electric cars will be important in the transport systems of the next decade. The other is the fact that the single biggest slice of the US$163*

billion green stimulus cash promised by the governments of major economies has been ear-marked for increasing energy efficiency.

All of this suggests that, in a rare moment in history, national and international political agendas are aligned with public opinion and pointing to the possibility of taking important steps toward sustainable development.

Notes

1 See OECD (2006) for a discussion on decoupling of economic growth, energy consumption and environmental impact.
2 Those who claim 'we have lived this challenge before' have perhaps failed to realize that, in the next four decades, global power consumption is expected to double, expanding by 15 terawatts, the same amount which the world has taken approximately 200 years to build up!
3 In 1972, *The Limits to Growth*, an influential study commissioned by the Club of Rome, warned that the elevated rates of economic and population growth would soon reach a ceiling due to the Earth's finite resources. Energy consumption, and fossil fuel use especially, became key concerns. While the anticipated growth ceiling has long been surpassed – owing in part to increased energy efficiency, decreased resource waste and increased productivity – the book's underlying message is still valuable.
4 This has also led to hefty military costs. According to the RAND Corporation (2009), American defence expenditure with the specific objective of protecting oil resources currently varies between US$67.5 billion and US$91 billion annually. These indirect costs amount to a further call for a diversification of fuel supplies.
5 OPEC, established in 1960, is the cartel for major petroleum exporting countries. As of 2008, the OPEC cartel is comprised of 12 countries: Algeria, Angola, Ecuador, Iran, Iraq, Kuwait, Libya, Nigeria, Qatar, Saudi Arabia, the United Arab Emirates and Venezuela.
6 In addition to CO_2, GHGs include water vapour, methane, nitrous oxides and CFCs.
7 The IPCC is an intergovernmental scientific organization created in 1988 by the World Meteorological Organization and the United Nations Environment Programme to study the risks of anthropogenic climate change. It has since issued four major reports as research and analytical efforts produced increasingly robust results. Despite persisting uncertainties, the *Fourth Assessment Report*, issued in February 2007, has come to be widely accepted as a reference for policymakers and others. It lays out four scenarios, with estimates of the increase in global temperatures ranging from 1.1°C to 6.4°C. The 550ppm by 2050 scenario referred to in the main text is relatively conservative, and does not include, for instance, the impact of melting polar ice caps.
8 COP15: 15th Conference of the Parties that, under the auspices of the United Nations, are negotiating global climate change policy and the successor measures to the Kyoto Protocol, which expires in 2012.
9 Another underestimated burden of the ICV is noise pollution. In densely populated urban areas, average noise pollution far exceeds human comfort levels. For instance, in Bangkok noise levels range from 75dB to 80dB, which is two to three times the human comfort limit (Cervero, 1998). To illustrate the point, this is roughly equiva-

lent to having a garbage disposal truck outside your door all day and night. Reader might think they have become accustomed to modern levels of urban noise pollution and thus be inclined to dismiss this as a significant externality of the ICV. However, ICV noise pollution was estimated to have cost the American real-estate market a total of US$9 billion in 1989 (or US$15.6 billion in 2008 terms) (Murphy and Delucchi, 1998). On a societal level this is a non-negligible economic cost.

10 A quick review of the literature on pollution from private transportation reveals a shift in emphasis away from the discussion of toxic pollutants towards CO_2. This may be a result of the progress made in meeting local air pollution standards over recent decades.

11 Notice that the exact volumetric fuel consumption disparity between ethanol and gasoline will vary depending on the specific vehicle. This is due to the fact that, despite the lower energy density, ethanol fuel has a higher octane rating and a lower combustion temperature compared to petrol. This allows engines to be design with a higher compression ratio, providing a 5 to 10 per cent increase in acceleration and top speed. Thus an engine designed for optimal ethanol performance can actually be marginally downsized without compromising performance and thus lowering fuel consumption.

12 Note that standard Brazilian gasoline is composed of approximately 20 per cent ethanol. If pure gasoline were used, CO_2 emissions would be higher, while CO, HC and CHO figures would be lower.

13 It is also worth noting that, while biofuels are said to be carbon neutral, widespread production of such fuels greatly increases the risks of deforestation, as crop land availability becomes more scarce.

14 Although this discussion is focused on private transport, it is worth noting that other modes of transportation – notably aviation and freight applications, which represent approximately 25 per cent of petroleum consumption in the transportation sector in the US – are well suited for a transition to biofuel-powered solutions.

15 Chapter 4 will demonstrate that batteries hold the most promise as a source of energy for EVs – consequently, this book focuses on the prospects of the battery EV.

References

Blanch, F. (2009) 'Oil could exceed $100 next year', *FT.com*, www.ft.com/cms/s/0/542bb6d6-c264-11de-be3a-00144feab49a.html, accessed 26 October 2009

Cervero, R. (1998) *The Transit Metropolis: A Global Inquiry*, Island Press, Washington, DC

The Economist (2008) 'The future of energy', *The Economist*, 19 June

Ehsani, M., Gao, Y., Gay, S. E. and Emadi, A. (2004) *Modern Electric, Hybrid Electric, and Fuel Cell Vehicles: Fundamentals, Theory, and Design*, CRC Press, Boca Raton, FL

Electrification Coalition (2009) *Electrification Roadmap: Revolutionizing Transportation and Achieving Energy Security*, Electrification Coalition, Washington, DC

Hughes, J. D. (2004) 'Can energy supply meet forecast world demand? Energy supply and demand trends, forecasts and implications for a sustainable energy future', Energy at Dalhousie Lecture Series presentation, Nova Scotia

IEA (International Energy Agency) (2007) 'Biofuel production', *IEA Energy Technology Essentials*, Paris

IEA (2009a) *World Energy Outlook 2009*, International Energy Agency, Paris

IEA (2009b) *Key World Energy Statistics 2009*, International Energy Agency, Paris

IEA (2009c) *Transport, Energy and CO$_2$: Moving Towards Sustainability*, International Energy Agency, Paris

IPCC (Intergovernmental Panel on Climate Change) (2007) *IPCC Fourth Assessment Report: Climate Change 2007 (AR4)*, IPCC, Geneva

Maslin, M. (2005) *Global Warming: A Very Short Introduction*, Oxford University Press, Oxford, UK

Meadows, D. H., Meadows, D. L., Randers, J., and Behrens, W. W. (1972) *The Limits to Growth*, Universe Books, New York

Miller, P. and Moffet, J. (1993) *The Price of Mobility: Uncovering the Hidden Costs of Transportation*, Natural Resources Defense Council, New York

Murphy, J. and Delucchi, M. (1998) 'A review of the literature on the social cost of motor vehicle use in the United States', *Journal of Transportation and Statistics*, vol 1, no 1, Bureau of Transportation Statistics (www.bts.gov), January, pp15–42

New Energy Finance (2009a) 'Huge variety in performance as clean energy shares rise in third quarter of 2009', press release, 1 October

New Energy Finance (2009b) 'Clean energy shares rebound by 36 per cent in Q2 on hopes for easing of credit squeeze and optimism about "green stimulus" funds', press release, 2 July

OECD (2006) *Decoupling the Environmental Impacts of Transport from Economic Growth*, OECD Publishing, Paris

Pecorelli, L. A.,???, J., Particelli, F. and Serra, J. V. (2010) [REFERENCE YET TO BE COMPLETED BY AUTHOR]

RAND Corporation (2009) *Imported Oil and National Security*, RAND Corporation, Santa Monica, CA

Stern, N. (2006) *Stern Review on the Economics of Climate Change*, UK Office of Climate Change (www.occ.gov.uk), available at www.sternreview.org.uk

Wachs, M. (1993) 'Learning from Los Angeles: Transport, urban form, and air quality', *Transportation*, vol 20, pp329–354

Part II

Technological Feasibility

3

Vehicle Propulsion

If we did the things we are capable of, we would astound ourselves.
Thomas Edison

Part I of this book looked at the rise of the ICV's technological dominance in the automotive industry over the course of the 20th century – and forecast its decline due to a combination of factors that are pointing towards a shift to electric propulsion in the near future. Part II will evaluate the merits of the electric solution, asking: *Can existing EV technology already provide an efficient and sustainable mode of transportation?*

The following two chapters compare the ICV and EV, providing the reader with an understanding of their basic operating principles, their limitations and the advances that can be expected in the near term for either type of vehicle. The discussion aims to demonstrate that the technology is available today to produce well-performing EVs and that the EV is indeed a superior machine. Chapter 5 will expand this evaluation to consider the infrastructure requirements and the broader sustainability of this technological shift.

A Few Basic Concepts

Engineers are trained to function in a world of acronyms and classifications. While this is generally extremely helpful when handling an array of variables and concepts, it often becomes a barrier to communicating with the outside world. Vehicle technology, and in particular EV technology,[1] is no exception. In this light, some basic references for the discussion will need to be established – decomposing the vehicle into its core components as well as defining efficiency from an engineering perspective, as this will be a key concept in the analysis of the ICV and EV technologies throughout the book.

Vehicle components

While a vehicle is made up of thousands of subcomponents – chassis, body, seats, mirrors, radio systems and so forth – this discussion is merely concerned with those components that are essential to its primary objective – motion. Figure 3.1 shows the core subcomponents required for ICV and EV operation. Throughout the discussion the author will refer to the vehicle propulsion (VP) and the energy supply (ES) systems – both of which are at the core of the automobile's function.

The VP system is more than just the motor or engine.[2] It can be thought of as the group of components that participate in the conversion of stored energy, supplied by the ES system, into kinetic energy at the wheels – in other words the energy that ultimately propels the vehicle. While the motor is the heart of this system, it would not be able to accomplish its task without complementary organs. These organs include the transmission, differentials, camshafts, crankshafts and more. It is essential to recognize the existence and relevance of these complementary organs in what follows, but they will not be discussed at length and the reader need not be concerned with understanding them in detail.

If the heart and other organs of a vehicle are its VP system, then the ES system can be thought of as the lungs, veins and arteries that supply the vehicle with energy. While the 'fuel' that is stored and carried is central to the ES system, it alone is meaningless without the mechanism by which it is transferred and controlled – much as the motor is necessary but insufficient to ensure propulsion. The ICV ES consists of the traditional combustion fuel and fuel tank arrangement, but EVs can have alternative configurations – comprised of batteries, fuel cells and ultracapacitors.

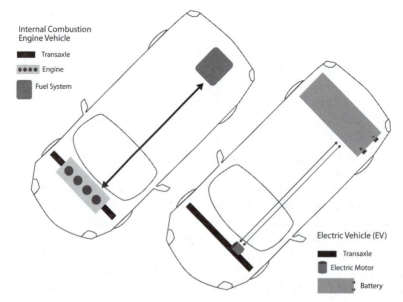

Figure 3.1 *Vehicle components*

Breaking down a vehicle's key operating systems into the VP and ES systems is meant to facilitate the analysis. The reader should keep in mind, nonetheless, that this is a somewhat arbitrary distinction, as these systems' functions interact and overlap.

Efficiency

Strictly speaking, the role of an automobile is to convert stored energy into useful work for the purpose of transporting someone or something including itself from A to B. This basic concept leads to the question: How much energy is needed to perform this task? At the heart of this discussion is the concept of efficiency, which, unless explicitly defined from the start, proves to be the source of unnecessary confusion. This text will refer to a variety of distinct efficiencies, making an explicit definition of the terms particularly pertinent.

In the eyes of the engineer, the concept of efficiency derives from the discipline of thermodynamics, which is effectively the study of energy conversion. Thinking back to secondary school science, the reader should recall an abundance of terms relating to energy – chemical energy, atomic energy, kinetic energy, potential energy, thermal energy, and the list goes on. Some may also recall how one type of energy may be transformed into another, as long as the process abides by the first and second laws of thermodynamics. The first law teaches us that energy cannot be created or destroyed, such that the amount of energy in a system can only change if energy is exchanged with an external system. The second law tells us that, as energy is transformed from one form to another, the amount of *useful* energy in a system – in other words energy that is available to do work – diminishes. This tells us that in the real world, some of the energy involved in a conversion process will invariably become useless heat energy, eventually lost to the surrounding environment.

Engineers are interested in energy conversion efficiency – how much of the energy input is actually converted into useful energy. Each type of energy conversion is burdened by different losses that vary depending on operating conditions. To evaluate a complex system – in which multiple conversion processes are occurring in succession, each having a different efficiency – it becomes important to break it down into clearly defined and manageable subsystems.

In automotive energy efficiency, this is especially relevant. A distinction has already been made between the VP and ES systems, examined in this and the following chapters respectively. Together, these encompass all of the energy conversion processes taking place *within the vehicle*. Tank-to-wheel (T2W) efficiency can be derived by taking the product of the corresponding VP and ES efficiencies. However, given that energy input for ICVs and grid-powered EVs are not comparable, a comprehensive efficiency evaluation will need to consider the efficiency of the energy system which feeds them, known as the well-to-tank (W2T) efficiency. Chapter 6 provides a W2T analysis, which is used together with the T2W efficiency to derive either vehicle's well-to-wheel (W2W) efficiencies.

One final distinction should be made at this point between conventional 'fuel economy' (mpg or km/L) and engineering 'fuel efficiency' (T2W efficiency). Notice that while T2W efficiency is a key determinant of fuel economy, they are not equivalent terms. T2W efficiency is a dimensionless number that indicates the ratio between useful energy output at the wheel and original energy input from the tank. In contrast, fuel economy is a ratio of distance travelled and the corresponding fuel consumption. Unfortunately, the term fuel efficiency is often used interchangeably to refer to T2W efficiency and fuel economy. In this book, fuel efficiency is used exclusively to refer to the engineering T2W efficiency.

With the general reader in mind, I shall avoid as much as possible references to equations and scientific minutiae regarding the behaviour of batteries, motors and so on. For those seeking such detail, this field is well endowed with high-quality technical publications. Throughout the discussion, wherever relevant, specific sources for further reading will be indicated. The goal here is to provide the reader with the technological foundation to enable him or her to evaluate the merits and limitations of current and potential EV solutions, as compared to the ICV. Let's begin with an evaluation of the latter, with which the reader is likely to be more familiar.

The Internal Combustion Engine Vehicle

At the heart of the ICV propulsion system is the internal combustion engine (ICE). This discussion begins with a brief explanation of how the ICE converts chemical energy contained in the fuel into kinetic energy to propel the vehicle. The following section demonstrates how ICEs are inherently inefficient and have effectively reached their technological peak. Finally, an examination of the ICE's torque and power characteristics uncovers the origin of its inadequate performance.

Operating principle

As its name suggests, ICEs rely on the process of combustion to convert chemically stored energy present in fuels into heat energy to perform work on the engine pistons, ultimately leading to motion. As combustion occurs, the hydrocarbon chains contained in any fuel split apart and react with the air in the combustion chamber, forming new chemical substances and releasing heat energy. However, the formation of each substance requires, or uses up, a specific amount of energy – this is known as enthalpy. The goal of any engine thus must be to release more energy (in kinetic form) from the break-up of the hydrocarbon chains and their reaction with air than is consumed by the production of the substances that exit through the chamber's exhaust valve (Figure 3.2).

ICEs come in a variety of flavours: four-stroke, two-stroke, Wankel rotary, to name but a few. By far the single most common ICE used for four-wheel road transport purposes is the four-stroke engine, on which this discussion focuses henceforth. This is appropriate not only due to the market dominance of the

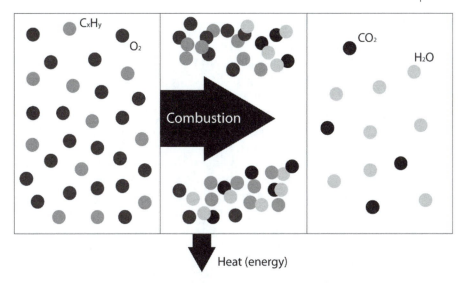

Figure 3.2 *The combustion process*

four-stroke engine, but also because no other combustion engine would provide a comprehensive advantage. As the name implies, the operation of a four-stroke engine involves four processes: intake, compression, combustion/expansion and exhaust; these are illustrated in Figure 3.3.

The reader is probably aware that an array of combustion fuels exist. However, as far as the present discussion of the ICE and the efficiency of the combustion cycle is concerned, these can be treated as one and the same.[3] Due to its supreme global dominance among combustion fuels for transportation, this discussion focuses on petrol, though the author will draw attention to other fuels where appropriate along the way.

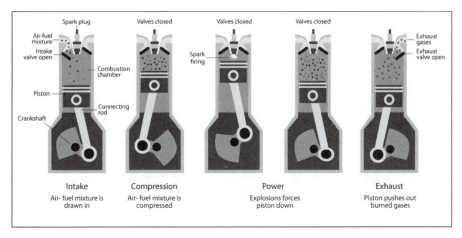

Figure 3.3 *ICE basic operating principle*

Cycle efficiency

The single most critical limitation of the ICE is that it is a heat engine. The reader might recall from secondary school physics that Carnot's Theorem can be used to show that an ideal heat engine fuelled by petrol would have a maximum energy efficiency of 73 per cent.[4] But while the Carnot Cycle is the basic conceptual building block of any heat engine, its underlying thermodynamic processes fail to hold in ICEs. The operation of petrol-driven ICEs is best described by the Otto Cycle (Figure 3.4), which has an ideal efficiency closer to 42 per cent, assuming, among a number of other conditions, that combustion occurs instantaneously and evenly, and that the combustion expansion process is adiabatic, which is to say no heat is lost to the surrounding chamber.

Before the reader gets either excited or discouraged by these ideal efficiency levels, it is necessary to draw attention to all the inevitable inefficiencies faced by a real heat engine compared to the ideal Otto Cycle. Just to give a taste of the challenge: combustion does not occur instantaneously or evenly as assumed by the Otto model, and the cycle is not adiabatic, with heat lost to the cylinder walls, reducing energy available to perform work on the piston. By this point, 40 per cent has already been shaved off the ideal Otto Cycle efficiency, despite having only considered losses in the cylinder.

Exiting the cylinder, valves are used for the intake of reactant gases as well as the exhaust of combustion products. The mass flow in and out of the cylinder occurs at such a rate (approaching the speed of sound) that fluid dynamic limitations cause a further 15–20 per cent reduction in efficiency.

Now recall that, while the ICE itself is the heart of the VP system, the system also depends on other organs in order to fulfil its ultimate mission. Alas, the VP system's complementary organs consist of hundreds of metallic moving parts – transmissions, camshafts, crankshafts and so on – rubbing and pulling and

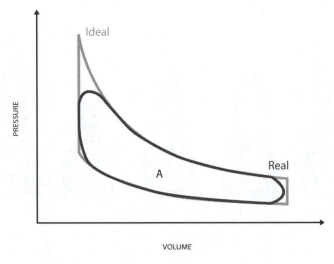

Figure 3.4 *Ideal Otto Cycle*

colliding into each other several thousand times per minute. Surprisingly, over the years engineers have managed to minimize the mechanical losses associated with these various interactions to around 15 per cent.

All things considered, the modern ICV's VP system gives around 15–18 per cent overall T2W energy efficiency! Depending on the analyst, foreseeable improvements could raise this by 20 per cent or 30 per cent (Boston Consulting Group, 2009; Credit Suisse, 2009). Do not be misled by these figures – such improvement would result in a still measly 18–23 per cent overall VP system efficiency. However, this would require, for instance, the use of expensive advanced ceramic materials to permit higher combustion temperatures within the cylinder. Thus it seems that efficiency improvements are reaching a practical limit in the case of the ICV.

To complicate matters further, combustion cycles are far from smooth processes, as VP components suffer enormous variations in stress and temperature caused by each individual explosion. From a mechanical standpoint, they are extremely complex.[5] No wonder a typical ICE's life expectancy is only around 200,000km before it presents serious problems. And to avoid early retirement from this short life, ICEs require periodic maintenance – oil and coolant change, transmission checks and so on. Interestingly, consumers have become so accustomed to these requirements that most do not realize how very expensive it is to merely maintain an ICE. Today's engines have been fine-tuned to ensure a mutually optimized performance in terms of energy efficiency and lifetime. There are no significant gains to be had.

Driving performance

The success of an automobile is rarely defined merely by its energy efficiency. If that were the case, ICVs would never have made it so far. Rather, driving performance – acceleration and top speed – tends to be the critical differentiating factor between any two vehicles. Indeed, while the ICEs used in conventional vehicles – petrol and diesel engines – are not based on the most efficient ICE cycles, they provide the only acceptable variable-speed operating performance.

Have you ever noticed how your engine behaves when you 'floor' it (in other words push the acceleration pedal to the bottom)? You should be able to observe that it becomes more responsive (you get more 'umph') as the rpm (engine speed in revolutions per minute) needle climbs, until it peaks at around 4000rpm. After that, the engine seems increasingly resistant to accelerate – 5000rpm, 6000rpm, 7000rpm – until, well, chances are you have shifted to the next gear because you were concerned with the engine's groans.

To understand driving performance one must begin with the concept of torque. Despite the popular misconception, it is not power, but rather torque, that best explains a vehicle's ability to accelerate. It is equally important to understand that peak torque is a poor performance indicator, since it is only achieved within a very narrow band of operating speed, as illustrated by a typical torque curve (Figure 3.5).

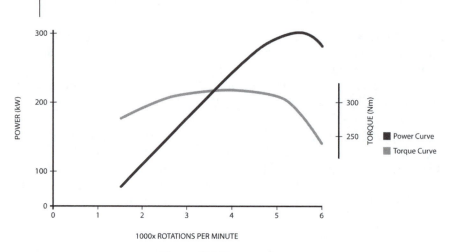

Figure 3.5 *Torque curve*

In practice, drivers require peak torque at low speeds, for example when accelerating away from a stop light. As driving speeds increase, torque requirements gradually decrease – once at high speeds, drivers rarely require full accelerating potential. It is clear from Figure 3.5 that ICE torque characteristics do not emulate driving performance requirements. To obtain better performance across typical driving speeds, engineers use multiple gears to match the ideal engine speeds with the wider vehicle speeds (Figure 3.6).

The point of this engine performance discussion is twofold. First, to highlight how, contrary to popular belief, ICEs have appalling performance – as will be shown, electric motors outperform ICEs hands down. More importantly, such limited performance characteristics impose the use of complex transmission solutions (multiple gears) on the ICE that ultimately restrict potential efficiency gains.

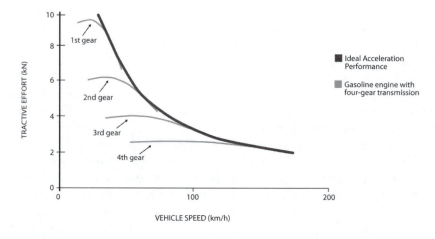

Figure 3.6 *Multiple gear torque curves*

The end of the road

It is undeniable that the ICE has played an invaluable role in the development of modern society and thus deserves a place among the greatest achievements of modern technology. The fact that ICEs are capable of withstanding such brutal self-abuse in itself is noteworthy. However, the fact that we rely so heavily on this self-destructive, inefficient (and polluting) technology should be disconcerting to all, even those hugely fascinated by this astonishing human achievement, such as the author himself. It is also clear that potential efficiency gains for the ICE seem to have reached a limit, at least as far as its VP system is concerned.

The Electric Vehicle

High efficiency, cutting-edge performance and environmental friendliness are just some of the advantages that EVs offer over ICVs. These benefits result from the substitution of the ICE-based VP system with an electric motor-based system. While the former involves a complex network of fast-moving components, the latter depends on the simple interaction between the electric motor, electronic control units (ECUs), and a drastically simplified transmission system.

Basic operating principle

At the heart of the electric VP system sits a device as universally prevalent in modern life as the Bic ballpoint pen – an electric motor (EM). Straight from the start of the day, you're probably awoken by an alarm clock operated by a simple EM. Then some of you use an electric toothbrush, electric shaver, hair dryer and so on. Eventually, you use the blender, fridge and so on to prepare breakfast. Get into your car and it runs at the turn of a key because of Kettering's electric starter motor (Chapter 1). At the office, you use an elevator or escalator to get to your floor that is kept at a comfortable temperature using an air conditioner, fan or central heater. You've finally sat at your desk where you turn on your computer, printer and other electronic devices, most of which depend in some way or other on EMs. Now look around as you busy yourself at work, enjoy your lunch or even after-work drinks – you should notice EMs everywhere. Indeed, without EMs modern life as we know it would cease to exist.

The EM's underlying operating principle is simple – an electric current flowing through a wire produces an electromagnetic field around it, which, when wrapped in a coil, temporarily exhibits the properties of a conventional magnet. If this coil, called an electromagnet, is placed in the proximity of another magnet, they will attract or repel each other, creating motion.

EMs are thus constructed by configuring such magnetic elements to produce a continuous rotational motion. As such, EMs consist of two fundamental elements – a stator (stationary element) and a rotor (rotating element) – which work together to convert electric current into kinetic energy. (This is the exact reverse of a power generator that uses kinetic energy to induce an electrical

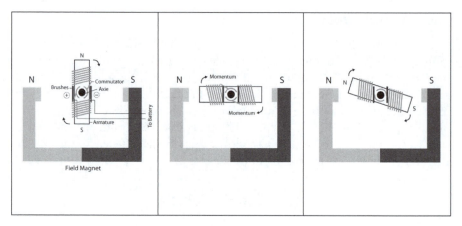

Figure 3.7 *Brushed DC motor*

current through a circuit.) The traditional brushed direct current (DC) EM is used here to illustrate the basic operating principle of an EM (Figure 3.7).

The EM is designed such that the electromagnetic field orientation continually varies in relation to the permanent magnet poles. This is crucial: uninterrupted rotation can only be achieved with the alternation of electromagnetic field polarity. If the electromagnetic field didn't alternate, the rotor would swing around 180° and stop as soon as the electromagnetic north aligned with the magnetic south, and vice versa. The switch in polarity is achieved by switching the direction of the DC current.

As Figure 3.7 illustrates, the brushed design is vital to ensure that the electromagnetic field polarity switches direction as the rotor swings 180° around the stator. The central flaw behind this direct current motor design is the brush-commutator connection. The presence of a physical contact between two components in relative motion reduces the motor's operational efficiency, life expectancy and reliability – here, however, in a far less drastic manner than in the case of the ICV.

Brushless EMs have existed since Nikola Tesla's 1888 invention of the alternating current (AC) motor. By using a permanent magnet as the rotor and an electromagnet fed by a variable power supply as the stator, the essential electromagnetic field variation was created without the need for additional parts to ensure continuous motion. Alas, given that batteries provide DC power supplies, EVs were restricted to the less efficient brushed EM designs until the development of power electronics.

Power electronics

From a technological perspective, modern EVs could be said to resemble a laptop more than an automobile. Indeed, what makes the modern EV competitive is largely the result of the late 20th-century microelectronics boom, which turned ECUs into a staple ingredient in our lives. They provide the brains for every electronic device we use and the mini-brains for each subcomponent within these devices. In the case of the modern EV, they have revolutionized EM power control technology.

ECUs are the devices that manage the amount of power/energy delivered to/consumed by the motor to drive the vehicle.[6] To do so, they vary the voltage, current and even frequency delivered to the EM, ensuring that the vehicle responds to the driver's inputs (how much he or she steps on the 'gas' pedal).

In the first battery EVs (BEVs), at the beginning of the 20th century, power control was achieved mechanically, using switches and rheostats (variable resistors). These mechanical systems were slow to respond to driver inputs, suffered from large amounts of energy dissipation (waste) and provided limited speed control. Today, ECUs activate power supplies in BEVs through digital commands, which provide infinitely faster response and smoother operating conditions. It is now possible to electronically manipulate both direct current and alternating current supplies into the exact signal required to meet driver requirements. This increase in operational control has provided engineers with a greater degree of flexibility in the design of modern EV motors. As such, the breakthrough that distinguishes BEV propulsion systems today with relation to those of early days is really the ECU.

The modern electric motor

The ECU's ability to manipulate the characteristics of the DC power that flows from a battery into an electric motor has allowed engineers to do away with the brush/commutator connection in conventional brushed DC motors. The lack of this physical contact between components improves motor efficiency, reliability (particularly at high operating speeds) and lifespan, while enabling maintenance-free operations. Thus there is now a strong trend towards brush-less solutions in automotive applications.

While the scientific principle behind the modern EM (the interaction between electromagnets and permanent magnets) remains unaltered, there is now a vast variety of EM design typologies, such that selecting an adequate solution for a specific application is no trivial task. This requires engineers to consider parameters such as operating speed range, power characteristics, reliability, efficiency, cost and life expectancy.

In the case of automotive application, EMs must meet, though not be limited to, some basic specifications, notably:

- power ratings around 100kW;
- torque ratings around 200Nm;
- good regenerative braking; and
- 10-year lifespan.

Modern EV development has homed in on three EM families that best suit these basic requirements – AC induction, AC switched reluctance and permanent magnet.

On paper, these solutions present very comparable performance, each offering marginal advantages in specific properties. A comprehensive and detailed technical evaluation of these three EMs alone could generate more than enough material for a book and technical EV texts typically dedicate entire chapters to this topic. In the next three paragraphs the author has attempted to provide a concise assessment of the three technologies.

AC induction motors have been the most widely deployed in a diverse range of applications and are thus the most mature and proven technology. Additionally, they are inexpensive and extremely reliable. However, their efficiency deteriorates at low load levels and they have a narrow constant power range. While induction motors provide a considerable step-up in efficiency compared to brushed motors, they still do not provide an ideal solution. This is the result of energy being consumed by the induction of current in the rotor, which is crucial to produce the induction motor's electromagnetic rotor motion. This current flow also heats the rotor, thus requiring more energy to keep it cool.

AC switched reluctance motors are also proving to be inexpensive and reliable, as a result of their simple construction. They also benefit from good torque/speed characteristics with wider constant power range. While ECUs permit the use of AC supplies in EV applications, however, both induction motors and switched reluctance motors continue to face difficulty in power control.

Finally, *permanent magnet motors* provide the highest efficiency levels among EM rivals. These motors can be broken down into AC synchronous and brushless DC types depending on the power controller used. Their advantage next to other brushless designs is that their permanent magnet rotor provides very high flux density without consuming any energy (as in the case of induction motors). Furthermore, the high energy density permanent magnet allows for a very compact motor design. On the downside, however, brushless permanent magnet motors are not cheap since the high energy density permanent magnets must be made from expensive rare-earth metals. Furthermore, they too suffer from a narrow constant power range.

The above provides a mere glimpse into these solutions. For further information, the reader should refer to Chan and Chau (2001), Ehsani et al (2004) and Hughes (2006). But having identified the most promising technologies, the discussion now considers how competitive these are next to the ICE systems.

Driving performance

It is important to put an end to the 'EVs are boring to drive' myth. The fact of the matter is that even the most stubborn petrol-head would be overwhelmed by the true colours of the electric VP system. For sure, when a former lecturer of mine first suggested that an EV was capable of outpacing a Ferrari 360 Modena and a Porsche Carrera GT, I thought he had inhaled too many fumes.[7] But it soon became apparent that, while sluggish battery development in the early 1900s may have put the brakes on EV performance, their underlying VP system has always been cutting-edge.

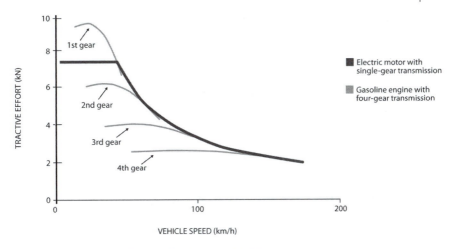

Figure 3.8 *ICE and EM torque curves*

At this point, readers are probably asking themselves: How can this be? How come society has always thought EVs were toys for mad scientists? Figure 3.8 compares the torque curves of an ICE and EM with comparable ratings.[8] The results could not be clearer.

To begin with, the EM offers peak torque from rest and sustains it up into the 6000rpm zone. This means this EV sustains full accelerating potential across half of the driving speed range without needing multiple gears. In contrast, the ICE has to build up torque at low speeds to a plateau between 2500rpm and 5000rpm, after which it rapidly deteriorates.

What does all this mean? Consider an EV with a maximum speed of 200km/hr at 14,000rpm.[9] This would require a gear ratio of 8.28:1 so that the wheel would turn approximately 1690 times per minute at maximum speed. With the same gear ratio, an ICV would have inadequate acceleration below 60km/hr – which is highly inconvenient in urban areas – and reach a maximum speed around 120km/hr.[10] Though an automotive engineer may be shocked by this crude simplification of the problem, the point holds: EMs are more responsive at all speeds and provide peak acceleration from rest up to high cruising speeds, whereas the ICE rarely does. Notice, then, that a given EM can achieve the same accelerating performance as a higher horsepower-rated ICE device.

California-based EV manufacturer Tesla Motors offers a perfect example of how this torque profile makes EVs fun to drive. Elon Musk, Tesla's co-founder and CEO, says that every time someone gets into the company's roadster, he asks the passenger to turn on the radio. He then accelerates right as the unsuspecting victim is extending an arm towards the radio controls. Invariably, passengers fail in their attempt due to the huge accelerating force that glues them to their seat-back. While that may not sound too pleasant to many people, it does say something about EVs being 'boring'.

The road ahead

The electric motor is the epitome of less is more. It delivers more performance, more efficiently and in a fraction of the space and weight of the ICE, without polluting its surroundings. Indeed, it is a fundamentally better product than the ICE. The historically poor perception regarding EVs is not due to limitations of its motor. Rather, the EM's fully mature technology has had to rely on under-developed battery technology, which, as will be discussed in Chapter 4, has ripened over the last two decades. Today it seems ever more likely that vehicle electrification will finally come to fruition.

Hybrids: The Electrification Spectrum

It is important that the reader understand that hybridization is not itself a distinct technology; rather, it is a middle ground between ICV and BEV technol-ogies – and this is what makes it particularly appealing. The key question in hybridization is determining how the ICV/EV VP and ES systems will interface and interact – in other words the vehicle architecture. Most drivers may not give this a second's thought, but, as will be seen, it is the vehicle architecture that largely defines a hybrid electric vehicle's (HEV's) performance. This section describes and analyses four vehicle architectures with distinct characteristics – parallel, series, series/parallel and complex VP systems. Each of these presents distinct characteristics, suiting specific vehicle solutions.

The parallel hybrid

ICVs and EVs ultimately drive their wheels in an identical manner – their motors produce rotational motion that is transferred through some sort of gear arrangement to the wheels. In a hybrid, the simplest solution is to have the ICV and EV VP systems connect to the transmission simultaneously. This is called a parallel system (Figure 3.9).

The benefits of parallel systems are not hard to identify. To begin with, they provide the simplest design and least capital-intensive solution that can be readily adopted by an automotive manufacturer. Furthermore, they allow either the ICE or the EM or both systems to directly power the wheels. This, in turn, allows the ICE to be downsized – in line with the introduced EM – without impacting vehicle performance. The smaller engine provides improved fuel economy and lower emissions. Splitting the power source into EM and ICE removes the burden of ensuring long-range self-sufficiency from the EV-based ES system and thus does not require a high capacity battery (Chapter 4).

However, the drawbacks can be identified with just as much ease. The solution continues to rely heavily on ICE technology. Indeed, with the exception of a valuable downsizing of the engine, the ICV VP system remains essentially untouched and thus remains maintenance intensive and inefficient. Notably, the ICE must still provide traction across its entire speed range and thus does not

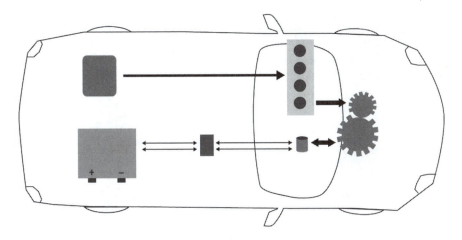

Figure 3.9 *Schematic diagram of parallel architecture*

take full advantage of the wide operating efficiency of EMs. Leaving the burden of range autonomy with the ICE-based ES system limits the EM's opportunities to contribute significantly to vehicle propulsion. As a result, parallel system development has dominated the ICE-biased part of the HEV spectrum, such as power-assisted HEVs and micro HEVs (see Appendix: Vehicle Classifications).

Unsurprisingly, the ICE typically accounts for at least 80 per cent of the vehicle's overall power rating – which is a reasonable indicator for its utilization factor. Consequently, the efficiency gain from parallel HEVs is likely to be around 15 per cent. Undoubtedly ahead of the curve, Honda's Integrated Motor Assist hybrid technology offers 32 per cent fuel economy,[11] providing a benchmark for what is economically achievable by parallel systems.

With the next chapter on ES systems in mind, it is important to highlight that parallel HEVs do not require significant electrical energy storage. As such, the ES system must be designed for maximum power delivery. While a natural evolution towards more EM-biased systems would provide further gains, parallel systems will always be limited by their association with ICEs. This configuration therefore plays a crucial but inherently limited role in EV adoption.

The series hybrid

Unless the reader is somewhat familiar with power generation technology, it may be difficult for them to conceptualize any other way of merging the ICE and EM systems. Fret not though, here's a hint: *Could an EM be used to supply energy to drive the ICE? How about the opposite?*

Driving an ICE requires some sort of combustion fuel. Obviously, the kinetic energy produced by EMs cannot be readily transformed into gasoline, ethanol or any other such combustion fuel. EMs, however, require electricity to produce kinetic energy. As seen in the previous section, the EM applies the reverse

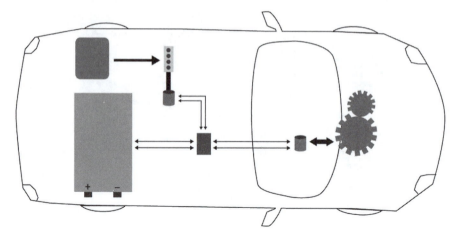

Figure 3.10 *Schematic diagram of series architecture*

principle of what occurs in a power generator, where kinetic energy produces electricity. Furthermore, EMs recover energy during braking – a concept called regenerative braking – by operating as generators. Since ICEs produce kinetic energy, would it not be possible to connect it to a power generator to produce electrical energy? In turn, that electrical energy could (re)charge the battery and thus drive the EM. As such, the ICE effectively becomes a complementary energy source to the battery and the EM becomes the lone direct driver of the wheels, thus creating what is referred to as a series (or serial) system (Figure 3.10).

Evaluation of series systems is not as straightforward as that of their parallel counterparts. By driving the wheels directly with the EM only, series configuration greatly reduces VP mechanical complexity, thus minimizing maintenance. Furthermore, since a high-power EM is required to fulfil peak power, the series system is in an ideal position to maximize regenerative braking performance. Beyond the EM power source, this architecture relies on an ICE generator set to guarantee reliable energy supply for extended range comparable with that of an ICV. While this configuration under-utilizes the individual component's cumulative power ratings, it minimizes the range burden on the battery, without reducing the role of the EM in driving the wheels.

Series architecture significantly alters the role of ICEs in automobiles, thus making room for improving on the existing technology. The generator set's role is to sustain the state of charge of the battery over long trips, allowing ICEs to operate at a stable power level independently of real-time driving behaviour. The battery acts as an energy buffer: if driving power consumption exceeds generator set production, the battery will discharge, but if it drops below production, then the excess will recharge the battery. Thus the generator set can be designed to operate within a very narrow speed band to maximize ICE energy efficiency, while eliminating the need for the ICV's complex (inefficient) variable gearing transmissions.[12]

The series architecture presents a unique opportunity to do away with the conventional petrol and diesel ICE altogether. This does not mean turning it into a BEV, however. The reader may recall that, while conventional petrol and diesel ICEs are not based on the most efficient cycle, they offer the only acceptable variable-speed operating performance. Having said that, in the case of HEVs, and notably of series hybrids, the ICE is used to activate a constant-speed generator, thus welcoming the use of other heat engine solutions. Microturbines, for instance, have very high energy efficiency within very narrow operating bands. Outside of these bands, their responsiveness deteriorates along with efficiency – clearly not suitable for driving a conventional ICV but perfectly compatible with serial HEVs. Indeed, successful replacement of existing ICEs with more efficient solutions could provide HEVs with a much longer than expected product life. However, with the exception of GM's 1999 demonstration of microturbine generators in the EV1 series hybrid, this possibility has remained largely unexplored.[13]

In theory, series hybrids are capable of providing the highest emissions reductions and fuel economy of all hybrid architectures, depending, of course, on the utilization rate of the generator set. To guarantee a low utilization of the generator set, it is necessary to use a large battery, which in turn compromises the series system's cost-effectiveness. The high utilization of battery energy for series systems pushes their application to the electric-biased extreme of the spectrum – notably plug-in HEVs or, more specifically, extended-range EVs. There is no question as to the compatibility between series architecture and future BEV targets. However, as will be examined in Chapter 6, series HEVs may not provide the most cost-effective response to global concerns in the short run.

The series/parallel hybrid

While parallel systems tend not to fulfil the desire for EM-biased HEVs, series systems under-utilize their installed power capacity. By merging these, the series/parallel system provides the key benefits of both solutions (Figure 3.11).

Indeed, the series/parallel system is often considered to provide the best of both worlds. It allows both the EM and the ICE to drive the wheels, as in the parallel system, such that the vehicle can exploit the combined output of all its power sources. As was the case with parallel architecture, this means that ICE and EM can both be downsized, yet still provide the same performance as a series HEV.

Note, however, that while still capable of being driven directly by the EM alone, a series/parallel architecture relies more heavily on the ICE when compared to a series system. This is inevitable since the EM in a series/parallel system will, by definition, always be rated below peak vehicle power. Consequently, while the EM in a series HEV can satisfy any driving condition, the series/parallel will require ICE assistance for high power performance. Nevertheless, series/parallel systems have the ability to limit ICE use to their most

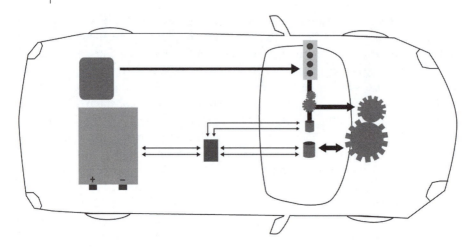

Figure 3.11 *Schematic diagram of series/parallel architecture*

efficient operating conditions – for example, ICEs are kept off until the operating speed reaches their optimal speed band. While the series/parallel design still requires the ICE to operate through a broad speed band – thus preventing the use of microturbines – it does allow for smaller more efficient engine designs. Notably, the Atkinson Cycle engine, which offers a 12–14 per cent increase in efficiency next to conventional ICVs, has established a strong position in this market.

All of this flexibility and control of power delivery reflects the series/parallel system's high opportunity for optimization. However, whether this can compensate for the reduced EM bias depends largely on the specific driving cycle and the exact vehicle specifications. Flexibility also brings a high degree of complexity. Indeed, the operational dynamics of the various interconnected motors and generators is not trivial and would not be possible without the use of a planetary gear.[14] Despite its cost and complexity, though, manufacturers have clearly considered series/parallel architecture as an acceptable compromise.

Toyota's Hybrid Synergy Drive is by far the most popular series/parallel solution on the market. And, with the demand for full HEVs expanding, it is to be expected that series/parallel automobiles will maintain or expand their presence in the market. Indeed, some plug-in HEVs, including Toyota's Prius and BYD's F3DM, are being introduced with the series/parallel architecture as opposed to increasing the EM bias through series systems.

The complex hybrid

A few architectures have emerged in the last couple of years whose characteristics, although distinct, present some common principles in design and operation. While the complex hybrid may resemble a regular series/parallel architecture, it distinguishes itself through its upgraded planetary gear set. In some versions, such as the Lexus RX450h, a two-axle propulsion configuration is used with

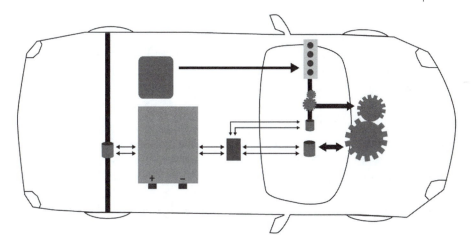

Figure 3.12 *Schematic diagram of complex architecture*

a hybrid branch (1) on the front axle and an EM branch (2) on the rear axle (Figure 3.12).

The complex architecture, perhaps better known by the industry misnomer 'two-mode hybrid', promises to provide improved high speed and high load efficiencies compared to series/parallel systems. This is achieved by incorporating a second (and often a third) planetary gear set, which provides greater flexibility for managing the proportion of mechanical and electrical power delivered according to operating speeds. As with series/parallel and series systems, the substitution of the Otto Cycle engines with Diesel or Atkinson Cycle engines has become commonplace.

It should be noted that the Atkinson Cycle does induce a low power density penalty. Even so, these engines ensure higher energy efficiency. What makes complex architectures particularly valuable is the fact that the EM is specifically designed to provide power assistance during peak demand. This ensures that consumers do not notice any performance dip due to the Atkinson Cycle's low power density.

Complex systems are bound to play an increasing role in this next stage of HEV development. However, this architecture is only reaching the market now and it has to prove itself against other lower-cost solutions such as Prius's series/parallel. The high load capability of complex systems makes these systems ideal for use with sport utility vehicles (SUVs) and urban trucks. No wonder GM and Chrysler were the leaders behind this technological development. But looking at the result of SUV/light truck hybridization shows that this is not enough.

GM, for instance, has claimed 25 per cent better fuel economy on its Yukon models, which, according to US Environmental Protection Agency (EPA) data, currently emit around $275 gCO_2/km$. Given the starting point, this would prove to be an insignificant improvement, taking Yukon emissions down to $205 gCO_2/km$. Notice that this is 70 per cent higher than the voluntary emissions standards for 2012 set by the European ACEA agreement – a benchmark which is likely to drive both American and EU emissions standards in the coming years. For sure, this should prove a laudable step forward in cleaning up SUV emissions. However, even with the wildest of performance improvements, hybridized SUVs will remain unsustainable.

The start of the journey

While pure electrification is the ideal and most likely long-term path for vehicle propulsion systems, one cannot ignore the importance of hybrid electric vehicles in this technological paradigm shift. As will be seen, BEVs are unlikely to be cost-effective in most market segments during the early stages of penetration. Thus hybridization represents a cost-effective transitional phase to the electric future.

Approaching a Verdict 1:
Better at the Core

Electric VP systems, regardless of design, offer some basic advantages over ICE systems: increased efficiency, reduced maintenance costs, design flexibility and high performance. All of these qualities stem from two basic design properties: mechanical simplicity and the nature of electrical operation.

Recall, for starters, the fact that EMs consist of merely one moving part: a rotor shaft which rotates in relation to the rest of the motor. Furthermore, by avoiding the combustion process, EMs do not suffer from the same self-destructive behaviour of ICEs. The design thus reduces overall wear and tear of the VP components – both due to the limited number of moving parts and the reduced stress between them. As a result, expensive motor repairs and regular maintenance are minimized – lubricants and working fluids are not required to ensure the ICV's health.[15]

As far as design is concerned, readers can take comfort in the fact that EVs do not impose any fundamental change in the design of a vehicle or in the manner with which the driver interacts with a vehicle. As Tom Hanks, an EV owner and enthusiast, recently put it during an interview on the *Late Show with David Letterman*:

> *They ask me all the time how [an EV] works. I say: well this is amazing, what you do with this electric car, Dave. You put the key in ... and you turn it [grins and nods]. Then there's this thing on the floor called the 'pedal', a pedal. And what you do is, you press on that and, believe it or not, that sucker goes! It will take you down the Pacific Coast Highway so fast you can get a ticket.*

Although the EV can look and feel much the same as an ICV, it is clear that their mechanical simplicity offers greater functionality and flexibility in car design if desired in the future. Mechanical simplicity means that EM-based VP systems can provide competitive performance in small and lightweight devices. Indeed, an AC induction motor can produce an astonishing 160hp with a mere 26kg of equipment, compared to a mammoth nearing 140kg for an equivalent ICE (not including other heavy VP components).[16] Sadly, manufacturers have yet to take full advantage of these benefits.

Finally, performance. As we saw above, ICEs have poor torque and power characteristics over a wide speed range. Variable gearing is thus fundamental in ICVs to ensure satisfactory vehicle performance across a range of speeds. Conversely, the transmission requirements for EVs are greatly reduced due to high energy conversion efficiency across a wide range of operating speeds. As a result, many EVs can forgo variable gearing, thus reducing transmission losses. Furthermore, EVs are increasingly switching to transmissions with more efficient and reliable electronic, rather than mechanical, differential controls. In some cases, where the EM is mounted directly onto the wheel, such as in some permanent magnet DC motors, EVs can forgo transmissions altogether.

All of this means that high mechanical losses inherent to ICEs and its accessories are negligible in EMs, such that electric VP system efficiencies can exceed 90 per cent compared to 15–18 per cent in the ICE VP systems. Undeniably superior to the ICE system, electric VP systems are constrained, however, by their association with suboptimal ES system solutions. This will be discussed in the following chapter.

Appendix:
Vehicle Classifications

Electric vehicle (EV): A vehicle driven by an electric motor. When we refer to EVs in this text we are deliberately *not* discriminating between the various types of EVs. Thus this is an all-encompassing terminology. Notice, however, that some authors use the EV terminology to refer specifically to pure-electric vehicles (excluding hybridization with ICVs) or, even more selectively, to refer to battery-powered EVs.

Battery EV (BEV): An EV powered solely by an electrochemical battery.

Fuel cell EV (FCEV): An EV powered by a fuel cell (FC). Given the properties of FC systems (discussed in the next chapter), these are likely to be hybridized with a battery or ultracapacitor power source.

Ultracapacitor EV (UCEV): An EV powered by an ultracapacitor (UC). Given the properties of UCs, these would necessarily be hybridized with a battery or FC.

Hybrid EV (HEV): Any vehicle which combines electric and combustion power sources. Notice that this excludes all-electric hybridizations such as fuel cell/

battery EVs and ultracapacitor/battery EVs. While not strictly accurate, this terminology has been informally accepted by industry and even academia, and is adopted in this book.

Grid-enabled EV (GEV): Any EV which can be connected to the grid for power exchange. This necessarily includes BEVs, PHEVs and UCEVs. In the case of FCEVs, this book *assumes* grid compatibility. It should be noted that FCs cannot be charged, so grid compatibility would be based on (a) FCEVs producing electricity for the grid or (b) a hybridized FCEV where the UC or battery may be recharged from the grid.

Plug-in HEV (PHEV): Any HEV capable of charging its batteries by directly connecting to the electrical grid. A PHEV can be driven directly by either one of its propulsion devices (the ICE or the EM). Though not an official requirement, it might be reasonable to expect these vehicles to have a minimum electric-only range of 20km (requiring a 4kWh lithium-ion battery pack).

Extended range EV (EREV): Covers PHEVs which can only be driven by their EM, as opposed to regular PHEVs which can be driven by either the ICE or EM. The distinction is made by the automotive industry so as to promote these as pure EVs rather than HEVs. In principle, EREVs should accommodate larger batteries (say 16kWh to produce a 64km electric-only range) to meet the vast majority of driving scenarios, particularly in urban areas.

Full (or strong) HEV: Describes HEVs capable of being driven by electric-only power for short distances, noting, however, that they cannot be recharged on the grid. Again, there is no official battery specification, though there is a consensus, in practice, that these would have NiMH battery packs of around 1.5kWh, which provide a couple of kilometres in electric-only range.

Power-assist HEV: HEVs with reduced EMs and batteries, such that their propulsion role is limited to assisting the ICE with torque boosts during heavy acceleration.

Micro HEV: ICVs which employ small but inexpensive EMs and batteries for the purposes of energy conservation through regenerative braking and ICE shutdown during vehicle idling. While these technologies provide a valuable improvement in ICV energy efficiency, we must highlight that they cannot provide any propulsion assistance. Consequently, many experts, including those at the Society of Automotive Engineers, disagree with their classification as HEVs. Indeed, recall that the underlying prerequisite to being a hybrid vehicle is the use of two or more power sources to drive the vehicle, thus disqualifying micro 'HEVs'.

Mild HEV: Sometimes used to define HEVs below full hybrid. This ambiguity has become an advertising tool to associate power-assist HEVs with micro HEVs, intending to enhance power-assist technology's HEV credentials.

Notes

1   For instance, the reader has probably come across a daunting array of 'EV' classifications, most of which are confusing at best. Much of the problem, in the case of EVs, stems from a lack of standardized terminology. The appendix to this chapter brings together all the vehicle classifications which are used in this text and can be referred to by the reader as needed.

2   While the term motor can be used generically to designate any mechanism that transforms potential energy into kinetic energy, the term engine is typically applied in reference to motors that rely on the combustion process. Thus we speak of steam engines, compression ignition engines, spark ignition engines and so on. Strictly speaking, it would not be incorrect to speak of an electric engine; however, the term electric motor is usually employed and when we say engine it is generally understood that this is a motor that relies on a combustion mechanism. In this discussion, we will keep with popular terminology.

3   Note, from the discussion on biofuels in the previous chapter, that each fuel may offer very specific performance improvements, such as higher energy densities or higher octane ratings. However, this does not affect the basic assessment of ICE performance conducted in this chapter. Where relevant it will be highlighted.

4   The efficiency of a theoretically ideal heat engine is given by:
    n(eff) = 1 − (exhaust temperature)/(combustion temperature).

5   If a psychiatrist were to treat an ICE patient, they would diagnose it with self-destructive behaviour.

6   The author has specifically chosen to treat ECUs as part of the VP system, as opposed to the ES system, because of its crucial impact on VP system evolution and design. However, it is important to recognize that given the ECU's function as the interface between VP and ES systems, this is an arbitrary selection.

7   If the reader is still suspicious of what is shown in Figure 3.8, search Google or YouTube for 'X1 Ferrari Porsche' and watch the Ferrari and Porsche supercars being left behind by the modest X1.

8   Horsepower (i.e. peak power) ratings vary greatly throughout the various LDV categories, from as low as 26kW (35hp) for the Tata Nano to upwards of 400kW (approximately 500hp) for high-end luxury sedans and sports coupés. More conventional vehicles such as Toyota Corollas and VW Passats fall somewhere around 120–200kW (approximately 160–250hp).

9   This example is based on the Tesla Roadster, which has a 63.43cm wheel diameter, which gives a travel distance of 1.992m per wheel revolution.

10 Thus ICVs typically have around five gear ratios, say for 0–20, 20–50, 50–90, 90–150 and 150–200km/hr.

11 When I say that a car has $x\%$ fuel economy I mean that it is an improvement in fuel economy compared to an equivalent ICE vehicle (i.e. same weight, design, power ratings, etc). In this case the comparison is based on the highway fuel economy of the Honda Civic Hybrid Sedan (45mpg) and Honda Civic Sedan (34mpg).

12 It is important to acknowledge that these gains are not entirely recoverable, since losses will result from charging the battery and operating the EM. Still, series architecture will always produce a substantial efficiency gain relative to conventional ICV systems.

13 Though less radical and promising for the long run, more immediate alternatives could take shape in the form of greater diesel engine adoption for American SUVs and light trucks or Atkinson Cycle engine adoption for sedans and smaller vehicles. While a technical evaluation of the Atkinson Cycle is not warranted here, it is worth a mention since it is being widely adopted by most HEV applications today, including the Toyota Prius.

14 Planetary gears are complex mechanical gear sets that combine multiple power devices and optimize their output based on the combined system requirement. Explanation of the operating principles of planetary gears is beyond the scope of this book.

15 Notice that, while EVs, in their modern incarnation, have a relatively short track record, EMs as such have a well-established record of reliability.

16 In comparing motor for motor, we are giving ICVs the benefit of the doubt! If you compare full VP systems, then the EV would include a lightweight, compact transmission and ECU, while the ICV would include full transmission, differentials, crankshafts, huge cooling systems and so on.

References

Boston Consulting Group (2009) *The Comeback of the Electric Car? How Real, How Soon, and What Must Happen Next*, Boston Consulting Group, Boston, MA, January, www.bcg.com/documents/file15404.pdf

Chan, C. C. and Chau, K. T. (2001) *Modern Electric Vehicle Technology*, Oxford University Press, Oxford, UK

Credit Suisse (2009) 'Electric Vehicles', *Credit Suisse Equity Research*, 1 October

Ehsani, M., Gao, Y., Gay, S. E. and Emadi, A. (2004) *Modern Electric, Hybrid Electric, and Fuel Cell Vehicles: Fundamentals, Theory, and Design*, CRC Press, Boca Raton, FL

Hughes, A. (2006) *Electric Motors and Drives: Fundamentals, Types and Applications*, Elsevier, Oxford, UK

4

Energy Storage

We can't solve problems by using the same kind of thinking we used when we created them.

Albert Einstein

The previous chapter showed how much better electric vehicle propulsion (VP) systems really are compared to their combustion counterparts. It was also shown that much of the improvement in electric VP systems was due to the advancement of microelectronics since the 1980s. The microelectronics boom has also proved crucial for the recent development in battery and other energy storage (ES) technologies. To date, however, no alternative to the combustion-based ES system has been able to offer equivalent performance and convenience at a competitive cost. Indeed, largely due to the effectiveness of conventional fuels, the internal combustion engine vehicle's (ICV's) ES system has always trumped other less tangible benefits of using alternative energy sources. If electric vehicles (EVs) expect to penetrate the transportation market, then the fossil fuel-based ES system will have to be replaced by a competitive alternative.

This chapter sets off by identifying the key parameters for evaluating an ES system and establishing a benchmark based on the ICV ES solution. It then examines three key EV ES technologies – batteries, fuel cells (FCs) and ultra-capacitors (UCs) – as potential substitutes for the combustion-based solution. Note that the discussion and the data presented do not refer to a specific product – rather they try to capture the current status of each technology. However, the evaluation against the ICV ES system focuses strictly on technologies that are already available in the marketplace. However, these technologies are undergoing rapid development, such that in each case, some attention is given to the most promising areas of research and development (R&D).

Energy Storage Performance Parameters

Simply put, ES systems are meant to store and deliver energy to the VP system readily and efficiently. The evaluation of ES systems thus involves two fundamental properties: specific energy and specific power. Specific energy is the amount of energy stored by the ES system that can be made available to propel the automobile,[1] measured in kWh/kg.[2] Specific power is the rate at which this energy can be delivered by the ES system, measured in kW/kg. It is worth briefly looking at how these properties effect vehicle performance, notably range, fuel or energy efficiency,[3] driving performance, and recharge rate.

Vehicle range[4] is the distance that can be travelled on a full tank of gas or fully charged battery, so it is a function of energy capacity (and fuel efficiency). Modern ICVs typically offer over 450km of autonomy, which is far above the capacity required by daily driving patterns across the globe. As will be discussed, even in America, average daily travel range remains below 50km and only about 15 per cent of all daily trips reach 100km (IEA, 2009). This observation will be central to the discussion throughout the rest of the book.

Driving performance – acceleration and top speed – is a function of the ES system's power delivery characteristics. Systems which rely on chemical reactions to deliver energy are sensitive to reaction rates. As is the case with ICEs, some ES systems respond adversely to variable driving loads. Alas, vehicles must be designed to meet the requirements of a typical urban driving cycle (Figure 4.1), characterized by frequent stop-and-go traffic.

This imposes short irregular bursts of acceleration and braking, which results in a momentary demand for peak power (rate of energy delivery) up to 16 times higher than the vehicle's average power requirements (Chan and Chau, 2001, p178). Acceleration and deceleration processes account for two-thirds of the energy consumption over an average driving cycle (Ehsani et al, 2004, p315). So as not to compromise vehicle performance, ES systems are typically

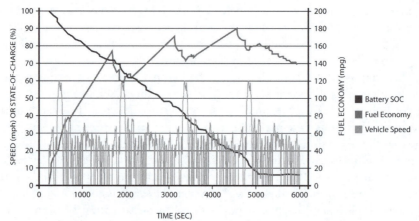

Figure 4.1 *Power requirement urban driving cycles*

Source: Imperial College London

Box 4.1 REGENERATIVE BRAKING

Consider a Honda Civic (approximately 1200kg curb weight) cruising along a highway at 120km/hr (33.3m/s). The vehicle approaches a traffic jam and brakes to a halt in tens of metres. In so doing, it uses up or wastes 0.19kWh (= ½ m·v²). For comparison, consider the Tesla Roadster, which also has a curb weight of approximately 1200kg. This vehicle has a range of 393km on a single charge of its 53kWh battery, consuming 0.13kWh/km (2.14km/MJ). What this indicates is that, during the Honda Civic's emergency brake, it wasted enough energy to power the Tesla supercar over 1.5km!

More common deceleration profiles might suggest braking to a halt from 50km/hr – or a waste of 0.03kWh. Roughly speaking, it might be said that for every four times an average vehicle, like the Honda Civic, brakes it wastes one kilometre of potential EV range. This adds up to more than 25 per cent energy loss in typical urban areas and can reach a shocking (no pun intended) 70 per cent in large cities such as New York (Ehsani et al, 2004, p334).

---

designed to meet the peak power output. Note however, that this implies a lot of built-in power capability that gets used only rarely.

Fuel efficiency (in other words tank-to-wheel, or T2W, efficiency) measures the proportion of stored energy that is successfully converted into useful energy for propelling the vehicle. Depending on vehicle technology, two elements may influence fuel efficiency: energy conversion efficiency and energy recovery. Independent of vehicle type, fuel efficiency is dominated by the vehicle's energy conversion efficiency, which is the product of the VP and ES system efficiencies.[5] The more performance is summoned by the driver, the faster and less efficient are the chemical reactions and the lower the fuel efficiency. In the case of EVs, the ES efficiency is closely linked to individual driving behaviour.

A substantial proportion of energy consumed during acceleration is subsequently used up (wasted) during braking (Box 4.1). However, as discussed in Chapter 3, EMs function as a power generator during braking and downhill situations, thus offering the unique opportunity of energy recovery – referred to as regenerative braking. Regenerative braking imposes two essential design conditions on ES systems. First, it requires an ES system capable of accepting electrical energy input. And second, the ES system must be capable of accepting high power input to maximize the vehicle's recovery potential.

Recharge rate has perhaps been the single most important obstacle to EV adoption. Fast and convenient recharging is not merely a function of vehicle technology, but rather depends extensively on the interface between the ES system used and the recharging infrastructure available. Given the dependence on infrastructure characteristics, this discussion will be further elaborated in Chapter 5. Meanwhile, this chapter will examine the recharging characteristics of each technology.

It is important to observe that the performance characteristics discussed above are all functions of energy and power, which themselves are co-dependent variables, as shown in Figure 4.2. This chapter will examine the combustion-based EV system and three EV-based ES systems, highlighting how the energy/power compromises shown in the figure play out under different options.

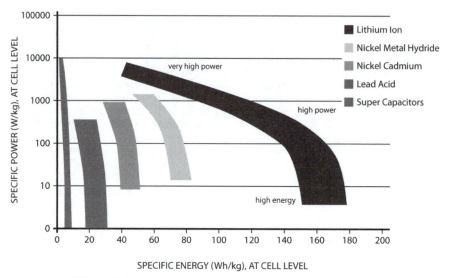

Figure 4.2 *Ragonne Curves: Energy/power compromise*

Combustion-Based Energy Storage Systems

For all its flaws, the ICE did manage to get one crucial thing right: it latched onto a plentiful energy source. Over the last century, the most effective method of supplying and storing energy for transportation purposes has been through combustion fuels (excluding, perhaps, modern rail-based transport). Broadly speaking, combustion fuels consist of any chemical substance formed by hydrocarbon (or carbohydrate) chains that are burned to obtain energy. Since the start of the Industrial Revolution, we have used everything from sperm whale oil to landfill methane gas to biomass-derived fuels to petroleum to make things flare up. Due to their supreme dominance, this discussion focuses on fossil fuels and especially on petrol.

There are three key factors that contribute to the widespread success of the combustion-based ES system. First and foremost is the extremely high energy density of combustion fuels. Even after taking into account the 15–19 per cent T2W efficiency of the ICV's VP system, every litre of combustion fuel still offers very high energy density at the wheel (ATW).[6] Since petrol at the station contains 12.9kWh/kg (46.44MJ/kg), the petrol driving an ICV has an energy density ATW of at least 1.94kWh/kg (6.98MJ/kg).[7] This provides the ICV with unparalleled range capabilities.

The second factor is the absence of chemical reactions throughout the ES system, as the energy content is stored and transferred exclusively through physical means. The physical transfer of energy content in and out of the ES system decouples much of the energy/power compromise burden. With the high energy density of combustion fuels, these systems ensure extremely rapid energy transfer to power the vehicle.

The third merit of the ICV's ES solution results from its physical simplicity, which translates into a crucial implication – low cost. The simplicity of combustion fuel storage – a fuel tank and some pipes to direct the fuel into the engine – is fundamental in an industry where competitive advantage has historically revolved around low production costs. Vehicle costs will be considered in greater detail in Chapter 5.

Electrochemical Battery Energy Storage Systems

For over a century, the electrochemical battery, popularly just 'battery', has been used to power EVs. Of course, a lot has changed since 1834, when Thomas Davenport used a non-rechargeable lead-acid battery to power the first EV. Today, most people are familiar with batteries in their day-to-day life, whether they are off-the-shelf AAs or AAAs used in remotes or perhaps bespoke batteries used in laptops or MP3 players. However, most people probably do not understand how these little cylinders make their calculators work, let alone their future supercars.

Operating principle

In contrast to the *open* energy conversion systems found in the ICV, batteries exchange (electrical) energy with their surroundings without exchanging matter, making them *closed* systems. Rather than being irreversibly consumed (used up and expelled) as in the case of combustion fuels, the system's chemical substances convert energy by changing states. In other words, batteries undergo reversible chemical reactions – converting electrical energy input into chemically stored energy during charging and inversely converting the stored chemical energy back into electrical energy for use in the motor during discharging.

A battery is composed of several electrochemical cells stacked together. These have identical electrochemical properties and operational characteristics and function as independent, modular subunits of the battery. Thus some cells may reach full charge/discharge before others, which leads to different problems depending on the chemical composition of the battery.[8]

A typical cell configuration will consist of three primary elements: a negative electrode (anode) and a positive electrode (cathode) that are immersed in an electrolytic (electrically conductive) substance. Consider the reactions taking place within a lithium-ion (Li-ion) battery, though the same basic principles apply to any other chemical composition. The anode typically consists of carbon in a graphite form, while the cathode is a transitional metal oxide, the exact composition of which is the key determinant of the battery characteristics. Both anode and cathode are intercalated compounds that permit lithium ions to slip in and out during charge/discharge cycles. The electrodes are immersed into the electrolyte solution – which consists of a lithium salt dissolved in an organic solvent – in which a separator (for example polypropylene) is introduced to prevent electrons from flowing between electrodes directly through the electrolyte (Figure 4.3).

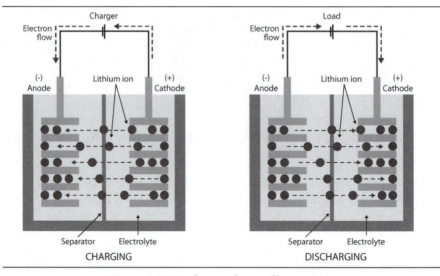

Figure 4.3 *Discharge/charge illustrations*

Note: The figure illustrates the chemical reactions taking place during discharging and charging processes, which are exact reversals of each other. During the discharging process lithium ions are released from the graphite anode and transferred to the metal oxide cathode through the electrolyte. The lithium-ion release coincides with an electron release from the anode into the circuit, which is captured on the other end by the cathode receiving the lithium ion. For all of this to occur, the anode and the cathode must be connected through an external circuit where electrical current travels. If an EM is connected to this electrical circuit, the current flow will deliver energy to drive the motor.

The fact that batteries operate as a closed system is a mixed blessing. On the one hand, it ensures zero emissions, minimizes resource waste during their operating life and allows regenerative braking. Indeed, the ICE VP system is unlikely to undergo any radical advancement to challenge the battery's advantage in any of these areas. On the other hand, the battery-based ES system is burdened by the hefty upfront payment of its lifetime fuel as well as the drag of continuously hauling around this fuel supply.

The battery pack challenge

Battery weight has been a major deterrent to EV implementation. Indeed most, if not all, of the weight reduction obtained from the switch between combustion-based and electrical VP systems is currently wasted on bulky battery packs needed to ensure suitable range. However, a brief look at the numbers is encouraging.

Figure 4.4 shows that only 26 per cent of a battery pack's overall weight is directly associated with the energy production process (Ehsani et al, 2004, p307). This is largely due to the need for a sealed casing to prevent harmful chemicals from leaking into the environment and to the wiring and electrical accessories. But the figure raises three questions:

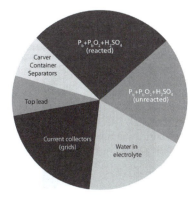

Figure 4.4 *Battery weight distribution*

Source: Ehsani et al (2004)

1 Is there not a more intelligent way to seal and encase a battery?
2 Are there not lighter materials available to replace some of the heavy pack components?
3 Why does the electrolytic solution account for such a large proportion of the pack weight?

Consider why a battery is designed the way it is. More specifically, why are most batteries cylinder shaped? Even the classic rectangular 9-volt battery is actually six AAAA cylindrical batteries enclosed in a rectangular case.

The sealed cylindrical cell was the first and remains to this day the most widely used 'household' battery design. Its widespread popularity can be attributed to its cheap and simple manufacturing process, high energy density and mechanical stability. However, the cylindrical shape does not offer optimal utilization of space, a factor that has become increasingly important in the world of microelectronics. What is more, cylindrical cells only exist in standardized sizes – AA, AAA, D and so on. These shapes are not ideal for the design of bespoke and especially large battery packs, such as those for EV applications.

In the early 1990s, the prismatic cell emerged in response to the perpetual search for miniaturization during the microelectronics boom. In a prismatic cell, thin wafers of cathode, separator and anode are stacked up. This arrangement provides for a vast increase in the utilization of space, at the expense of slightly reduced energy density and increased manufacturing costs. Consequently, prismatic cell battery packs are always built as bespoke solutions – standardized prismatic packs are not available in the aisles of the local convenience store. If the reader is curious to see what one really looks like, some digital cameras use prismatic battery packs, as do most mobile phones (Figure 4.5).

Over the past decade, automotive manufacturers have increasingly switched from cylindrical to prismatic cells. In part, this is because lithium compositions are particularly suited for prismatic designs – in fact, lithium polymer batteries

As would be expected, high maximum energy and power are both desirable qualities. However, as observed in the HEV discussion in the last chapter, different BEV/HEV solutions impose different requirements on the battery. The reader might recall how parallel HEVs need not concern themselves with energy capacity, since these are typically intended to be power-assist HEVs with combustion fuel covering the bulk of the energy storage task. Rather, it is peak power that concerns them. As the degree of electrification increases, the focus rapidly shifts to energy capacity. In the case of pure BEVs and plug-in HEVs, high energy density is particularly important, since the battery is the sole (or primary in the case of plug-in HEVs) energy source for the vehicle.

Historically, EVs have relied on lead-acid battery solutions as their power source. While lead-acid may be able to satisfy the limited power requirements of a weak power-assist HEV, it is not suited for stronger levels of electrification. The wave of HEV development at the turn of the millennium allowed manufacturers to take advantage of the new battery compositions that had emerged during the previous decade. Nickel-based compositions, developed during the 1990s, and notably nickel metal hydride (NiMH), offered vast improvements in battery energy capacity and life expectancy. Indeed, NiMH has permitted the development of commercially viable full HEVs, raising hopes of a new era of grid-enabled EVs. NiMH may technically permit the demonstration of plug-in HEVs and even pure BEVs; however, achieving a range of just 160km would require a 500kg battery. Alas, the NiMH battery fell decidedly short of expectations.

In 1991, Sony launched the first Li-ion battery, opening the door to a flood of similar compositions. However, early Li-ion compositions posed a critical safety challenge. The reader may recollect how laptop manufacturers – including Sony, Dell, HP and Apple – had to recall their products due to multiple 'spontaneous combustion' Li-ion battery incidents. Needless to say, it would not go down well if cars started self-igniting. Fortunately, battery manufacturers, including Sony, have long solved the initial problem and developed Li-ion designs suitable for EV applications (Dhameja, 2002, p12).

Indeed Li-ion batteries are now thought to be the modality that holds the most potential for EV applications. As the previous graph showed, Li-ion batteries already offer more than double the energy density of the most advanced NiMH batteries, making a BEV range of upwards of 400km technically achievable. Furthermore, as highlighted earlier, it is expected that they can nearly double their current limit to reach energy densities of 300Wh/kg (1.08MJ/kg), making extended range even more of a reality.

Beyond superior energy and power densities, Li-ion batteries virtually eliminate maintenance concerns. The reader can probably recall the days when they bought a laptop with 'great' battery life, but six months down the road, the factory-installed two-hour battery dwindled down to five minutes. Fortunately, current Li-ion batteries do not suffer from the memory loss that causes this capacity deterioration. What is more, Li-ion compositions benefit from very high energy efficiencies, of around 80 per cent, which ensure T2W efficiencies of 75–78 per cent (compared to 15–18 per cent for the ICV).

However, it must also be recognized that Li-ion compositions are still relatively untested technologies, particularly in the unrelenting operating conditions of the automobile. Furthermore, though technically possible, an economically feasible method of recycling Li-ion batteries remains to be demonstrated. The current wave of EV prototypes is predominantly based on Li-ion compositions and presents encouraging results. On that note, the evaluation now looks more closely at the most promising Li-ion compositions.

Modern lithium batteries

As opposed to lead-acid and NiMH, which are very specific battery cell compositions, the term 'Li-ion' refers to a broad range of battery chemistries. This section identifies and evaluates the four Li-ion chemical compositions (Table 4.1) that demonstrate the greatest potential for automotive applications:

1   NCA (lithium nickel cobalt aluminium);
2   LFP (lithium iron phosphate);
3   LMO (lithium manganese spinel or lithium manganese polymer); and
4   LMO/LTO (lithium titanate).

As can be seen from Table 4.1, no composition offers absolute supremacy in all areas. However, each technology may offer better solutions to specific problems.

The NCA composition may be expensive and require restrictive operating controls to ensure safety. However, its high power density and especially its long lifespan make it ideal for power-assist HEVs. Costs can be managed by the small size of the battery. Furthermore, HEV batteries are unlikely to ever approach full depletion. Rather charge/discharge cycles will tend to be shallow but very frequent. This means that the low state-of-charge utilization factor is acceptable for HEVs and that the high cycle life is desirable.

Meanwhile, LFP presents the opposite opportunity. With the rise in production volumes, LFP is expected to become the most cost-effective composition on the market. The improved built-in stability and safety offered by this composition minimizes the failure risks and reduces the cost of pre-emptive safety measures. Additionally, the high state-of-charge utilization factor and the low deterioration of energy capacity over the lifetime of the battery mean that manufacturers need not design oversized units to ensure adequate performance. Finally, LFP uses relatively inexpensive raw materials, making these compositions extremely suited to EV and plug-in HEV applications, where energy capacity utilization needs to be high.

LMO and LTO/LMO compositions present intermediary solutions between NCA and LFP and are also likely to mark their presence in the full HEV and plug-in HEV markets. At this point, however, it would be premature to predict which of these technologies, if any, is likely to dominate the growing automotive battery market – growth and development is expected to maintain a rapid pace, and breakthroughs are always looming on the horizon.

Table 4.1 *Lithium-ion battery characteristics, by composition*

	NCA	LMO	LMO/LTO	LFP
Energy density (Wh/kg)	170	150	150	140
Power density (W/kg)	Highest	Good	Good	OK
Maturity	Most proven	Safety and durability needs proving	Safety and durability needs proving	Electronic monitoring needs proving
Life expectancy	Good Demonstrated: 15 years & 350,000 cycles	OK Capacity fading concerns	Very good	Very good
Cost	High (cobalt and nickel)	High	Highest	Lowest
Safety	Least thermal stability High charge thermal runaway	Better than NCA Some thermal instability expected	Better than LMO and NCA	Best Least risk of overcharge
Operating temperature characteristics		Capacity fades above 40°C Poor charging at low temp	Capacity fades above 40°C	Poor cold temperature performance
Usable charge range	Degrade at high charge Approximately 30–70%	Capacity fades with cycling Approximately 30–70%	100% charge	10–100% charge
Application	Power-assisted HEVs, because of high power density & cycle life	HEV	HEVs, because of long life, low energy but high power	PHEV and BEV

Battery cost structure

It is widely assumed that, for the Li-ion battery composition to establish itself as the dominant automotive power source, its cost must come down at least to US$500/kWh. Understanding the battery cost breakdown is important to assess the potential to reduce overall battery costs. As can be seen in Figure 4.7, there are three bits of the data that stand out: scrap rate, 'chemical substances' (cathode, anode and electrolyte materials) and R&D.

Above all else, what stands out immediately from Figure 4.7 is the enormous scrap rate, which is estimated to contribute around 25 per cent of total pack cost.[9] To help put this measure of wasted material in context, while automotive industry standards require scrap rates below 0.1 per cent, battery manufacturers have been found to operate with rates of up to 60 per cent (BCG, 2010, p6)! This may be largely explained by the relative lack of experience in manufacturing EV-grade batteries, a problem that is likely to take care of itself as the market expands, pushing aside those with lower quality standards.

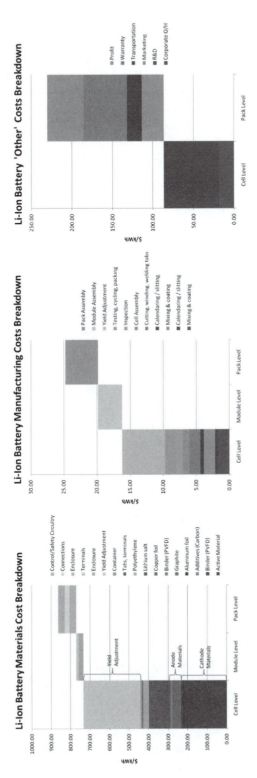

Figure 4.7 *Battery cost breakdown*

Source: Anderson (2009)

The next big expenditure item is 'chemical substances', mainly the cathode material. Obviously, one cannot expect to eliminate these costs, since they cover the fundamental elements of the battery. However, there are ways to shave off some of the expenditure. The development of new active materials – either replacing or dramatically reducing the use of expensive elements such as cobalt and nickel – has attracted attention from the recent wave of clean R&D funding that recognizes that this is key to low-cost BEV feasibility. Perhaps more likely than a breakthrough discovery are potential savings from economies of scale – the market value of expensive elements found in lithium-ion batteries is sensitive to order volumes, and as battery production expands, so will raw material volumes.

As with any nascent technology, R&D costs represent a disproportionate burden against the product's negligible sales. Market growth will be key to diluting this burden. However, battery manufacturers are expected to continue spending hefty amounts on R&D. Governments, in turn, have already played a role by injecting funds into R&D programmes and are likely to continue to do so. Indeed, since the 2008 financial crisis, governments around the world have collectively set aside over US$500 billion of their economic stimulus packages for green investments. There are signs that key beneficiaries of this money have been and will continue to be battery and smart grid technologies.

It is also worth noting that steep price drops are not unprecedented in the battery industry. Between 1991 and 2005, Li-ion microelectronics battery prices dropped by 91 per cent from US$3170/kWh to US$280/kWh. While EV batteries are also based on Li-ion chemical compositions, their higher level of complexity means they still have a great deal to gain in terms of economies of scale.

Waste disposal

A major environmental argument against batteries is that they contain chemical substances – such as acids and lithium – which, if improperly disposed of, can be damaging to the surrounding environment. While this cannot be contradicted, it must be qualified.

A battery is a closed-system device. Thus, by definition, the chemical substances it contains never escape into the surrounding environment during its operating life, unless the battery is improperly tampered with. Once the battery reaches the end of its operating life, the substances present at the outset remain securely stored.

Lithium-ion batteries enjoy a very high recycling potential (Figure 4.8) and an economically feasible recycling mechanism is expected to be developed before the first generation of EVs reaches the end of the life cycle. As such, in the long run, lithium markets are likely to rely heavily on recycled resources.

By following a battery-leasing approach, as discussed in Chapter 5, the waste management process can be regulated and more easily monitored by government authorities. In contrast, an ICV fleet, in which chemical substances, such

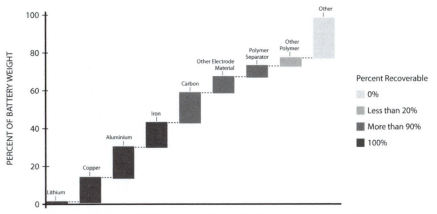

Figure 4.8 *Recyclable material in a lithium-ion battery, by weight*

Source: Electrification Coalition

as lubricating oils, are handled by millions of individuals over the course of its useful life, is a far greater waste management and enforcement challenge. While it is difficult to quantify the potential environmental impact, it can be argued that the EV system is inherently more amenable to effective waste management. Consequently, toxic/chemical waste issues, if adequately addressed by governments, in no way tarnish the EV's claim to environmental friendliness.

The threat of lithium dependence

One of the core concerns of EV critics is that the production of batteries depends on geographically limited lithium reserves. While, like petroleum, lithium is undoubtedly a scarce and geographically limited resource, EV battery markets are unlikely to be threatened by supply constraints. A brief look at the geography of reserves shows that, although emotionally enticing, the argument has poor foundations.

The Middle East of lithium reserves is surely Latin America,[10] where 80 per cent of global reserves are found. However, EV battery technology is currently being developed and produced primarily in the US and China, where only 4 per cent and 10 per cent of global lithium reserves are found respectively (Figure 4.9).

According to a Credit Suisse study (2009), lithium consumption is expected to more than double between 2008 and 2020, driven primarily by the nascent EV battery industry. As a result, the EV battery industry is expected to represent the single largest end market (40 per cent) for lithium raw materials. However, based on planned supply expansions by major suppliers in the major producing countries (Chile, China, Argentina and the US), capacity utilization rates will remain below 80 per cent until 2015. While there are no formal expansion plans for the second half of the decade, if the Credit Suisse forecasts prove accurate, the major suppliers are expected to have ample capacity still available for development. Note that these expansions ignore unharnessed Bolivian resources.

Figure 4.9 *Lithium reserves map*

Meanwhile, consumers should feel reassured that EV ownership does not lock them into a scarce resource market like the ICV does with petroleum. On the contrary, the battery is an initial investment and not an ongoing expense. Having acquired a battery, the owner's exposure to lithium supplies becomes negligible. And, while lithium is expected to provide the best chemical composition for EV batteries today, ongoing battery research can be expected to offer competitive alternative solutions.

Consequently, EVs do not impose a de facto dependence on lithium resources nor can their natural resource market risks be compared to those currently faced by ICVs. On the contrary, one of the EV's key advantages is indeed to ensure greater resource independence worldwide.

Fuel Cell Energy Storage Systems

The hydrogen fuel cell (FC) began to claim an important role in future transportation technology in 1970, when John Bockris coined the term 'hydrogen economy'. Since then, hydrogen energy technologies have come and gone from the spotlight in an emphatic manner. As polemic as the hydrogen FC solution may be, it cannot be neglected in any EV discussion.

Operating principle

A fuel cell (FC) is akin to a battery in the sense that it converts chemical energy into electrical energy via an electrochemical reaction. However, the similarities end there. In fact, the rest of the FC ES system, notably the handling of the chemical fuels, more closely resembles the open combustion-based ES system, since this ES must include a replenishable fuel (H_2) reservoir.

Strictly speaking, a FC is a single galvanic electrochemical cell. In practice, we erroneously use the term FC to describe an FC stack, which, as the name

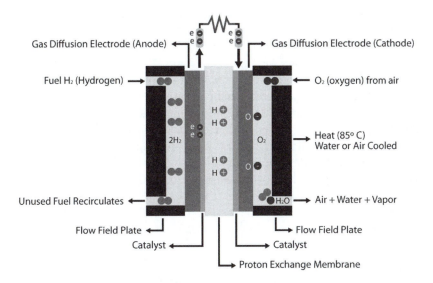

Figure 4.10 *Chemical reactions in a fuel cell*

suggests, is a pile of individual FCs that operate as an integrated energy conversion device. Given its widespread use, the FC misnomer is adopted as the standard terminology in this book.

Initially, a typical single cell structure closely resembles that of an individual battery cell, with a negative electrode (anode), a positive electrode (cathode) and an electrolyte substance. However, as the individual cells take on their functional shape and join to form a stack, they quickly lose all resemblance to their battery counterparts. Figure 4.10 illustrates the processes taking place in a typical cell within a proton exchange membrane FC (PEMFC).

FCs themselves do not undergo chemical alterations, but are designed to induce the chemical reaction of fuels flowing across their surfaces. At the anode surface, hydrogen gas (H_2) is split into two hydrogen ions (H^+) and two electrons (e^-). The electrons flow to the cathode plate through an external circuit that then powers the motor. Meanwhile, the hydrogen ions flow to the cathode plate through the proton exchange membrane (the electrolyte), which is only permeable to positively charged ions. At the cathode, the hydrogen ions, electrons and oxygen molecules (from the ambient air) react to form water that is exhausted out of the vehicle.

Anode: $2H_2 \longrightarrow 4H^+ + 4e^-$

Cathode: $O_2 + 4H^+ + 4e^- \longrightarrow 2H_2O$

The reactions in each individual FC produce electrical power at 0.6–0.85V. They are then connected in series, thus forming a FC stack, to ensure adequate operating voltage (100s of V). To ensure the reactions produce electrical power at suitable current levels (100s of A), each individual FC cross-sectional area must be suitably large (100s of cm^2).

The PEMFC technology described in Figure 4.10 is the uncontested FC technology for the automotive industry. First, it offers good specific power (kW/kg) while operating at ambient temperatures. Additionally, its cathode is only reactive with oxygen, so PEMFCs allow the intake of ambient air without any need for purification or separation of the oxygen. Finally, the polymer membrane is very thin, allowing PEMFC units to be compact. These characteristics make the PEMFC ideal for automobiles.

The FC system provides an interesting compromise between battery and combustion systems. On the one hand, it takes advantage of the efficiency and environmental benefits of the electricity-based VP system. On the other, it benefits from an open ES system, thus ensuring fast refuels, reduced fuel load and no upfront fuel expenditure.

However, every compromise has its drawbacks. Notably, being an open system, the FC reactions are not reversible – while the battery switches between electricity charge and discharge modes, the FC cannot switch between the production of electricity and hydrogen. This prevents the FC from benefiting from one of the EV's greatest merits – regenerative braking.

Furthermore, to ensure environmentally friendly operations, FCs use pure hydrogen fuel. While hydrogen is often credited with being an abundant, readily available and clean fuel source, this overlooks one fundamental issue – pure hydrogen fuel is simply not found in nature and must be produced. Neglecting this minor detail is rather like forgetting that a tiger has sharp teeth.

The hydrogen storage challenge

Hydrogen fuel has the highest specific energy (kWh/kg) of any automotive energy source and recharge rates depend only on the flow rate of the fuel into the pressurized tank, in a manner that is directly comparable to ICVs. However, it also has the lowest energy density (kWh/L) of any fuel, making storage anything but trivial. Currently, there are two approaches to storing hydrogen: compressed gas and cryogenic liquid.

While cryogenic liquid offers greater energy density than compressed gas, it must be stored in temperatures below –253°C. Even with the best insulation – which requires heavy materials – keeping the cryogenic hydrogen appropriately cooled ends up being very energy intensive. In practice, this constraint severely limits the use of liquid hydrogen for automotive applications.

Consequently, compressed gas tends to be the storage mechanism of choice in the automotive industry. To minimize the storage space occupied, the gas is compressed to either 350 or 700 bars. The more compressed (700 bar) cylinders provide better energy density, but require thicker casing. In turn, this not only adds to the weight of the car but also increases the space used up for fuel storage in the vehicle.

Compressed gas also proves to be the cheapest hydrogen storage mechanism on an energy capacity basis. Even so, to ensure ICV comparable range, hydrogen tanks are estimated to cost around US$12,000–15,000 per tank, though with increased production this could rapidly fall below US$2000 (IEA, 2007). Alas, although providing the best overall compromise, 700-bar hydrogen gas only provides 42 per cent of the energy density offered by compressed natural gas (CNG) used in ICVs, so this is still not an ideal solution.

Research into alternative hydrogen storage mechanisms has increased over the past decade. Much attention has turned to chemical substances that offer increased hydrogen density compared to pure hydrogen gas. While these have spurred interesting laboratory results, there is still no indication that any of the alternatives being considered can be integrated into an energy system that outperforms compressed hydrogen gas.

Fuel cell prospects

One of the key advantages of FCEVs is the fact that the energy source and power source are decoupled. Hydrogen energy is stored physically in the pressurized cylinders, while power is produced independently by the FC stack. As noted above, this ensures fast recharge rates and acceptable range capabilities. But what does that say about driving performance and fuel efficiency?

PEMFCs do not offer competitive performance or efficiency at equivalent cost to battery technologies. The theoretical efficiency for a PEMFC is 65 per cent, but, according to the IEA, real applications achieve only 35–40 per cent efficiency. Note that, even at 35 per cent stack efficiencies, FCEV overall vehicle efficiency would still be more than double ICV efficiency. However, compared to typical BEV efficiencies, which range between 55 and 80 per cent, PEMFC-based solutions do not provide encouraging results.[11]

Worse, PEMFC stack costs may exceed US$1800/kW for low-volume production. This would give the Honda FCX Clarity's PEMFC a whopping price tag of US$180,000! Yes, that is *just* for the PEMFC stack. Granted, costs are plummeting and the IEA estimates that mass production PEMFC costs should drop to US$100/kW, or US$10,000 for a 100kW stack, but this still means that once prices have dropped for PEMFC stacks and hydrogen storage tanks, FCEV consumers would expect to incur an overall ES system capital cost of at least US$12,000. Furthermore, the IEA's timeframe for this evolution looks to be at least two decades into the future, making the economics of FCEVs very unfavourable.

Ultracapacitor Energy Storage Systems

Batteries are proving to be reliable energy sources, but remain relatively ineffective power sources (Figure 4.2). That is to say, they can hold a substantial amount of energy but they have difficulty converting energy quickly. Ultracapacitor (UC) technology has received increased attention because of its ability to efficiently deliver and accept high power levels. However, due to their fundamental physical properties, such systems do not provide suitable levels of energy content.

Operating principle

UCs are similar to batteries and FCs in that they are a source of electrical energy. They are closed energy sources just like batteries and can be recharged by the power grid. Otherwise, these systems are as similar to one another as solar panels and wind turbines. UCs store and supply energy in a fundamentally distinct manner which does not involve any form of chemical conversion, as occurs in batteries and FCs.

Let us consider the lightning phenomenon to better understand the physical properties at play in an UC. While our understanding of lightning remains a matter under study, some of the principles are thought to be understood. Lightning is thought to occur largely as a result of the behaviour of ice particles in storm clouds. During a storm, ice particles continuously collide with each other, which results in electrons being displaced from one particle to another, thus creating electrical differentials between different particles. Gradually, positively charged ice crystals begin to rise to the top of the storm clouds and negatively charged ice particles and hailstones drop towards the lower layers (Figure 4.11).

Capacitors are based on this same principle – of physically separating electrically charged electrodes to prevent electron flow. If the UC is connected to a battery, electrons will flow into one plate, polarizing it and repelling electrons away from the opposing plate. By preventing the current flow between the plates, an electrical potential difference (PD) is produced – positive on one side and negative on the other. For a capacitor to store electrons, it is crucial that no current flows between its two plates during the charge accumulation phase. Thus, while the goal is to build up as much charge as possible, it is vital that

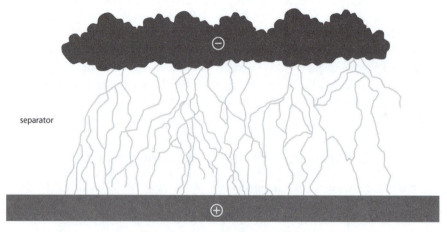

Figure 4.11 *Lightning analogy*

the relative charge between these plates never overcomes the resistance of the insulating material separating them.

To use the stored energy in an UC, one must simply reverse the circuit – in other words remove the battery and connect the EM to power. The PD between the plates acts as a pressure differential, inducing the electrons to flow from the negative plate towards the positive plate through the EM.

The clear advantage of UCs over batteries and FCs is that the energy is not stored chemically and thus can readily accept or deliver high power transfers. However, the UC's physical storage mechanism greatly limits its energy capacity, as discussed next. As will be seen later, the need to compromise between power and energy objectives in ES systems creates some opportunities for UCs.

The nanotechnology potential

The author has already stated that capacitors have limited energy capacity because of their physical storage mechanism. But given that the energy density of the best Li-ion batteries sits around 10 per cent of petrol's energy density ATW, just how much more 'limited' can capacitors be?

A conventional capacitor uses what is called a dielectric material to separate the polarized plates. Dielectric materials are characterized by the fact that they can be easily polarized, which is crucial to create the PD between plates. Unfortunately, there are also practical limits to how thin the dielectric material can be, ultimately restricting the miniaturization of conventional capacitors. Box 4.3 shows that conventional dielectric capacitors are not an acceptable solution for energy storage.

As seen in Box 4.3, to evaluate the energy storage potential of a capacitor, one must consider two things: the amount of charge (Ah) that can be stored and the maximum PD (V) that can be created between the plates. The amount of charge stored is determined by the physical space available for electrons to occupy, which is a function of the plate dimensions and its material properties. The maximum PD is limited by the properties of the separator material. These physical parameters prove to be extremely restrictive, currently limiting the use of capacitors to applications with very low energy requirements.

However, with the development of nanotechnology, ultracapacitors began to appear around the turn of the 21st century, allowing for much greater energy storage potential. While the underlying physical principles governing the UC remain unchanged, its molecular structure is distinct from traditional capacitors. Major advances in EV applications become possible.

In place of the conventional plate–dielectric–plate arrangement, UC technology advances are building on the principle of electrical double layers (Figure 4.13) – parallel layers of ions forming along the surface of an object submerged in a liquid substance. By stacking two layers of a substance with nano-porous surface texture (like a minuscule sponge) in place of the dielectric material, the surface area available for storing charge can be dramatically increased, while minimizing the thickness of each plate pair.

Box 4.3 30,240 CANS OF TUNA

Capacitance, or the energy storage potential of a capacitor, is measured in farads. A one farad (1F) capacitor can store one coulomb (1C) of charge at a PD of one volt (1V), allowing it to release a charge of one amp (1A) during one second (1s). Depending on the maximum PD, a 1F capacitor will be somewhere between the size of a can of tuna and a 1 litre bottle.

Putting this into perspective, consider a pair of AA batteries powering a Nintendo Wii remote control. Together they store 2.8 amp-hours (Ah) – or 10,080 amp-seconds (As) at 3V. So, how many capacitors would be needed to power this remote? Assume three 1F capacitors each with a 1V maximum PD, which are connected in series to get a ⅓F capacitor at 3V maximum PD, then connecting 10,080 of these in parallel to obtain the 2.8Ah charge storage. So, assuming a 1F capacitor the size of a tuna can operating at 1V, we can deduce that a Wii remote would require 30,240 cans of tuna. If these capacitors were laid out on the surface of a king-sized bed, they would stack up more than two and a half metres (Figure 4.12).

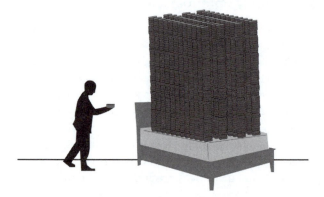

Figure 4.12 *King-sized bed of tuna*

Notice that this result overestimates the capacitors' capabilities. In reality, every capacitor has a minimum voltage below which it can no longer release energy. Thus one would need substantially more charge storage to be able to release the 10,080As before the minimum voltage cut-off.

Soon we will probably have mastered the nanotech manufacturing processes, allowing optimized UCs to be perfected and mass-produced. In theory, it is possible to develop a UC using carbon nanotubes or other nanotech-based solution to create the ideal electrical double-layer conditions that would offer energy capacity equivalent to or better than modern batteries. Texas-based UC and battery experts EEStor Inc. claim to have developed an innovative UC, called EESU, that can match or exceed Li-ion energy capacity levels at a fraction of the cost. Thus UCs could replace batteries and FCs as an independent energy source. However, for the time being, such solutions are not commercially available.

Hybridization

Despite their current limitations, the merits of UCs are undeniable: they hold excellent potential to deliver high power. As a result, hybrid ES system designs

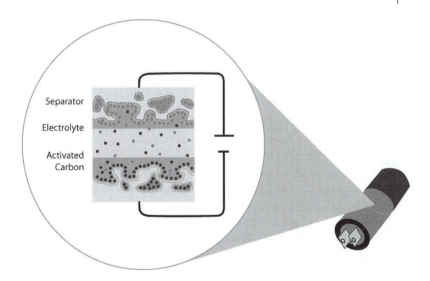

Figure 4.13 *Inside an ultracapacitor*

are being developed using battery energy sources complemented by UC power sources. In this format, the battery power can be designed to meet average power output while the UC provides the surplus peak power.

In fact, such a battery/capacitor hybridization design is not new. For quite some time now, flash photography has used a similar scheme. In this case, while the camera's battery cannot deliver the peak power required to operate the flash, the capacitor can. However, the capacitor has an insignificant energy capacity, so it needs to be recharged by the battery after every flash – this is why we have to wait a few seconds between clicks when using the flash.

Alternatively, compare the UC/battery EV with a water network. Figure 4.14 illustrates both systems.

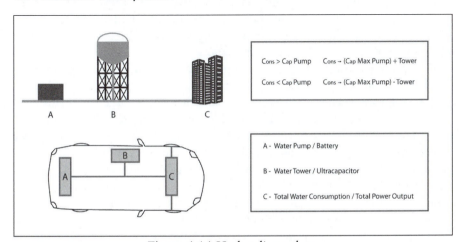

Figure 4.14 *Hydraulic analogy*

Notice that by using a water tower, the water company can install a water pump to meet average flow rates while the water tower responds to the real-time fluctuations in water demand. Just as water towers are used to assist water pumps in water distribution networks, dramatically reducing the capital cost of pumping equipment, UCs can be used to respond to real-time load fluctuations in EV circuits. This would effectively decouple energy and power activities, greatly simplifying the design of ES systems.

Consider a 1200kg Honda Civic, for instance. Say the driver needs to reach highway speeds (130km/hr) with optimal ultracapacitor efficiency (90 per cent) and that they live in a city with hills no higher than 100m. Using the principles of mechanical energy,[12] one can deduce that the maximum energy required for simultaneous acceleration and hill-climbing with the Honda Civic is 610Wh. Based on commercialized technology (~5Wh/kg), this would require a UC system of at least 150kg. Note, however, that there have been a flood of news releases promising dramatic energy capacity improvements, some as high as 60Wh/kg (0.22MJ/kg).

What is more, while batteries are capable of operating across a wide spectrum of power levels, battery power efficiency decays exponentially as the discharge current increases to deliver more power. In contrast, UCs offer exceptionally high conversion efficiencies (>90 per cent) across their operating spectrum. Ideally, batteries would be designed to meet merely base load (constant speed) operations, while the UC would meet the fluctuations (acceleration, deceleration, hill-climbing and so on). This would allow engineers to design batteries for optimal energy capacity and maximized cycle life, and supplement them with UCs to ensure peak power.

Approaching a Verdict 2: Closing the Gap

No alternative to the combustion-based ES system thus far has been able to offer equivalent performance and convenience at a competitive cost. However, recent technological advances are beginning to offer alternatives to the century-old ICE. Battery technology, in particular, offers a competitive alternative based on energy efficiency and driving performance.

However, electric ES systems continue to fail two major challenges: vehicle range and recharge obstacles. Vehicle range is related to storage capacity and thus to the capital cost of the vehicle. This, in turn, is largely a question of economies of scale. As each of the three ES systems reviewed above gain scale, one can expect to see considerable cost reductions. However, in the case of the battery, and perhaps the UC as well, the 'fuel substance' is built into the system, so increasing range will always have a direct impact on the vehicle price tag. The next chapter looks at how this also provides very low operating costs for BEVs, with favourable implications on the net present value of the BEV option. In addition, new chemical compositions have provided batteries with major leaps in energy capacity, with further advances still expected to ensure they remain the most cost-effective electric ES system overall.

As mentioned at the start of this chapter, recharging is not so much a question of vehicle technology (and storage capacity) as an infrastructure interface challenge. Granted, there are batteries on the market that achieve partial charge (up to 115km) in around 10 minutes. Alas, compared to the direct physical transfer of high energy-content fuels, chemical reactions stand very little chance of matching ICV refuelling rates – now or ever.[13]

Recharging infrastructure solutions have emerged, drawing on the BEV's inherent merits, which address both the battery's capital cost and range problem through innovative business models. This is addressed in detail in Chapter 5.

Notes

1   In most systems, energy capacity and usable energy capacity are identical measures. However, batteries must never be fully discharged, so usable energy capacity is some fraction of total (i.e. the battery's nominal) energy capacity.

2   Notice that the appropriate metric for energy, according to the International System of Units, is the joule. However, given the widespread use of kWh, for instance in electricity bills, this book provides all EV energy-related measures in both kWh and MJ. In the case of conventional ICVs, where energy capacity is more commonly measured in volumetric terms (litres or gallons of fuel), the book provides all ICV energy-related measures in both litres and MJ.

3   Recall that in this book, fuel efficiency refers to the strict engineering terminology, i.e. it is a dimensionless parameter that relates energy input to energy output in any given system.

4   Energy, as noted previously, is a measure of a system's capacity to perform work on something. In the case of the automobile, motion is the result of work being done by the VP system on the road surface, such that the distance travelled by a vehicle is proportional to the amount of work done by the VP system.

5   We already know the ICE and EM VP system efficiencies to be 15–18 and 92–97 per cent respectively; we will use these to obtain overall energy conversion efficiencies throughout the chapter.

6   Energy density ATW is defined as the amount of energy (expressed in kWh) per unit of fuel (expressed in litres or kg) that effectively performs work on the wheels to move the vehicle.

7   This compares, for instance, to Li-ion batteries that store 0.150kWh/kg (0.54MJ/kg).

8   For instance, as a battery pack discharges, the pack voltage eventually drops to a point which no longer meets minimum operating conditions, even though some cells might still have energy available. Alas, if nickel cadmium cells are not fully discharged on a regular basis, then the non-discharged chemical substances crystallizes, reducing that cell's energy capacity. This phenomenon, called the memory effect, is what used to rapidly reduce battery life back in early laptops.

9   This estimate is obtain by summing the material and manufacturing yield adjustment costs (approximately US$300/kWh) and dividing it by the total battery pack cost (US$1126/kWh)

10 Signs point to greener pastures. While President Evo Morales has tightened control of Bolivia's natural resources, these policies have proven less radical than

initially expected and cannot be compared to those practised by the government of Venezuela. Meanwhile, Chilean politics has proven stable and reliable since the 1990 return to democratic rule.

11 If one expands the analysis from T2W to W2W, these discrepancies accentuate the advantage of BEV over FCEV and ICV.

12 Mechanical energy is the sum of kinetic energy ($\frac{1}{2}mv^2$) and potential energy (mgh).

13 While a 115km charge range in 10 minutes may seem quite reasonable, it does not even begin to compare with the ICV's 480km range refuelling in just five minutes.

References

Anderson, D. L. (2009) 'An evaluation of current and future costs for lithium-ion batteries for use in electrified vehicle powertrains', Master's thesis, Duke University, Durham, NC

BCG (Boston Consulting Group) (2010) *Batteries for Electric Cars: Challenges, Opportunities and the Outlook to 2020*, Boston Consulting Group, Boston, MA, January, www.bcg.com/documents/file36615.pdf

Chan, C. C. and Chau, K. T. (2001) *Modern Electric Vehicle Technology*, Oxford University Press, Oxford, UK

Credit Suisse (2009) 'Electric vehicles', *Credit Suisse Equity Research*, 1 October

Dhameja, S. (2002) *Electric Vehicle Battery Systems*, Newnes (Butterworth-Heinemann), Elsevier Group, Oxford

Ehsani, M., Gao, Y., Gay, S. E. and Emadi, A. (2004) *Modern Electric, Hybrid Electric, and Fuel Cell Vehicles: Fundamentals, Theory, and Design*, CRC Press, Boca Raton, FL

IEA (2007) 'Fuel cells', *IEA Energy Technology Essentials*, International Energy Agency, Paris

IEA (2009) *Technology Roadmap: Electric and Plug-In Hybrid Electric Vehicles*, International Energy Agency, Paris

5

The Electric Vehicle
Recharging Infrastructure

Fundamental progress has to do with the reinterpretation of basic ideas.

Alfred North Whitehead

Innovation theory says that a technology alone is worthless to the mass-market consumer unless it can be transformed into a 'whole product solution' (Moore, 1999), in other words one that encompasses the broad range of complementary goods and services required for the typical consumer to feel comfortable in its use. Oh, and yes, they usually need to feel that it is a bargain or, at least, clearly worth their money. But what distinguishes a good technology – such as WordPerfect, UNIX and BetaMax – from a successful whole product – MS Word, Windows and VHS?

Needless to say, a major factor behind the dominance of ICV technology has been the development of a successful, widespread recharging infrastructure network. Drivers can fill up their gas-guzzler almost anywhere on the globe. In contrast, the recharging concern is probably the most critical obstacle to EV adoption.

The EV recharging system concern is generally overstated, since modern EVs can meet average daily travel distances in urban as well as in rural areas with an ample margin. However, even if the consumer 'accepts' that range autonomy is not a real problem, when they reach the dealership to buy their brand new, energy-efficient, high-performance EV, they are likely to think 'but what if?' For instance, on their annual long distance trip, once the charge depletes, will the family be stuck for several hours waiting for the car to recharge? For that matter, where will they be able to recharge?

For whatever reason – whether the economic crisis or concern over global warming – the EV industry, in the last five to ten years, has received an influx of fresh ideas and players, along with the financial resources to support them. Innovative solutions are emerging rapidly and promising good results, not just in terms of the individual vehicle but, crucially, in terms of the energy system needed to support the EV solution.

This chapter will examine the two recharging approaches being proposed and how different market architectures might influence their performance. In addition, it examines how this new infrastructure will interact with the existing power network. The purpose here is not so much to identify an optimal set of solutions but rather to highlight the current trends in business behaviour that show a fundamental shift from previous EV developments. The author has selected what are seen as the most promising global ideas, to present their merits, risks and limitations in a unified discussion. With that in mind, this chapter begins by examining the one dominant characteristic that will need to guide the development of any effective recharging system.

Energy Services

As noted previously, the ICV's greatest asset is its association with combustion fuels that are supremely effective energy carriers and around which the refuelling infrastructure was built. Indeed, as vehicle capital costs began to drop from the early 1920s, the automotive and petroleum industries jointly ensured that the infrastructure was both operationally convenient and widespread.

Operational convenience was guaranteed first by designing an industry standard interface between the fuel supplier and the vehicle. The fuel hose provided a simple design and a safe physical solution to the problem. Coupled with the high energy-content characteristics of combustion fuels, this ensured fast refuelling for a long driving range.

Meanwhile, liquid and gaseous fuels had to be transported via a network of tankers, trucks and pipelines, which meant distribution costs grew with decreasing scale and increasing proximity to individual consumers. Consequently, fuel distribution logistics were optimized to reduce the cost of transporting supplies to the consumer while ensuring the convenience of widespread availability. By standardizing the supplier/vehicle interface, distribution costs could be shared between several fuel suppliers.

The result is that, over the years, the ICV energy solution has provided consumers with fast and widespread refuelling at low capital cost for the consumer. This energy system solution transformed the ICV from mere technology into a whole-product offering.

These same characteristics currently play against EV implementation, which has held the industry at a stalemate in the development of sustainable transport. While speed of refuelling is basically a technological issue, optimal location of refuelling sites requires a departure from the ICV infrastructure solution.

The following section examines how the recharge market might evolve. It begins with a redefinition of what a whole-product solution for electric recharging services should involve. It then provides a description of the physical mechanisms being considered to provide a fast recharge service and highlights their technical advantages and limitations. It then discusses solutions with respect to their spatial distribution so as to ensure a widespread and reliable infrastructure. Finally, it considers how different market architectures might impact the success of such solutions.

A battery whole-product solution

In the early EV world, the battery was viewed as an integrated component of the vehicle – equivalent to an ICV's fuel tank. This approach imposed three significant obstacles on EV marketing: high capital costs, slow recharge rates and unreliable infrastructural solutions. However, batteries are increasingly regarded as a self-contained fuel pack independent of the EV. Such a perspective transforms the battery and its energy content into an integrated *quasi-service* as opposed to two distinct elements – a product and a recharging service.

The purpose of marketing the battery separately from the vehicle is, first and foremost, to dilute the initial capital cost over the vehicle's lifetime, by means of various financing arrangements. Rather than owning the battery outright, the consumer would pay a battery service provider (BSP) for the service that the fuel pack provides. According to management consultants Frost & Sullivan (2009), 75 per cent of EVs are expected to be marketed through some form of battery-energy financing scheme. Beyond diluting the battery costs, this proposition also reduces the consumer's exposure to the risk of battery-related failures. Beyond the initial battery cost, battery reliability and life expectancy is a further concern for prospective buyers.

Notice, however, that even if an alternative technology is desirable and profitable, breaking from tradition usually requires a new entrant into the market – such as Xerox (Box 5.1) – or strong government intervention – as in the London Sewage System case (Introduction) and the Brazilian ethanol case (Chapter 1) – to turn things upside down. Even then, a suitable business model must be found to market the 'new' product. The Xerox case presents lessons that are extremely relevant to the study of EV implementation. It shows how the company came to dominate the photocopying industry using a technology that had been rejected by every major industry player because of high initial capital cost. Their secret weapon: an innovative business model to support the new superior technology (Chesbrough and Rosenbloom, 2002).

Just like Xerox in 1959, the EV industry offers an improved technology which must be turned into a whole-product solution through innovative business models. While the role of an adequate business model in the success of a technology is no major insight in and of itself, it is important to recognize that cognitive lock-in is a dangerous but common state among established businesses. Willingly or not, Big Auto[1] has left space for new investors to compete for a

---

Box 5.1 Xerox case study

Before 1960, photocopying in offices was done through one of two processes: wet photographic (high-quality) or dry thermal (low-quality). In both cases, photocopiers were commercialized through the so-called 'razor-and-razor-blade' business model. The idea was to sell photocopying devices at a marginal mark-up over their already relatively cheap cost, in turn ensuring long-term revenue streams from supplies that were sold at a substantially higher mark-up. However, in 1959, Xerox (at the time called Haloid) introduced its first photocopying device based on electrophotography technology.

Electrophotography offered three basic improvements: higher image quality, faster copying and no need for specialist copying paper. However, these improvements came at the very high capital cost of US$2000, more than six times the cost of a typical photocopying device at the time. Furthermore, despite not needing special paper, variable costs per copy were equivalent to those of typical office copiers.

Xerox sought an established photocopying industry partner to market its product but was unanimously rejected by every major manufacturer on the basis that the product lacked comparative advantage in any specific application. From their perspective, consumers would not make the additional investment to obtain the machine's 'marginal' performance improvements.

Nevertheless, Xerox believed in the technology's inherent value and invested in developing a different business model to support it – notably by redefining the terms of its service and the associated revenue architecture. As opposed to selling the expensive device, Xerox proposed to offer it to consumers on a monthly lease. For US$95 per month, consumers could make up to 2000 copies and Xerox provided all the supplies and technical support. If consumers exceeded their 2000-copy allowance, they paid US$0.04 per additional copy.

This business model offered a cheap, efficient and high-quality copying solution for the office. The appeal was far beyond anyone's expectations – the first customers averaged 2000 copies per day. Xerox's revenues shot from US$30m (1959) to US$2.5bn (1972) – a compound annual growth rate of 41 per cent over little over a decade. These results led ultimately to the complete collapse of the long-standing 'razor-and-razor-blade' business model.

The lesson to be taken from this case is that, too often, technologies are inappropriately assumed to be uncompetitive simply as a result of the analyst's inability to consider them through the perspective of an unconventional business model. The unfortunate consequence is that businesses often miss out on exploiting the latent value of their technological creations. In the Xerox case, rivals recognized the fundamental merits of the new technology, but were unable to identify the possibility of changing the whole-product solution and its cost structure, thus failing to perceive a compelling reason for consumers to buy the new 'product package'.

---

share of the battery service market. While Big Auto focused on the incremental improvements of essentially the same vehicle formula for half a century, newcomers are targeting the long-neglected EV energy systems challenge. In this context, much like in the Xerox case, what the industry is witnessing is a redefinition of the EV energy system business model to ensure more attractive pricing, faster recharge rates and widespread supply availability.

Fast recharge service mechanisms

To date, EV recharging has relied solely on plugging in the vehicle into low-voltage power supplies. Given that the average daily driving distance in the US is 50km (Davis and Diegel, 2007) (Figure 5.1) and assuming drivers plug in their cars overnight, they would basically never have the hassle of fuelling them

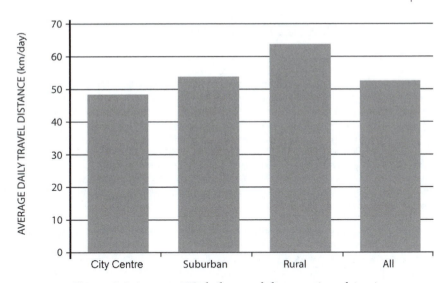

Figure 5.1 *Average US daily travel distance (per driver)*

Source: Davis and Diegel (2007)

up en route to work or in the midst of daily activities. This means that concerns over the reliability of recharging systems, more commonly known as the range anxiety issue, are largely of a psychological nature. By allowing EVs to recharge overnight at home, during the day at the office and at all other locations where vehicles remain parked for extended periods of time, it will be possible to accommodate the vast majority of an EV's energy requirements, particularly in urban settings.

Undoubtedly, slow-charge will end up being a fundamental piece of the overall recharge puzzle. However, slow-charge cannot provide consumers with the same level of service as the existing ICV infrastructure (i.e. fast recharge), despite access to low-voltage electricity being inherently widespread, and businesses have come to terms with the fact that the traditional slow-charge infrastructure will not suffice.

In their search for a solution beyond slow-charge, businesses appear torn between fast-charge plug-in and battery swapping as the best approach to providing convenient and reliable energy to move EVs. The discussion now turns its attention to understanding how these can work to provide competitive energy provision.[2]

Fast-charge plug-in

The most obvious method of increasing the recharge rate is to use a high-power energy supply so that greater volumes of energy flow into the battery in a given period of time. By using a supply of 50kW, recharge times could theoretically be dropped to a matter of 30 minutes for a 25kWh battery. This is the equivalent of supplying 5.5km of range per minute of charge. However, the solution has drawbacks.

BOX 5.2 OVERLOADING THE GRID

Consider a modern EV, such as the BYD e6, whose battery packs have 72kWh energy capacity. According to BYD, the e6 will reach 50 per cent SOC in just 10 minutes. To achieve these charge rates, the e6 will need access to a power supply of 216kW – highly ambitious by today's standards. While it is unlikely that all e6s hook up simultaneously to the fast-charge infrastructure, utility companies fear that many other EVs will soon be on the roads, thus increasing the demand for fast charge at any given time. This needs to be put into perspective.

Based on preliminary production schedules, sales volumes of 10,000 units per model are expected in the first year. By 2015, there could easily be over 100,000 state-of-the-art EVs on American roads. If 5 per cent of these vehicles (5000 EVs) simultaneously hooked into fast-charge infrastructure, they would induce a brief 1080MW load on the power grid, equivalent to instantaneously calling for a large-scale power plant to provide electricity for a ten-minute period. But is this a plausible scenario?

While one might expect 5 per cent (or so) of total trips to require a daytime fast recharge (to meet long distance travel needs), it is also reasonable to expect that these fast-charge loads would be distributed over the course of the day. If loads were evenly spread over a ten-hour period, they would create a relatively stable additional 18MW demand[3] (negligible next to US installed capacity of 1130GW in 2008). Even assuming that fast charging is not as evenly spread out as suggested above, it is clear that the impact on the grid of this additional demand is not catastrophic.

Chapter 4 (Box 4.2) found that the rate at which energy can be injected into batteries is limited by the rate of chemical reactions occurring in the battery. Batteries accept high power levels at a low state of charge (SOC). However, as the SOC increases, so does the internal resistance within the cells. Consequently, high power input cannot be sustained at high SOC, to avoid overheating the battery and permanently damaging the pack. What is more, most batteries available today have not been developed to receive high power input such as that indicated above.

The solution also raises concerns over impacts on the power grid. Indeed, if future battery compositions achieve ultra-short charge times, as is promised by China's BYD and California's Tesla, it is feared that the impact on the grid could be dramatic. But as demonstrated in Box 5.2, these concerns may be overstated. Other impacts of the EV on the power grid will be discussed later in this chapter.

For these reasons, fast-charge systems require advanced monitoring equipment to ensure that the power input is adjusted according to SOC and to prevent overload conditions on the power grid. Such high power levels would also require stringent operating regulations to avoid fatal accidents at the point of recharge. This means trained personnel, thus restricting the application to specialist fast-charge stations.

Moreover, even BYD's technology 'only' provides 150–200km for every 10 minutes of charge, which is about a fifth of the rate of ICV fuelling. Indeed, truly fast charging relies heavily on technological advances, particularly in terms of battery compositions, which could take a matter of maybe 10 years to become available.

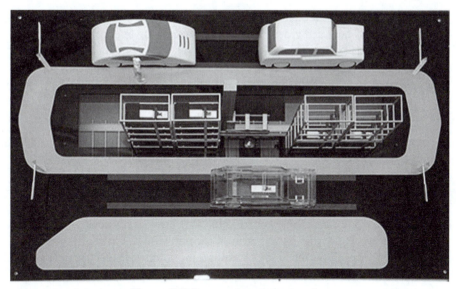

Figure 5.2 *Battery-swapping station*

Source: Better Place

Battery swapping

The greatest advantage of the battery-swapping alternative is probably that it does not depend on future technological innovation, as required by fast charging. In contrast with plug-in solutions, energy is not converted into the car through a charging process – rather it is physically transferred without any change of state, by merely changing the pack. This is analogous to the way we manage batteries in remote controls, cameras, calculators, etc.

However, to be successful, such a system depends on a vast network of battery-swapping stations, each of which maintaining on hand enough charged batteries to meet real-time demand (Figure 5.2). This would require multiple battery packs to be available per EV operating in the network. Needless to say, the deployment of such a network would be very capital intensive, such that failure to build up a corresponding customer base with an elevated rate of utilization could lead to catastrophic financial results for the supplier.

Since companies do not disclose data on planned storage, it is difficult to make a reliable concrete evaluation of this issue. But let's assume that, during the first five years, they must store one battery for every two vehicles on the road and approximately one for every four vehicles thereafter. This would inflate their initial battery investment costs by 50 per cent, while simultaneously shrinking each battery's utilization factor. This is the equivalent of increasing an EV's battery capacity by 50 per cent without increasing average travel distances. As will be seen in Chapter 6, this would have a severe impact on an EV's lifetime profitability.

Looking ahead, consider what happens if, in maybe 20 years, fast charge (minutes) and ultra-high energy content (500+km range) electrical storage devices do become available at competitive prices. Why would anyone need to swap batteries? These are indeed risks which battery-swapping businesses will need to address as their networks evolve. Still, the battery-swapping proposition can take advantage of existing refuelling stations, assuming petroleum distribution businesses recognize the trend towards the EV.

Widespread recharge service infrastructure

A suitable recharge mechanism should be able to ensure both fast and slow recharge rates, as discussed above. However, an additional concern for consumers is having easy access to the EV energy system whenever needed. Recall the question at the opening of this chapter: *Where will EVs be able to recharge?*

It is often claimed that the power grid is inherently widespread, making it an excellent automotive energy source. However, how many sockets do drivers come across every day just sitting around for public use? For that matter, how many of these are compatible with EV recharging solutions? Electricity is indeed widespread and could come to provide a reliable charging network, but the power system, as it is today, does not ensure the same level of vehicle energy service as the petroleum refuelling system. So how might the infrastructure problem be addressed?[4]

As the controllers of the power grid, utilities are the natural heirs to the BSP throne. Indeed, they have the opportunity to expand their markets while taking advantage of their existing infrastructure and of synergies that will be discussed later in this chapter. Ironically, though, utilities run the risk of a similar cognitive lock-in vice as Big Auto: EVs are not their core business – they would need to explore the unknown. Having said that, many utilities are stepping up to the challenge. The gates have also been opened by risk-seeking investors who are more willing to break with tradition. Obviously, they have no intention of taking over the utilities' core business, but hope to act as system integrators, providing the interface between automotive manufacturers, energy providers and consumers.

The discussion examines what is already being done by BSPs to provide widespread energy services and the potential drawbacks to the two main approaches – charge spots and battery stations. Keep in mind that these solutions are not necessarily mutually exclusive.

Charge spots

The most common BSP model is the age-old plug-in charging mechanism, except widespread and with a high-power electrical supply option for fast charging. This solution will not provide an equivalent recharge service to ICV fuelling stations, at least not in the foreseeable future.[5] However, it is less capital intensive than battery swapping and should prove to be an adequate solution for the vast majority of situations.

The first advantage of the charge spot is its relative ease of dissemination. Assuming a basic level of plug and socket design standardization, so that an EV is capable of plugging into any available charge spot, deployment can effectively be achieved by a broad range of independent investors. The second advantage is the vastly reduced capital expenditure requirements. A standard power supply charge spot will cost US$2000. Such a charge spot should suffice for the vast majority of applications – from office building to on-street parking to shopping complex parking spots.

In the few cases where conventional charge spots are insufficient – say an interstate trip – a high-power, fast-charge spot, for instance offered by a (retro-fitted) gas fuelling station, should prove reliable.[6] In contrast to the simple, basic charge spot, a fast-charge spot will incur an estimated cost of US$100,000, and thus deployment must be carefully planned to avoid runaway development costs. In addition to the high initial capital requirements, fast-chargers should not be implemented by independent investors. Rather, a regulated business is required to ensure safety conditions for consumers and personnel, as well as to avoid stressing the electrical grid with unpredictable and excessive power loads.

Governments and businesses around the world are already investing billions of dollars to put in place widespread charging networks. London Mayor Boris Johnson, for example, promises to have deployed 25,000 charge spots across the city by 2015, to support the 100,000 EVs he expects to populate the English capital's roads (Jha, 2009). The French government have decided on a more comprehensive revamping of the recharge market, beginning with a US$2.2 billion programme to put in place improved infrastructure across the country. In parallel, they promise to make charge spots obligatory in new apartment blocks from 2012 on and in all office parking lots by 2015 (Salton, 2009).

Across the Atlantic, in the US, despite less stringent vehicle emissions regulations, EV charging infrastructure is taking off as well. Tesla Motors has partnered with solar power specialists SolarCity and Deutsch-based Rabobank to develop the first EV charging corridor. Five charge spots have been installed between San Francisco and Los Angeles along the 680km stretch of Highway 101. Meanwhile, ECOtality has been working on a 180km corridor linking Tucson and Phoenix, Arizona. Recently, the company was also awarded a US$100 million grant by the Department of Energy to install 12,750 charge spots on the East and West Coasts of the US to coincide with Nissan's LEAF EV launch (Motavalli, 2009).

Again, the EV is all about thinking outside the box, where business models are concerned. While traditional power utilities and governments may be the obvious candidates for deploying charge-spot infrastructure, an unexpected class of investors has emerged with a particularly attractive proposition: parking spots with free electricity for your EV. As unprofitable as it might sound, it is spreading fast across both Europe and the US, with McDonald's and Sainsbury's (the British grocery chain store) leading the way.

The business principle is simple. It is a cheap and easy way of attracting customers. Rather than spending money on advertising campaigns, the local movie theatre installs several conventional charge spots for customers to use free of charge. As an EV customer going to the movies after a long day of

Table 5.1 *Free charge*

	Units	Theatre	Fast food HGWY	Grocery
Capital cost	US$	2500	10,000	10,000
Cost original advert	US$/cust	1.00	0.50	1.50
Avg space utilization	hrs/day	6	12	12
Operation period	days/wk	4	7	7
Avg parking time	hrs/vehicle	2.5	0.5	0.75
No. vehicles daily	vehicles/day	2.4	24	16
Charge power drawn	kW	1.9	7.2	7.2
Electricity cost	US$/kWh	0.09	0.09	0.09
Electricity cost per vehicle	US$/vehicle	0.43	0.32	0.49
Customer per vehicle	cust/vehicle	2	2	1
Cost per customer	US$/cust	0.21	0.16	0.49
Savings per customer	US$/cust	0.79	0.34	1.01
Annual savings	US$/year	785	5906	5906
Payback	yrs	3.2	1.7	1.7

Note: HGWY = highway.
Source: Credit Suisse (2009)

chores, you think: I can top up my car for free here or go to another theatre and pay to charge it at home later. You take the deal, relax and watch your movie while the theatre sells more tickets despite reducing its advertisement bill. Table 5.1 illustrates how the money saved on marketing can quickly make up for the charge-spot investment and running costs.

Crucially, charge station infrastructure deployment rate will need to keep up with EV penetration. In fact, assuming manufacturers and consumers can reach a compromise regarding suitable vehicle range, a network of dispersed recharging stations can be expected to soon complement and gradually replace the gasoline station system as transportation fuel supplier.

Battery-swapping stations

The battery-swapping business model is based strictly on systems integration. It is no coincidence that Better Place was founded by Shai Agassi, a former SAP executive and software systems integration entrepreneur. And no surprise that the company has committed to developing several multi-billion dollar projects around the world based on the swapping concept.

Beginning in 2010, Better Place plans to gradually deploy its stations according to EV penetration rates – with commitments in Israel, Denmark and Japan, as well as in Canberra, Ontario, California and Hawaii. To ensure service reliability, they propose to deploy one swap station for every 100 vehicles sold during the first five years and one for every 1000 vehicles thenceforth.

The company has selected each project location carefully, ensuring not only the support of local governments and population, but also the predictability of driving range patterns. By doing this, Better Place is able to plan its networks with greater certainty and thus minimize excess development costs. Even so, development costs are not encouraging, with estimates for a swap station at US$500,000. These networks are designed to support an EV fleet with the same comfort level as existing petrol networks offer the ICV. If this is confirmed, consumer confidence and market penetration can be expected to boom rapidly in supported regions.

While the Better Place model is based on effectively identifying niche markets with favourable conditions, it does not necessarily create a platform for scaling up or replicating the business. Indeed, proof of concept of the Better Place model in Israel, or even in California, will not make deployment in Middle America any more likely, given the distinct topographic conditions and the strategic importance of reducing petrol dependence in these locations. In addition, by the time their model is scaled up, battery costs may have dropped – reducing the need for battery financing and perhaps even making long-distance travel a reality on a single charge. Battery swapping could become redundant.

The isolated nature of most Better Place projects ensures physical boundaries that help control costs at an early stage, but it subsequently limits the possibility of gradual geographical expansion of the network. Battery swapping has high initial capital costs, so global penetration can be expected to stagnate prematurely unless barriers to entry can be overcome. In such an event, investors and politicians would have to collaborate closely to ensure widespread deployment of battery swapping, especially in emerging economies.

This evaluation is not meant to tarnish the swapping model in the reader's eyes. Indeed, the author believes that battery-swapping networks will flourish in distinct markets. However, it does not provide a silver bullet to the EV energy system challenge. Indeed, fast-charging and battery-swapping systems are not mutually exclusive solutions. It is likely that each will thrive in specific situations and in many cases may even complement each other. For example, battery swapping could be used on highways – for example Rio de Janeiro to São Paulo, San Francisco to Los Angeles, Boston to Washington, London to Manchester – to allow for long-range travel, while currently available (semi) fast charge could provide rapid range extension in urban areas – for example allowing taxis to top up during coffee breaks and buses at major terminals.

Market architecture

By offering more comprehensive solutions as opposed to just the electrical charge, BSPs can expand their business scope. In defining the structure of a BSP business, an investor must consider three variables: initial investment costs, operating costs and externalities. As has been seen, different recharge service solutions impose very different initial costs, depending on the level of battery financing offered as well as the type of recharge mechanism adopted – US$2000 per slow-charge spot, US$100,000 per fast-charge spot and US$500,000 per battery-swapping station. In Chapter 6 it will be demonstrated that the energy cost per kilometre for an EV is a fraction that of ICVs – around one-quarter in the US and closer to one-seventh in the EU. Furthermore, EVs may exploit

---

Box 5.3 PAYG versus contract

As we all know, cell phone companies offer two options: pay-as-you-go (PAYG) and contract. By equating mobile phone talk time to automobile kilometres driven, one can derive two pricing policies that are analogous to the familiar mobile phone solutions.

1 **PAYG:** A fixed tariff is set between a lower limit, determined by the provider's average lifetime cost per kWh, and an upper limit, equivalent to the cost per kilometre of petrol. Notice that the average lifetime cost per kWh would encompass not only the immediate electricity price, but also the capital cost of the battery amortized over its life.
2 **Contract:** Alternatively, consumers could select a monthly consumption plan consisting of a fixed and a variable component, similar to the way mobile phones are contracted rather than 'bought'. The fixed component would be set relative to the average lifetime cost per kWh of the battery provider and the preset monthly consumption level. In the event that the consumer exceeds the monthly allowance, an inflated tariff would set in, equivalent to PAYG. In the event that the consumer does not consume the full allowance, they continue to pay the fixed component (a month-to-month mileage rollover policy could possibly also apply).

---

various opportunities arising from externalities associated with both the power grid (vehicle-to-grid energy sales, discussed earlier in this chapter) and the technological switch from ICV to EV (carbon trading and other environmental incentives, discussed in Chapter 6).

A BSP can exploit the operating cost discrepancy between EVs and ICVs to recover its initial investment costs – of the battery and recharging facilities – and generate a profitable business. Drawing on an analogy with the mobile phone market, Box 5.3 provides an outline for how businesses might structure an adequate pricing policy.

One can begin to see how there are different solutions to address the EV/ICV cost discrepancy. Pursuing the contract modality a step further, Table 5.2 illustrates four kinds of policies that might be adopted. Indeed, BSPs might profit from being more than just energy providers, but rather, like the mobile network operators, provide an array of financing solutions – from energy to

Table 5.2 *Sample tariffs*

	Model 1	Model 2	Model 3	Model 4
Type	Energy pack	Maintenance pack	Part subsidy	Full subsidy
Cover	Partial battery lease + electricity maintenance	Energy package + insurance + maintenance package + 50% discount	Maintenance package + 100% discount	
Energy	Monthly bill	Fixed: <2000km/month	Fixed: 25,000km/year	Fixed: 30,000km/month
Contract	n/a	n/a	4 years	7 years
Subsidy	n/a	n/a	50% car	Free car
Monthly lease	<€150	<€300	€500–€800	€900–€1500

Source: Frost & Sullivan (2009)

Table 5.3 *Market structure matrix*[7]

Market Type	Payment	Candidates	Regulation standardization	Grid optimization	Supply optimization
Competitive	PAYG	Private sector agents, preferably with an inbuilt scale advantage and marginal cost of building in additional services, e.g. shopping centres, cinemas, parking lots	Industry collaboration for product standardization or commoditization	None	Pricing minimization (potentially unprofitable!); supply imbalance
Monopoly	Contract	State-owned discos or independent specialized BSPs or partnership thereof	Regulation to ensure competitive pricing and service quality	Full	No price optimization; supply equilibrium
Mixed	Contract	???	Naturally imposed by disco	Fully optimized by monopoly disco	Pricing optimization through supply auction

Note: disco = regional/provincial power distribution company.

vehicle purchase to maintenance – drawing in consumers while maximizing earnings potential.

The resulting market structure will depend partially on government orientation as well as on the prevailing power sector market structure. Table 5.3 summarizes the key aspects of the three basic market structures that are likely to prevail. It should be highlighted that the following models are hypothetical – none have been explicitly promoted by prospective BSPs. Nevertheless, they provide insight into the service options that will tend to prevail under different business environments and how governments might want to promote certain arrangements.

Competitive markets

The most similar structure to the present combustion-fuel market structure sees several independent BSPs simultaneously offering energy services. To ensure a competitive market, this requires the adoption of an industry-wide specification for battery and charge interface design such that all EVs in a region are compatible with all BSP equipment. Furthermore, in the case of the battery-swapping approach, a consumer has to be free to exchange a battery at any BSP, regardless of what battery they have on board.

Given that electronic instrumentation is standard practice with modern EV batteries, achieving high levels of compatibility and exchangeability is technically feasible. However, suppliers would also have to have access to some sort of coordinated, periodic stock reappropriation process, even if only on a virtual level (Box 5.4). Note that this could prove to be an insurmountable obstacle to a perfect competition battery-swapping network.

Box 5.4 Virtual reappropriation model

Stock reappropriation processes are not uncommon in energy markets. One good example of this is the Brazilian gas canister market. Rather than owning the canister itself and periodically refilling it with gas, consumers purchase the gas and the temporary use of a canister. At each order, the gas provider replaces the empty canister for a pre-filled unit.

To ensure market competition, gas providers are obliged by law to replace any empty canisters, regardless of the original canister proprietor. However, since each proprietor is solely responsible for safe operation of its canisters, this proprietor and its licensed provider partners are permitted to sell and install only their own canisters. To fulfil the necessary stock reappropriation requirements, each provider must return other providers' canisters to a reappropriation centre and subsequently collect their own canisters from the same centre.

One key problem may be expected when applying this solution to battery markets. The throughput of batteries swapped every day needs to be maximized for BSPs to profit. Ideally, empty batteries would immediately connect to the grid for recharging according to anticipated demand. But this would not be possible with batteries from multiple BSPs, since only the proprietor may recharge and sell their own units.

Suppose, however, that two BSPs (call them Shell and Petrobras) supply standardized batteries from the same manufacturer and with the same life expectancy. On a given day, a Petrobras battery with 1900 remaining cycles is exchanged at a Shell station and a Shell battery with 1800 remaining cycles is exchanged at a Petrobras station. The companies exchange proprietary titles for the batteries and Petrobras receives 100 cycles of credit from Shell. Over time, the credits will tend to cancel each other out or can be traded according to a pricing methodology.

This virtual reappropriation of battery-energy stocks should induce the operation of a more fluid and optimal market. A further problem, however, would need to be addressed – batteries are sensitive devices that must be handled and stored carefully, raising concerns that some companies may be inclined towards cutting maintenance costs. Thus this model would only work well if strict maintenance standards were upheld by regulators.

The key merit of competition is that, given product standardization and a high number of suppliers in the market, consumers will tend to benefit from the lowest possible price for service. This reduces the BSP's ability to forecast demand and thus exposes them to the risk of poor investment decisions. In turn, it could lead to increased price volatility according to supply/demand imbalance. Finally, unless they are actively encouraged by utilities, BSPs are unlikely to pay much attention to optimal battery/grid integration, while, in turn, utilities are unlikely to be attracted to individual BSPs because of their small scale.

Indeed, it seems that battery swapping based on competitive markets has limited advantages when compared to the complexity of the operations and the potential risks for BSPs. For that matter, from the consumer's perspective, a marginal price discount due to increased competition probably does not justify the potential unreliability of supplies and the risk of price volatility compared to the other alternatives.

In contrast, a plug-in solution based on competitive markets should not be expected to suffer the same disadvantages. The comparatively low investment cost of installing individual charging posts (in the US$1000s), as compared to developing a battery-swapping station (in the US$100,000s), makes the plug-in market attractive to relatively small-scale investors such as shopping centres, cinemas and roadside restaurants.

Monopolistic markets

At the other extreme, a single BSP could control the entire market. While the thought of monopoly control may scare the free-market enthusiast inside many readers, EV energy markets, particularly battery swapping, may prove to be a case of natural monopoly and thus would benefit by being managed as such. This approach would of course come naturally in countries with centralized governments and/or predominantly publicly owned power utilities.

Such a geographical monopoly market is well suited to a long-term contract approach (Box 5.3). From the consumer's perspective, this ensures system-wide standardization and compatibility, as well as guaranteeing long-term service availability. This is crucial in the early stage of development of a new market, which runs abandonment risks. For example, recall that during the late 1980s and early 1990s, Brazilian ethanol suppliers temporarily reduced production due to a combination of low oil and high sugar prices. While the Brazilian ethanol market thrives today, this slump left ethanol-dependent consumers temporarily stranded. Indeed, long-term contracts 'naturally' ensure that BSPs cannot simply abandon consumers overnight.

From the BSP's viewpoint, long-term contracts guarantee a minimum revenue level. Contracts provide a predictable demand and thus enhance the BSP's planning ability, reducing the risks of over/under investment/supply that are likely in competitive markets. Since the BSP controls all supplies, it need not worry about a complex stock reappropriation process. Furthermore, in a monopoly market, a utility would be drawn to a partnership with – or perhaps direct management of – the BSP to capture potential smart grid savings. Consequently, battery and grid operations would be mutually optimized to take advantage of economies of scale, resulting in lower overall costs of both services.

On the down-side, monopolies are prone to inefficiencies. Since consumers have no substitute for the service, the price and overall service quality could suffer. As a result, government regulation is vital to ensure optimal results.

Mixed markets

In many countries, power sector structure is a mix between monopoly and competition. On one hand, the power distribution business is typically monopolized by a regional/provincial company (a 'disco') that ensures a standardized interface with consumers and prevents redundant development of power lines. On the other, the power *generation* business is competitive, with several companies able to produce and sell power directly to a regional (usually state-owned) transmission grid that supplies the discos, thus ensuring low-cost energy supplies.

An analogous structure could be used for EV energy systems in many countries. Batteries would be owned by several businesses and supplied to consumers through a single battery disco, the BSP. This structure provides a compromise between the previous two alternatives, thus ensuring the benefits of both. A regulated auction system would guarantee that the BSP acquires only the lowest-priced supplies. The BSP would then be limited to a marginal price upscaling to cover business costs. As with the monopoly system, utility and BSP are drawn to a mutually beneficial battery-grid optimization, thus reducing overall system costs and rental price.

Once again, long-term contracts can be used to the advantage of consumer and BSP alike, reducing the risk of supplier abandonment, guaranteeing minimum revenue level and improving supply/demand balance. However, unlike the cost incidence under a monopoly model, battery investment costs are shared by various suppliers. As such, this model greatly reduces market risks – particularly at the crucial early stages of implementation. By minimizing both capital cost and risk exposure while optimizing operational costs, this model is likely to ensure the lowest long-term price for consumers.

Impact on the Power Grid

EVs rely entirely on electricity for energy supply – be it directly through plug-in charging or indirectly through battery swapping. Given the importance of maintaining a healthy power grid, much research has gone into evaluating potential impacts of EVs on the grid. This section considers two key impacts – harmonic distortion and load variation – and suggests that the development of the EV market would present major benefits to the quality of power supply overall, which could be captured and internalized by utilities.

Harmonic distortion: Confused grids

Harmonic distortion is the single most complex technical issue surrounding EVs. From a power utility's perspective, it has the potential to gravely hamper the quality of power supply and thus represents a direct threat to the utility's core business. What is more, different from batteries, which are an established part of modern life, harmonics are a sort of extra-terrestrial life form – even to many 'old timers' in the sector.

Think of the crisp clean sound produced by a good CD player as the typical power supply flowing through the grid. Along comes your friend, who decides to turn the music up. As the knob is turned, the volume increases without affecting the quality of the sound, until all of a sudden, the music begins to lose that velvety feel to your ears. This is due to harmonic distortion. But what actually changed to distort the signal?

In the case of the sound system, what happens is relatively simple. A CD player sends a wave signal to a device that amplifies the signal into the speakers. Amplifiers are typically evaluated based on how much power they can deliver – which is directly related to their maximum volume. An ideal amplifier is said to be a *linear* electronic device, which merely means that the frequency of the output signal matches that of the input signal, such that all it does is increase the signal's magnitude. In reality, as the device approaches its operating boundaries, its subcomponents gradually reach saturation and exceed their practical

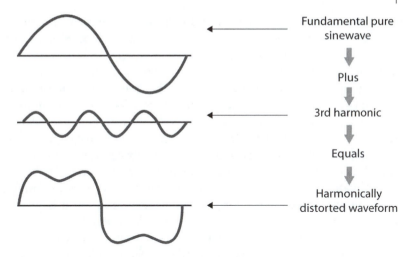

Figure 5.3 *Amplifier clipping*

output limits. At some point, the amplifier is no longer capable of replicating the input signal characteristics faithfully, and we begin to notice imperfections in the sound, as shown in Figure 5.3.

While the sound distortion described above highlights equipment limitations, EV charging distortions are actually induced. This is because batteries are compatible only with unidirectional direct current (DC) power, while the grid is a bidirectional alternating current (AC) power source. Battery chargers must thus convert the AC power input into a usable DC supply. They do this with a rectifier, which clips and inverts the AC power supply's negative components. This results in a distortion in the fundamental characteristics of the power signal, such that the output signal consists of a complex agglomeration of waveforms at different frequencies, each of which is an integer multiple of the fundamental input frequency.

So what does all this mean in practice for the power grid? Well, harmonic distortion results in a range of undesirable effects. Those less keen on the scientific minutiae might simply imagine the electrical grid and its components as avid and sensitive audiophiles who suffer migraines (transient failures) or hearing loss (permanent damage) if exposed to distorted sounds.

Transient failures are those resulting from the temporary presence of harmonic distortions. To begin with, there is a range of electronic equipment that relies on the fundamental frequency of the power supply (either 50Hz or 60Hz, depending on the country) in order to operate properly. Power measurement devices, variable-speed industrial motors and digital clocks are just some devices which are calibrated to a given grid frequency. Their accuracy relies on stability of that frequency. In addition, harmonic distortion produces higher frequency signals that face greater resistance in power lines, occasioning overheating and thus increasing system energy loss. Since these failures only occur while distortions are present, they do not impose permanent damage to the power grid but can nevertheless represent a significant opportunity cost to the utility in terms of energy sales forgone.

Transient voltage and current spikes can overload other devices in the system, resulting in temporary failures, irreversible damage or complete breakdown of a device. Indeed, readers are probably all familiar with surge protectors that are used to avoid the impact on sensitive electronic equipment from just these sorts of events. Even when electronic equipment is protected by an alarm or trip device, once they are triggered, someone must evaluate the failure and reset or replace the device, thus using up valuable time and money.

As with many things in the EV debate, the harmonic distortion obstacle is a poor and overstated excuse for not pursuing EV development. It is erroneous to think that harmonic distortion is a recent obstacle imposed by the adoption of EV technology. Quite the contrary, it has been around since the early 20th century – initially due to the use of vacuum tubes or thermionic valves. However, it became an inevitable hot topic following the dawn of the power electronics industry in the 1980s.

Assuming society has no intention of abandoning pretty much all its electronic devices (PCs, TVs, iPods, sound systems and the rest), dealing with harmonic distortion is an unavoidable issue for power utilities, EV or no EV. Harmonic distortion compensation technology is under way. While a dominant mature solution has yet to emerge, existing concepts can be considered adequate given the current market size, and it is improbable that EV charging in the near future will have any negative impact on power quality. Rather, in the long run, the increased investment in compensation technology for EVs should have an indirect positive impact by spilling over onto other harmonic distortion sources currently present on the grid.

A more in-depth evaluation of the impacts of harmonic distortions and the compensation technology that is being developed is beyond the scope of this book, but the discussion has hopefully provided the reader with a rough appreciation of how harmonic distortions work as well as a sense of their relevance as a problem to be contended with in implementing the EV solution.

Load variation: Smart grids

Utilities have historically viewed EVs merely as additional electricity demand, often fearing that they would impose high power loads that would be difficult or uneconomical to service. The risk of overloading the grid is perhaps the key reason why utilities have been slow to promote an EV market. Indeed, if charged during peak hours of the day, EVs could overload the power system, thus becoming an additional driver of system capacity expansion. However, if charged during the off-peak hours of the night, EVs could actually improve the capacity utilization factor of expensive power plants and distribution networks.

It is worth noting that the system-wide average utilization factor for power plants is a mere 57 per cent (Kempton and Tomic, 2005a). The American power

---

Box 5.5 From the kettle effect to random loads

British researchers Bunn and Seigal (1983a and 1983b) observed a peculiar behaviour in load variations during television broadcasts. They noticed a momentary spike in load that coincided with commercial breaks. Why?

Assume it is a typical evening and thousands of people are watching their favourite shows or news programmes after work. Suddenly, the commercial break comes on and everyone jumps off their seats to quickly take care of household and personal activities – such as preparing a cup of tea – that they have been postponing. In the British case, these results were most apparent during major sporting events, as millions of sports fans simultaneously turned on their electric kettles, thus producing a distinct blip in the load curve. According to National Grid,[9] electricity demand soared by 2110MW during the 2003 Rugby World Cup final half-time break – which equates to more than two million kettles simultaneously boiling water for tea.

However, with individuals watching different programmes, commercial breaks do not necessarily occur simultaneously. The resulting spikes in the load distribution curve become less distinct, albeit more frequent. This analysis can further be extended to other daily events: cooking, hot showers, listening to music, reading with a bedside light. Each and every single appliance that consumers turn on will draw energy from the grid. As the complexity of the scenario increases, it becomes clear how unpredictable load distributions really are. In fact, consumers take an awful lot for granted, starting with the mere fact, for instance, that they can simply flip a switch and a light comes on instantaneously!

---

industry would be able to power 158 million grid-enabled EVs (equivalent to 73 per cent of the current American passenger vehicle fleet) using existing capacity at full utilization (Kintner-Meyer et al, 2007). While this should not be seen as a concrete possibility, it shows how grid-enabled EV markets have the potential to drastically improve system-wide efficiency.

Grid-enabled EV and power grid complementarities stretch beyond additional load and greater utilization factors. Over the course of a day, utilities continuously manage power supplies to meet random fluctuations in demand (Box 5.5). This market segment, called 'ancillary services', is complicated by a few key characteristics of the underlying fluctuations:

- *Randomness*: Though daily trends in electricity demand, such as regular daytime peaks, are very predictable, instantaneous (second-by-second and minute-by-minute) variations are unpredictable and cannot be planned for;
- *Responsiveness*: Given that the electrical grid has negligible electrical storage capability,[8] utilities must manage their systems so as to match real-time demand, continuously adjusting power supplies in order to avoid brown-outs; and
- *Low utilization*: Accumulated over time, these fluctuations amount to negligible energy consumption compared to the supply capacity requirements they impose on the grid.

To meet these variations, the power sector typically employs small-scale power generators on a standby basis. Since generators cannot be switched on and off instantaneously, they must be left idling to be able to respond to instantaneous demand variations. This is a necessary but highly inefficient operating procedure: despite only fulfilling an estimated 1.4 per cent of consumption,[10] ancillary services account for 5 to 10 per cent of total electricity cost or, in America, US$12 billion per year (Kempton and Tomic, 2005b).

Ironically, in addition to this random *load* variation dilemma, the power sector will be increasingly troubled by a random *source* variation dilemma, caused by the growing use of weather-dependent power supplies, such as solar and wind. Of course, utilities can continue to adjust generators to meet surplus load. In the reverse situation, where supply surges due to random weather patterns, the surplus supply is 'taken for dead', since the power grid is incapable of storing any significant quantity of energy. In this context, keep in mind that ultracapacitor banks could be used to store energy off the grid at acceptable power levels and then provide rapid power delivery to EVs upon request.

This load/supply imbalance, coupled with the characteristics of the EV, presents a very interesting opportunity – vehicle-to-grid (V2G) or smart-grid operations. EVs are designed to provide frequent and intense power fluctuations, thus making them ideal power sources for ancillary services, in place of the conventional generator. Indeed, by their very nature, batteries allow both instantaneous power delivery (production) and acceptance (consumption) according to the load/supply connected.

At first glance, the reader might have serious doubts about V2G's functionality. First, this would consume some of the energy content of the battery, which would not go down well with range-anxious consumers. Second, EVs must be parked to perform ancillary power services, making them immobile power stations and not attractive to consumers on the move. But neither of these concerns is actually relevant.

Once connected to a smart grid, the EV might either demand or supply energy to balance grid conditions. When grid load surges over supply, the EV discharges to supply energy to the grid, and when grid supply exceeds load, the EV draws power to charge its battery. Crucially, since these variations are very small and very short-lived, the cumulative impact would be negligible on the overall SOC of the EV battery (Figure 5.4). Thus, the first concern can be put aside.

Turning to the second concern, while many might expect EV energy to be seldom available for use, because vehicles are constantly on the move, this is far from reality. The fact is that vehicles only spend an average of 4 per cent of their time on the road (Kempton and Tomic, 2005b). Even during rush hour, 92 per cent of existing vehicles are parked and theoretically available for grid connection (Kempton and Tomic, 2005b). Assuming that a large proportion of vehicles in the future will be capable of V2G operations, then the system would never depend on the availability of any one vehicle.

What is more, electronic controls (Figure 5.5) can allow drivers to determine how much energy they will require for their next trip – thus restricting V2G operations if necessary. Indeed, smart grids would allow consumers to programme vehicle recharge according to their driving requirements and the

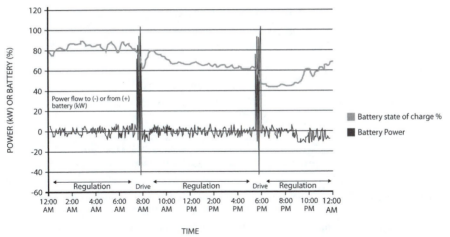

Figure 5.4 *Ancillary services and SOC*

system's energy tariffs. For example, a consumer could arrive home and plug in their car at 5.00 p.m. during peak electricity tariff time, but programme the charger to only activate when the off-peak tariff applied, say around midnight. Thus consumers need not have the hassle of remembering when to plug in, while the grid can avoid millions of cars arriving home and recharging simultaneously during the evening peak hours.

In this scenario, 'valley filling' of the grid load curve can be expected to occur anywhere that distinct peak/off-peak pricing policies exist. Consumers will simply set their EV recharging systems to operate during off-peak hours, while restricting peak-hour charging to necessity-only – good for the individual consumer and a boost to the capacity utilization factor of the utility's system.

Note that participating in V2G operations has costs for the vehicle owner that are often overlooked. First and foremost, there is the cost of producing each unit of energy. This consists not only of the expense incurred in charging

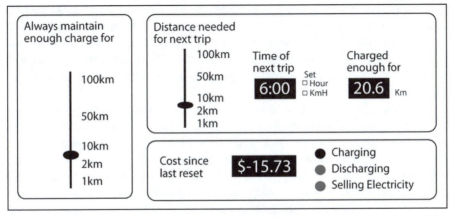

Figure 5.5 *The smart V2G dashboard*

Table 5.4 *V2G cost analysis*

	Toyota RAV4 EV	Comments
Capacity tariff (US$/kWh)	0.04	
Electricity tariff (US$/kWh)	0.1	
Power output (kW)	15	P(mains) < P(vehicle)
Contract duration (hrs/year)	6570	18 hr/day & 365 day/year
Dispatch-to-contract ratio	0.1	
Revenue (US$/year)	4928	([Capacity tariff] + [Electricity tariff] * [DtC ratio]) * [Power output] * [Contract duration]
Conversion efficiency (%)	75	
Battery capital cost (US$)	20,300	[US$1000/kWh] * [20kWh] + [10hr install labour] * [US$30/hr]
Battery life expectancy (kWh)	131,520	2000 deep discharge cycles (as tested) is equivalent to 6000 shallow discharge cycles
Battery degradation (US$/kWh)	0.15	[Battery capital cost] / [Battery life expectancy]
Energy production cost (US$/kWh)	0.283	([Electricity tariff] / [Conversion efficiency]) + [Battery degradation]
Annual energy cost [US$/year]	2790	[Energy production cost] * [DtC ratio] * [Power output] * [Contract duration]
V2G capital cost (US$)	1900	On-board incremental costs US$400 Wiring upgrade US$1500
Capital recovery factor (CRF)	0.16	$c_{ac} = c_c\,\text{CRF} = c_c\,\dfrac{d}{1-(1+d)^{-n}}$ where *d* is discount rate (10%) and *n* is lifetime (10 years)
Annual V2G capital cost (US$/year)	304	[V2G capital cost] * [CRF]
Cost (US$/year)	3094	[Annual energy cost] + [Annual capital cost]
Profit (US$/year)	1834	[Revenue] – [Cost]

Source: Kempton and Tomic (2005b)

the battery to begin with, but also includes the marginal depreciation caused by additional battery utilization. In addition, the incremental capital costs imposed by V2G-compatible equipment have to be considered. Thus participation in V2G only makes sense for the driver if the ancillary services remuneration outweighs the V2G costs.[11] Table 5.4 provides an example of the expected cost structure.

Given a suitable pricing structure, smart grids can simultaneously minimize a utility's marginal generation costs, supply losses and administrative costs associated with ancillary services, while providing low-cost electricity for both EV and conventional consumers. As such, they can be thought of as yet another dimension of a 'whole-product' concept. In the American scenario, replacing all ancillary services with V2G would mobilize approximately 1.3 million EVs or 0.75 per cent of the total vehicle fleet in 2007.

Clearly, V2G implementation that provides both ancillary services and valley-filling has the potential to bring about annual savings of tens of billions of dollars for American utilities. What is more, V2G operations could drastically reduce the cost of unexpected power failures, which are estimated to cost the American economy US$100 billion/year or 1 per cent of GDP (Kempton and Tomic, 2005a).

Approaching a Verdict 3:
A Ripe Whole-Product Solution

Hopefully, this part of the book has established that the EV offers a technically competitive alternative to the well-established, but outdated, ICV transportation solution. It should now be clear that the technology is available to produce EVs with overall comparable performance to ICVs. Moreover, as seen in this chapter, businesses are positioning themselves to provide services that address the EV's key energy system drawbacks, while promoting its benefits.

The current energy infrastructure trend is to regard the battery as an independent component of the vehicle and thus to finance it through a long-term energy contract. This both dilutes consumers' upfront costs and reduces their exposure to battery failure. Meanwhile, both fast-charge and battery-swap systems provide a potential response to historically slow recharge times and are both likely to enjoy market success depending on specific context. And, while insufficient infrastructure remains an issue, growing infrastructural deployment and improved GPS support can be expected to dampen concerns regarding availability of recharging stations. Finally, governments are starting to collaborate with industry in a transparent manner to define the BSP market architecture and guidelines, and ultimately stimulate adequate levels of investment in the recharging infrastructure and the power grid.

Projections of total investment requirements vary greatly depending on the assumptions of what system will prevail – notably, the degree of penetration of slow-charge, fast-charge and/or battery-swap solutions. But there are hints of what to expect based on already confirmed commitments and estimates from experts in the field. The Brattle Group, for instance, estimates that the US alone will have to spend US$900 billion over the next two decades (Hargreaves, 2009), while according to Shai Agassi, CEO of Better Place, the development of an adequate recharge system will require annual global investments of up to US$500 billion (Agassi, 2008).

Indeed, each individual solution presented in this chapter has the potential to thrive given adequate market and geopolitical conditions. Hopefully this discussion has demonstrated that the new EV industry is arriving with a range of competitive whole-product solutions.

Meanwhile, the power sector is becoming increasingly aware of the potential benefits of grid-enabled EV deployment. Notably, grid-enabled EVs could help to smooth load variations and improve ancillary service efficiency. What is more, concerns over harmonic distortions have been shown to be both exaggerated and, to some extent, irrelevant, since these distortions will need to be addressed regardless of grid-enabled EV penetration. In fact, increased investment in grid-enabled EVs has merely accelerated the development and deployment of harmonic filters, to the benefit of the entire power grid.

In sum, the EV industry has evolved and matured to the point where both technology and infrastructure development are being seriously addressed to meet consumer demands. On that note, the third and final part of the book shifts away from the narrow technological focus on the EV and its recharging issues and looks more broadly at the conditions for EV market penetration, developing a roadmap for its widespread adoption. In other words, it defines long-term objectives, establishes short-term targets leading to those objectives based on the technology outlined in previous chapters, and finally identifies policies to support this development path.

Notes

1 Interestingly, in recent years, rather than muscling the newcomers out – not that they would have been in a position to do so – some of the traditional manufacturers, notably Renault-Nissan, have shown they are happy to form development alliances. However, Big Auto's role overall may be insignificant in the rest of the energy system discussion.
2 The reader might notice that the fast-charge mechanism, in contrast to the battery-swap mechanism, does not necessarily require a battery-leasing marketing approach, as proposed in the introduction. Nevertheless, as will be observed over the course of this analysis, such an approach is desirable.
3 This assumes 60 ten-minute periods which make up the 10 hour day, each period serving approximately 83 vehicles with 216kW demand.
4 Complementing the need for a widespread recharge infrastructure, various solutions are being promoted to prevent driver stress regarding charge availability. GEVs are designed to closely monitor the SOC of their battery. When the charge reaches a certain point, a GEV's computer system can provide the driver with an array of solutions. GPS is used to locate nearby charging or swapping stations. In the case of long-distance travel, the GPS can be used to plan ahead, locating stations en route to a given destination. Reva, the India EV manufacturer, has recently developed an emergency charge solution for its new Li-ion battery EVs. The driver can request that their Reva momentarily accesses the Li-ion battery's reserve charge. Fully discharging a Li-ion battery occasionally does not reduce its life expectancy significantly and thus provides a suitable reserve. Nevertheless, the ultimate solution will require the deployment of an extensive charging infrastructure, not just quick-fix emergency solutions.
5 The reader should recall the technical limitations associated with fast-charge systems, discussed above and in Chapter 4.
6 Using average driving statistics, a vehicle with 100km range in the US will only exceed its range on 15 per cent of days. Assuming drivers never stop at regular charge spots during trips – a conservative assumption, as they may well charge during lunchtime or at the office or at any other pitstop – one can deduce that fast-

charge stations will be used for a maximum of 15 per cent of charging scenarios.

7   Later in this chapter it is discussed how vehicle-to-grid operations can minimize power grid losses if the EV fleet and grid are adequately optimized.

8   There is an inbuilt margin of 2.2 per cent of capacity within the transmission and distribution network.

9   National Grid plc is one of Britain's primary electrical utilities companies.

10 This estimate is based on the California market, where ancillary services represent around 17 per cent of the total power capacity (4100MW of 24,000MW system-wide power capacity). According to Kempton and Tomic, the utilization factor for ancillary services is extremely low – around 0.2 per cent for spinning reserves and 8 per cent for regulation up/down. Thus this estimate uses a conservative 8 per cent ancillary service average utilization factor.

11 Currently, the pricing of ancillary services is based on the availability of spare energy, rather than actual delivery of that energy. As such, a large proportion of ancillary service remuneration reflects how much energy is readily available and the period over which that availability is contracted. V2G arrangement could change the nature of this pricing policy.

References

Agassi, S. (2008) 'Future of transportation', press release, Better Place, Palo Alto, CA

Bunn, D. W. and Seigal, J. P. (1983a) 'Forecasting the effects of television programming upon electricity loads', *Journal of the Operational Research Society*, vol 34, pp17–25

Bunn, D. W. and Seigal, J. P. (1983b) 'Television peaks in electricity demand', *Energy Economics*, vol 5, issue 1, pp31–36

Chesbrough, H. and Rosenbloom, R. S. (2002) 'The role of the business model in capturing value from innovation: Evidence from Xerox Corporation's technology spin-off companies', *Industrial and Corporate Change*, vol 11, issue 3, pp529–555

Credit Suisse (2009) 'Electric vehicles', *Credit Suisse Equity Research*, 1 October

Davis, S. C. and Diegel, S. W. (2007) *Transportation Energy Data Book: Edition 26*, Oak Ridge National Laboratory, Oak Ridge, TN

Frost & Sullivan (2009) '360 degree analysis of the global electric vehicles market', white paper, Frost & Sullivan, www.frost.com/prod/servlet/segment-toc. pag?segid=9832-00-0D-00-00

Hargreaves, S. (2009) 'A \$2 trillion bet on powering America – The stimulus plan might jump-start new energy investments, which could drastically change how we use electricity', *CNN Money Online*, http://money.cnn.com/2009/01/06/news/economy/ smart_grid/index.htm, accessed 10 January 2011

Jha, A. (2009) 'London Mayor – 100,000 electric cars for capital: Boris Johnson announces commitment to making electric cars "first choice for Londoners", pledging £20m of the GLA budget', *The Guardian*, 8 April

Kempton, W. and Tomic, J. (2005a) 'Vehicle-to-grid power implementation: From stabilizing the grid to supporting large-scale renewable energy', *Elsevier Journal of Power Sources*, vol 144, issue 1, pp280–294

Kempton, W. and Tomic, J. (2005b) 'Vehicle-to-grid power fundamentals: Calculating capacity and revenue', *Elsevier Journal of Power Sources*, vol 144, issue 1, pp268–279

Kintner-Meyer, M., Schneider, K. and Pratt, R. (2007) 'Impacts assessment of plug-in hybrid vehicles on electric utilities and regional US power grids – Part 1: Technical analysis', Pacific Northwest National Laboratory, Richland, WA, November

Moore, G. A. (1999) *Crossing the Chasm: Marketing and Selling High-Tech Products to Mainstream Customers*, HarperCollins Publishers, London, UK

Motavalli, J. (2009) 'The world's first charging "corridors" for EVs attack the range problem', *BNET*, www.bnet.com/blog/electric-cars/the-world-8217s-first-charging-8220corridors-8221-for-evs-attack-the-range-problem/876, accessed 29 September 2009

Salton, J. (2009) 'France to spend US$2.2 billion on network of electric car charging stations', *Gizmag*, www.gizmag.com/france-two-billion-electric-car-charging-stations/13041/, accessed 12 October 2009

Part III

Electric Vehicle Roadmap

6

Electric Vehicle
Cost-Effectiveness

I conceive that the great part of the miseries of mankind are brought upon them by false estimates they have made of the value of things.

Benjamin Franklin

By now, the reader should feel reassured that the battery-powered EV is a valid alternative to the ICV even today. But does the fact that battery-powered EVs are a superior technology prove that they are more environmentally friendly and sustainable than ICVs? And even if they are, are they the most cost-effective solution for providing sustainable transport?

What is known for sure is that the battery-powered EV does not directly emit CO_2 and other harmful exhaust gases, that it does not rely solely on oil as an energy source, and that it converts the energy content stored within the vehicle more efficiently than ICVs. Looking beyond the vehicle itself and considering how it is 'fuelled', can it be said that it avoids scarce resource depletion and dependence? Does it guarantee less environmental impact overall – from well to wheel? Will the battery-powered EV really prove to be the most economic solution to sustainable transport for consumers? Or would it merely redistribute the way we incur such costs?

By the end of this chapter, the reader should see that, despite some uncertainties, the balance is already decidedly in favour of the battery-powered EV solution. The chapter begins with an evaluation of the capital cost of an EV's key components – notably the battery and the electric VP system. The next section compares the operating costs of battery-powered EVs and ICVs, expanding on the tank-to-wheel (T2W) analysis from Part II. The chapter then shifts into a well-to-wheel (W2W) analysis to compare the social costs of battery-powered EVs and ICVs, considering first energy-efficiency and economic gains then taking into account environmental externalities. Finally, the author uses these three broad cost categories to develop a vehicle lifetime cost model using various global scenarios to interpret the results.

Capital Costs

This analysis is concerned with determining how soon parts suppliers will be able to deliver the key components to meet growing consumer interest in EVs at acceptable cost. It should be clear by this stage that this is a market witnessing radical change. Indeed, it is impossible to forecast which options will prevail and when they will be commercially 'dominant'. While companies and governments have recently put implementation of new business models and financial incentives on the fast burner, it is still difficult to quantify exactly how much of an impact they will have on the EV's final cost to the consumer.

Given this is a rapidly changing market, by the time the reader flips through these pages, market conditions are expected to have evolved further. As such, this discussion avoids making static cost evaluations, but focuses on medium-run projections and trends.[1] The following discussion considers how these parameters are likely to evolve, highlighting ranges rather than precise estimates.

Vehicle propulsion system costs

Analysts often understate the degree to which battery-powered EVs – and to a lesser extent some HEVs – are mechanically simpler relative to their ICV counterparts. In fact, far too often a vehicle base price (excluding battery) is overlooked by non-automotive industry analysts. Even when these costs are differentiated, they are done so as a constant in time.

As we saw in Chapter 3, the VP systems for ICVs and BEVs have very little in common. The Electrification Roadmap (Electrification Coalition, 2009) study provides a breakdown of grid-enabled EV and ICV costs by component (Figure 6.1). It illustrates how much simpler electric components are and how these are still in the development phase. This is both a constraint, for consumers who want to switch to electric today, and an advantage, for consumers to benefit from the drop in vehicle price in the future.

While the ICV's complex mechanical systems limit its ability to achieve marginal cost reductions, the cost of a battery-powered EV's core components are expected to nearly halve over the next two decades. Indeed, just as one cannot neglect the additional cost of the battery in an EV, one also should not ignore its reduced VP system costs, or its ability to accelerate the drop in overall vehicle sticker price in the medium run.

Meanwhile, HEVs do not enjoy the same VP cost benefits as battery-powered EVs. While their core components are identical, the HEV is contaminated by the additional ICE components. However, HEVs are not a straightforward summa-

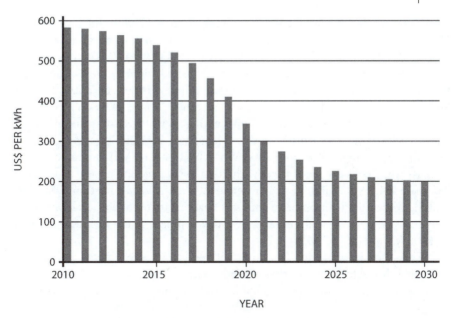

Figure 6.1 *Battery costs*

Source: Electrification Coalition (2009)

tion of ICV and battery-power EV components, since they enjoy downsized ICEs and simplified transmissions compared to ICVs. While HEVs have the highest VP system costs, these are currently more than compensated by their downsized batteries.

Battery costs

The development of the battery market is considered the primary make-or-break element in the EV puzzle. As discussed in Chapter 4, modern battery technology can satisfy all our automotive requirements – range, top speed, acceleration, long lifetime and safety. Unfortunately, this is achieved at a hefty upfront cost that most consumers will not look favourably upon.

In the absence of competition, one must estimate costs based on data provided by suppliers and product development assumptions. Of course, this does not provide for robust quantification and, not surprisingly, lithium-ion battery cost estimates range from US$500/kWh (US$139/MJ) to US$2000/kWh (US$556/MJ), depending on the reference.

A major problem behind battery cost estimates is the lack of transparency with which analysts tend to quote their valuations. It is often difficult to determine exactly what the 'battery cost' comprises. Is it the cost of the battery cells or of the battery pack? Does it include the cost of the full energy management system? Is it a cost target set by a manufacturer? Is it the cost for a unit purchase or of a large batch? Unless otherwise specified, the values quoted in this text will refer to the full manufacturing costs of the complete battery pack.

Recent studies by the Boston Consulting Group (2009) and Credit Suisse (2009) present the two highest battery cost estimates, at US$2000/kWh (US$556/MJ) and US$1200–1600/kWh (US$333–444/MJ) respectively. Both claim that quick cost reductions are expected, though their quantitative forecasts remain conservative next to other sources. In March 2009, Frost & Sullivan (2009) presented a 2008 cost evaluation of US$1000/kWh (US$278/MJ) and suggested steep cost reductions, with a 2010 forecast around US$750/kWh (US$208/MJ). McKinsey & Co. (Hensley et al, 2009) displayed greater uncertainty in their US$700–1500/kWh (US$194–417/MJ) quote, but their forecast was decidedly aggressive, with 2015 costs reaching as low as US$420/kWh (US$117/MJ). Finally, in November 2009, the Electrification Coalition[2] (2009), a group of automotive industry leaders focused on accelerating the shift to electric, presented an aggressive development plan, with costs around US$600/kWh (US$167/MJ).

While the Electrification Coalition will tend to underestimate battery costs, since they hope to promote their agenda, battery costs have indeed dropped rapidly since the microelectronics boom, and continue to do so, as discussed in Chapter 4. Thus a deliberate undervaluation may actually prove to be accurate by the time it is published and used. As EVs have gradually come to market, starting in late 2010, the real battery costs should quickly become transparent. Since the bulk of the market analyses performed on EVs are likely to be done by consulting and market research teams, greater transparency should help to relieve some of the uncertainty hanging over this option.

Perhaps the best indication of battery costs can be derived through a comparative sticker price analysis of EVs against their direct ICV rivals. Such is the case with the Nissan Leaf EV and Nissan Tiida (or Versa in the American market), both built on the same Nissan B platform. The Leaf, launched with an MSRP (manufacturer's suggested retail price) of US$33,720, is US$15,000 to US$20,000 more expensive than its Versa counterpart in the US market. Notice that individual consumers actually only pay somewhere around US$20,000–US$25,000, since the Leaf enjoys federal tax credits of US$7500 and a range of state tax rebates. Given a 24kWh battery, one expects battery prices to be in the US$625/kWh (US$174/MJ) to US$830/kWh (US$231/MJ) range.

While it is likely that Nissan is selling the Leaf at a loss, to promote consumer interest, much as Toyota did with its initial Prius hybrids, these figures remain a positive indication that real battery prices are at the lower end of the price spectrum. If, for instance, battery prices were actually US$1200/kWh (US$333/MJ) to US$1600/kWh (US$444/MJ), as suggested by Credit Suisse (2009), then Nissan would be making a loss of roughly US$15,000 to US$20,000 per vehicle. Given estimated annual production capacity of 500,000 Leafs globally by 2012, that would suggest Nissan are prepared to risk an annual loss of up to US$10 billion on the Leaf – this for a company whose 2010 profits amounted to US$3.3 billion. More likely is a per vehicle loss of around US$2000 to US$5000, which still exposes the company to potential annual losses of US$1–2.5 billion. These figures suggest that battery prices stand at between US$710/kWh (US$197/MJ) and US$1050/kWh (US$292/MJ).

Beyond ensuring greater price transparency, the deployment of EVs should provide a boost in battery sales volumes, leading to a much-needed increase in economies of scale. As a result, McKinsey expects annual cost reductions of 6–8 per cent over the next decade. As will be seen in the last section of this chapter, this scenario would provide a break-even subsidy-free lifetime cost for EVs within the next couple of years in European markets.

The cost reduction offered by a breakthrough technology, though difficult to estimate, is actually expected to be much greater than the gradual reductions expected from economies of scale. If technological breakthroughs are considered, and EV battery prices fall by as much as 72 per cent by 2015, as expected by McKinsey, this would provide a break-even subsidy-free lifetime cost for GEVs even in America!

As Figure 6.1 illustrates, EVs may reach competitive lifetime cost conditions as battery capital costs shrink in the short run. At this point, economists will claim that, given a suitable discount rate, consumers would make the rational decision and opt for the GEV's lifetime savings. Unfortunately, the sad fact of life is that consumers are not always rational. The vast proportion of potential buyers are unlikely to perform even a back-of-the-envelope lifetime cost valuation of an expensive good or service before acquisition. As such, the industry cannot rely on the consumer's mathematical prowess to prove that GEVs are indeed a cost-effective solution, despite their premium price tag.

If a BEV has a sticker price of, say, US$15,000 more than an equivalent ICV, but proves less expensive than its rival over 10 years at a 15 per cent discount rate, it would seem obvious that a rational consumer should opt for the BEV. After all, at that discount rate, they could easily take out a bank loan to finance the purchase and still profit, without ever having to part with their own capital. However, once the consumer considers the lower upfront cost of the ICV, who is to say that rational thinking will prevail.

Operating Costs

Vehicle running costs are a straightforward function of two variables: vehicle fuel economy and fuel price. Consider two vehicles with equivalent performance and design. The first, an ICV, has a fuel economy of 11km/L (26mpg),[3] while the second, a BEV, has a fuel economy of 0.15kWh/km. Now assume an oil price of US$0.73/L (US$2.75/gal) and electricity price of US$0.13/kWh – values that are a good representation of US market conditions at the beginning of 2010. This results in ICV and BEV operating costs of 6.6¢/km and 2¢/km respectively. In other words, ICVs cost around 3.3 times more to operate than an equivalent EV. And notice that this is in a market where fuel prices are notoriously cheap.

The battery-powered EV's low operating cost is perhaps the single most appealing characteristic for the typical cost-conscious consumer. As such, it is vital to have a good understanding of what drives vehicle fuel economy and fuel price, and how these are likely to change in the future.

Fuel economy

Beyond T2W efficiency, fuel economy is a function of the vehicle's aerodynamics, weight and rolling resistance, not to mention driving habits. To make this distinction clear, according to Amory Lovins et al (2004), only 1 per cent of the energy consumed by the vehicle is actually used to move the driver, while the rest is 'wasted' in moving the vehicle and its heavy accessories. An SUV and a station-wagon equipped with the same engine will have different fuel economy, since the station-wagon requires less fuel to move its lighter and more aerodynamic body. Indeed, fuel economy is far from a standardized commodity across vehicle classes.

Since this field is under significant pressure to change, analysts often choose to make calculated overvaluations of fuel economy to account for what they believe to be imminent technological improvements. Thus they frequently use 30+mpg (12.8+km/L) as a benchmark. For instance, the Credit Suisse market study mentioned earlier assumes petrol and diesel ICVs to offer 32mpg (13.6km/L) and 38mpg (16.2km/L) respectively. However, one must provide concrete justification for such optimistic benchmarks.

According to the US EPA,[4] the 2010 Toyota Prius is not only the first vehicle to reach the 50mpg (21.3km/L) combined fuel-economy milestone,[5] it is also one of only three vehicles[6] on the market to offer fuel economy above the 40mpg (17.0km/L) mark. All three are HEVs.[7] The most fuel-efficient ICVs on the American market are the Smart fortwo coupé and Smart fortwo convertible, that achieve 36mpg (15.3km/L) combined fuel economy as a result of their small size. There are only seven other ICVs on the American market that achieve combined fuel economy above 30mpg (12.8km/L). In fact, of the thousands of vehicle models on the American market, only 143 vehicle models offer fuel economy above 25mpg (10.5km/L), many of which are hybrids.[8] Thus it seems unjustified to use anything above 30 mpg (12.8km/L) as a benchmark for evaluating lifetime costs of ICVs.

The 25mpg (10.5km/L) fuel economy benchmark referred to above is particularly pertinent to this discussion. As the Credit Suisse report explicitly points out, 'energy efficiency of the transportation sector has not materially increased in the past two decades … fuel efficiency of vehicles reached a plateau of roughly 25 mpg'. In fact, the highest historical annual average fuel economy for cars on sale in America was achieved in 1987 (with 26.2mpg, 11.1km/L)!

It is worth noting that low oil prices during the 1990s put fuel economy progress on hold – and even reversed some of the former progress – since consumer preferences moved back to gas guzzlers such as SUVs. Over the last decade, oil prices have soared, dragging vehicle operating costs along for the ride, and once again making fuel economy a key consideration.

However, progress has been limited. Consider, for instance, vehicles such as the 2010 Toyota Camry, 2010 Honda Accord or 2010 VW Golf, which all offer around 25mpg (10.5km/L) fuel economy. The fuel economy of each in 2001 had already reached 24mpg (10.2km/L). In other words, over the last decade, a period during which Honda and Toyota meticulously perfected their products to improve fuel economy, these ICVs have achieved a mere 4 per cent improvement!

According to Boston Consulting Group, if the automotive manufacturers incorporated all potential ICE efficiency-improvement technologies, average fuel efficiency for diesel and petrol ICVs would improve by a maximum of 10 and 20 per cent respectively. Such advanced ICE technologies would result in a cost increase of US$1400 per diesel engine and US$2100 per petrol engine and are thus widely considered to offer the least expensive emissions reduction solution for the short run. Focusing on the petrol ICV, based on a current 25mpg (10.5km/L) benchmark, average petrol ICV fuel economy would peak at 30mpg (12.8km/L).

In that light, it is reasonable to say that, while some ICV fuel economy improvements are likely to emerge in the next decade, it will be the hybridization of vehicles that will provide substantive progress in this regard. Indeed, power-assist HEVs are capable of offering a further 10 to 15 per cent gain in fuel economy for a further US$2100. One step up, full HEVs offer a more substantial 25 to 30 per cent gain in fuel economy. According to Boston Consulting Group, this comes at the hefty price of US$7000 – though it is expected to drop to US$4000 by 2020.

Fuel price

The second key determinant of a vehicle's operating cost is fuel price. With the exception of the years following both 1970s oil crises and the current financial downturn, petroleum consumption has only known one direction: up, up and away. Looking into the future, there are no signs of change.

According to the IEA's *World Energy Outlook 2009* report (IEA, 2009a), global petroleum consumption is expected to expand by 20 million bbl/day between 2008 and 2030 – 97 per cent of which will come from transport! As noted previously, the global LDV fleet is expected to triple by 2050 (IEA, 2008), driven primarily by growth in China, India and other emerging markets. Alas, while LDVs account for little over half of the transportation sector's oil consumption, the other chunk – medium and heavy trucks, aviation, marine and other – currently holds no real promise in replacing their oil-based power sources (Figure 6.2).

As discussed in Chapter 2, biomass may be capable of displacing some of this expanding demand in parts of the world. However, its chances of capturing a significant share of the combustion fuels market on a global scale are limited. Meanwhile, cheap petroleum resources are widely considered to have already been discovered, such that supply expansion will come at ever higher costs. Such is the case, for instance, with the Brazilian pre-salt deep-sea oil fields and the Canadian tar sands. Not only are discoveries becoming more scarce and inaccessible, the proportion of oil supplies originating from national oil compa-

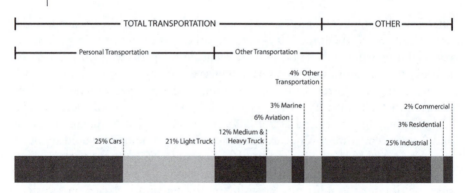

Figure 6.2 *Oil consumption breakdown by end use*

Source: Electrification Coalition (2009)

nies (NOCs) is due to climb to around two-thirds, thus increasingly the risk of price volatility.

Government policy is likely to be increasingly aimed at reducing environmental impacts, thus putting oil in an unfavourable position. As climate change strengthens its hold on political agendas globally, particularly in the US (Figure 6.3), tighter policies can only be expected to increase the final price of oil to consumers.

Indeed, the price of oil will remain volatile but in the long term will rise steadily, compromising ICV operating costs. According to IEA projections (Figure 6.4), in a business-as-usual scenario, oil prices would once again reach the annualized 2008 average price by the middle of this decade. Even if society adopted policies to dampen average annual energy growth rate from 1.4 per

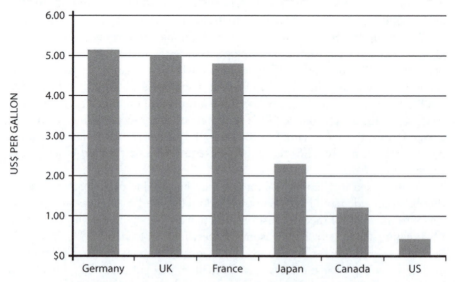

Figure 6.3 *Average gasoline taxes, March 2008 (US$/gal)*

Source: Electrification Coalition (2009)

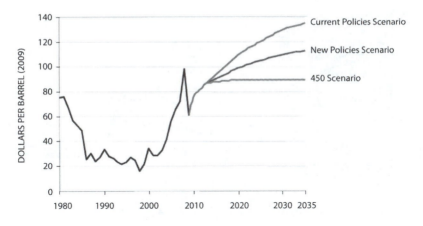

Figure 6.4 *IEA oil price forecasts*

Source: IEA (2010)

cent to 1.2 per cent, we would still reach 2008 oil price peaks by the end of the decade. It is worth highlighting that even in the extreme scenario where policy managed to reverse the growing trend of greenhouse gas emission, so as to stabilize concentrations at 450 ppm, oil prices would still remain around triple the low oil prices which society was accustomed to between the late 1980s and the early 2000s (approximately US$90/bbl compared to an average US$30/bbl).

On the other hand, while the price of electricity may rise faster than historical trends, driven by initial investments in green energy sources, the mere fact that it does not rely solely on one scarce natural resource should be enough to ensure a weaker price inflation than in the case of oil. Given a widening gap between oil and electricity prices coupled with the fact that neither ICV nor BEV T2W fuel efficiencies are likely to achieve significant gains, it is likely that the operating cost gap between BEVs and ICVs will widen further.

Social Costs

Well-to-wheel efficiency

As demonstrated in Chapter 4, BEVs benefit from a T2W fuel efficiency of about 75 per cent compared to 15 per cent for the ICV. However, comparing BEVs and ICVs solely on this basis overlooks a substantial fraction of the vehicle's energy supply chain. After all, electricity and gasoline are not equivalent energy sources. Total energy (i.e. W2W efficiency) is composed of both T2W and well-to-tank (W2T) efficiencies, which includes extraction, refining and distribution of the fuel itself.

Keeping in mind the various stages of energy consumption implicit in moving an automobile, it is now possible to evaluate W2W energy efficiency on a quantitative basis. Figure 6.5 shows that when the entire supply chain – from

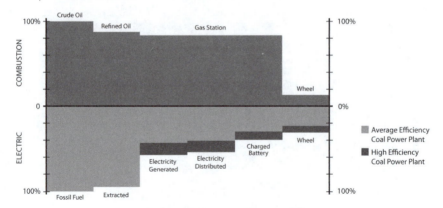

Figure 6.5 *BEV vs. ICV W2W efficiency*

primary fuel resource extraction to final consumption in the vehicle – is considered, BEVs are always more energy efficient than ICVs.

In the unlikely event that the additional power required for BEVs were to be generated using petroleum, the shift would result in annual energy savings of 38 per cent. Based on 2005 consumption figures and a US$92.58/barrel (January 2010) crude oil price, BEVs would provide annualized savings of US$118 billion for the American economy alone. If the price of petrol returns to the 2008 peak levels, these savings would escalate to a whopping US$185 billion/year (Figure 6.6).

However, real life can get even better. In reality, BEVs would not be powered by oil-fuelled power plants – except, perhaps, if owned by Middle Eastern sheiks. Early BEVs are likely to be moved predominantly by surplus night-time supplies from existing base-load power plants with very high electricity production efficiency, providing a W2W efficiency gain over ICVs of up to 123 per cent – a BEV W2W efficiency of 29 per cent vs. a W2W ICV efficiency of 13 per cent (Figure 6.5).

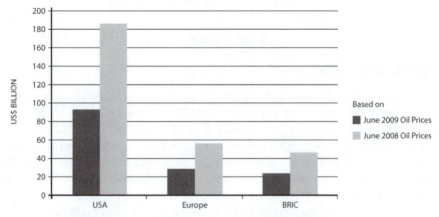

Figure 6.6 *Annualized savings on petrol bill due to EV use*

Note: BRIC = Brazil, Russia, India and China.
Source: statistics from the Energy Information Administration (US Dept of Transport)

Box 6.1 Hydrogen fuel cells W2W supply chain

Fuel cells, as the reader may recall, are fuelled by hydrogen, the most abundant element in our natural environment. However, hydrogen is typically found as part of a chemical compound. Thus the diatomic hydrogen gas form needed for FCs must be derived through the separation of the hydrogen carrier substance. Research has focused on developing and testing techniques for efficiently producing (in other words separating out) useful forms of hydrogen. The most common mechanism to date remains the age-old process of electrolysis, which uses electricity to separate water into hydrogen gas and oxygen. So why not just use electricity to charge batteries?

Indeed, when one compares the W2W energy efficiency of a BEV and an FCEV, the result is clear. Figure 6.7 shows the distribution of primary energy consumed along the supply chain of both systems. The FCEV has a W2W[9] efficiency of 19–23 per cent, compared to 69 per cent for the BEV. Assuming either vehicle is supplied with an identical 22.5kWh of generated energy, the FCEV travels a mere 42km compared to the BEV's 130km.

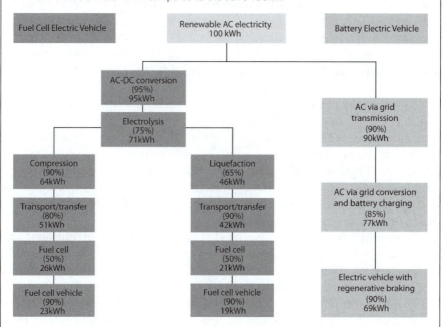

Figure 6.7 *BEV vs. FCEV W2W efficiency*

Source: Bossel (2006)

In this context, Professor Ulf Bossel (2006), leading expert at the European Fuel Cell Forum, has an important message:

Because of the high energy losses within a hydrogen economy, the synthetic energy carrier cannot compete with electricity. As the fundamental laws of physics cannot be changed by research, politics or investments, a hydrogen economy will never make sense.

Energy conservation and diversification seems not only important but inevitable. Furthermore, with oil prices expected to climb again in the medium term, the cost of petroleum dependence can only increase, hampering sustained growth in the future. In this light, it is lucky that BEVs are *prêt à porter* – an already available solution to the problem of energy dependence.

But before moving on, the reader might ask about fuel cells and the hydrogen economy, often hailed as the way of the future. Box 6.1 provides a brief discussion and a W2W comparison of FCEVs and BEVs. The results speak highly in favour of the latter.

Carbon emissions

Battery-powered EVs have been considered for a long time now as an attractive solution by those concerned with the environment, in terms of both climate change and local air pollution. But while BEVs do not result in any tailpipe emissions, it would be inaccurate to claim that this makes them zero-emissions vehicles. And on this basis critics claim that estimates of BEV emissions reductions (of both CO_2 and other forms of air pollution) wrongfully neglect emissions associated with power generation. However, the 'dirty power' argument against BEVs is based on a questionable foundation:[10] coal is dirtier than oil, thus coal-powered BEVs are dirtier than petrol-powered ICVs. The question really is: *How much do BEVs and ICVs pollute per kilometre travelled?*

As seen in the previous section, the BEV travels further on a unit of energy, and thus enjoys superior W2W efficiency, than the ICV. This section demonstrates how this W2W efficiency ensures that BEVs offer emissions reductions in virtually every real-world scenario. The W2W emissions calculations are divided into two manageable parts – upstream (well-to-tank) and downstream (tank-to-wheel). While W2T figures alone favour the ICV, it is important not to come to a premature conclusion, since the BEV's T2W efficiency more than makes up for any upstream inefficiencies.

To quantify the emissions associated with power generation, one must first specify an energy matrix for the country or region in question. In other words, the proportion of energy which is produced from each given energy source available in the country or region[11] must be determined.

To drive the point home, consider a mega-polluting country with 100 per cent coal-based power generation using existing coal-fired thermal plant technology. The combustion of 1kg of coal produces 2930 grams of CO_2 (gCO_2) emissions and 2.7kWh (9.7MJ) of energy available at the outlet.[12] This, in turn, means $1083gCO_2$/kWh ($301gCO_2$/MJ) of electricity consumed. To put this hypothetical country into context, none of the major global economies, including India and China, produce power with this level of carbon intensity (Figure 6.8).

An analogous analytical approach shows that $2710gCO_2$ is produced by every litre ($79.2gCO_2$/MJ) of gasoline consumed.[13] The evaluation can be further extended to consider the use of commercially available biofuels. With the exception of Brazil, ethanol fuel is only commercially available in blended form – typically E10 and E25.[14] Assume that the ethanol proportion of the fuel is carbon-neutral, but the fuel mix is consumed at a faster rate because ethanol

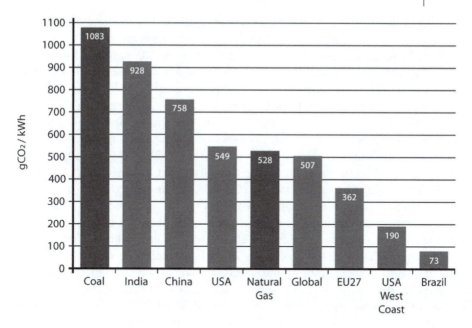

Figure 6.8 *Power source carbon intensity*

has lower energy content than gasoline. In this case, ICV CO_2 emissions drop by 1.5 per cent and 16.5 per cent with E10 and E25, respectively.

At first glance, coal-dependent BEVs would appear to be dirtier than ICVs. In fact, up to this point, ICVs appear better than all but the cleanest of power supplies. However, the BEV distinguishes itself by offering a paramount level of energy efficiency within the vehicle itself.

Table 6.1 presents a summary of results for vehicle emissions in different scenarios. It is important for the reader to recognize that these ICV fuel economies are optimistic (recall the fuel economy discussion above).

Table 6.1 *Vehicle emissions ratings (gCO_2/km reduced)*[15]

gCO_2/km saved	10km/L or 23.5mpg	Crude Oil 14km/L or 32.9mpg	21.25km/L or 50mpg	E25 14km/L or 32.9mpg	E10 14km/L or 32.9mpg
Coal	108.4	31.0	−35.0	50.0	46.5
Natural gas	191.7	114.3	48.3	133.3	129.8
US	188.5	111.1	45.1	130.2	126.6
US West Coast	242.3	165.0	99.0	184.0	180.5
EU27	216.5	139.2	73.2	158.2	154.7
China	157.1	79.8	13.8	98.8	95.3
India	131.6	54.3	−11.7	73.3	69.8
Brazil	259.9	182.5	116.5	201.6	198.0

Note: The rows indicate the given EV power source while the columns indicate the fuel economy when compared to alternative ICV fuels. The results are presented in terms of gCO_2/km avoided by the EV compared to the ICV alternative, so a positive and higher result indicates greater emissions avoidance by the EV.

According to this analysis, BEVs would ensure CO_2 emissions reduction in nearly any conceivable scenario. Indeed, except when it is driven in China, India and the hypothetical mega-polluting country, even the 50mpg Smart fortwo, the most fuel-efficient ICV on the market, proves less environmentally friendly than a BEV hooked up to a conventional 'dirty' power grid.

Based on travel data from the US Department of Transport, Americans drive approximately 3 trillion miles annually (4.8 trillion km/yr). If the entire American fleet switched to BEVs using conventional power, assuming a 23.5mpg (10km/L) benchmark fuel economy, it would save 773MtCO$_2$ annually. Even if a 50mpg (21.25km/L) benchmark fuel economy were assumed, switching to a BEV fleet would still generate savings of 84MtCO$_2$ annually.

Note that the use of ethanol blending does not provide any substantial alteration to these results. This is particularly relevant for the Brazilian context, where gasoline receives a mandatory 20–25 per cent ethanol blend, and is also increasingly relevant in the US and the EU, where small proportions of biofuels are gradually being introduced into conventional gasoline. In other words, the impact of ethanol blending in gasoline is less significant than might be expected from a CO_2 emissions reduction perspective, although it may continue to be of relevance from a fuel-diversification, dependence-reduction perspective.

Furthermore, this analysis has been developed to evaluate the worst-case scenario presented by modern power grids. However, the power sector is undergoing a similar transformation to the transportation sector, where the medium- to long-term direction is towards a lower emission energy matrix. Aside from the intensifying shift towards renewable or zero-emissions power sources for the long term, emission control technologies, such as carbon capture and storage (Box 6.2), are being pitched as an intermediary solution to decarbonizing existing polluting power sources.

Environmental criticism against the BEV on carbon emissions grounds is, at best, unfounded. Even after taking into account grid inefficiencies and embellished primary-energy carbon intensities, one finds that BEVs are virtually always cleaner than ICVs. It is undoubtedly possible to identify specific scenarios with conditions that do not justify early investment in BEVs. However, what is clearly demonstrated is that BEVs can offer widespread environmental benefits, both local and global, even in less-than-ideal market conditions such as China, where electricity is carbon intensive, and Brazil, where widespread ethanol use already provides a low-carbon transport solution. Indeed, it would be fallacious to argue against a shift away from the oil-consuming ICVs in the direction of BEVs based on the existing power grid.

Cost-Effectiveness of Electric Mobility

Predictably, the analysis now addresses the elephant in the room: Do the economics of electric transportation make sense? The reader knows that a BEV in the showroom costs more upfront than an equivalent ICV because of the

Box 6.2 Carbon capture and storage

Carbon capture and storage (CCS) is a three-stage process (Figure 6.9) involving (i) the separation and subsequent capture of CO_2 from a fuel or exhaust source, followed by (ii) the transportation of this CO_2 to a given location and finally (iii) storing the CO_2 in a geological formation away from the atmosphere for a long period of time. CCS has the potential to provide enormous cuts in CO_2 emissions from large-scale stationary emissions sources such as coal power stations. The expected geological storage potential for CO_2 is extremely high, with estimates for total capacity ranging from 2000$GtCO_2$ to possibly greater than 10,000$GtCO_2$ – which represents 80 to 400 years of emissions at today's rates.

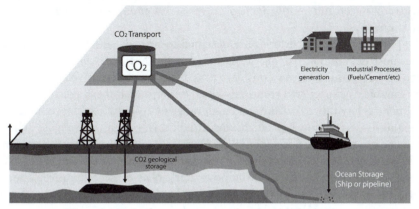

Figure 6.9 *Carbon capture and storage schematic*

Source: IEA

Typically, the primary cost burden of CCS is associated with the CO_2 capturing stage, since considerable energy is consumed to execute the capture and compression. The consequence is an 8 to 12 per cent reduction in overall plant efficiency. However, the system is estimated to be highly effective, capable of avoiding 85 to 95 per cent of CO_2 emissions. After accounting for the drop in plant efficiency, one finds a net reduction of 80 to 90 per cent in CO_2/kWh. Crucially, each individual stage in the CCS process is well developed and uses proven technologies. However, the solution is still largely unproven as a cost-effective integrated system and demonstration projects are only now gaining momentum. The success of these CCS demonstration projects is vital if CCS technology is to become a cost-effective carbon mitigation tool to prevent climate change.

high capital cost of its battery. However, the BEV runs at a fraction of the cost of the ICV. Furthermore, in a world where environmental concerns increasingly influence markets – be it through consumer preferences or government policy – electrification offers even greater value over a vehicle's life.

Private costs of battery electric vehicles

The relative lifetime cost of an EV against an ICV is extremely sensitive to four key variables – average daily travel, vehicle range, oil price and battery capital cost. These variables will vary across different countries, urban and suburban areas, as well as with time.

Average daily travel varies significantly according to geography. In continental Europe, for example, 50 per cent of trips remain below 10km and 80 per cent below 25km. Meanwhile, in the UK, 97 per cent of all trips do not exceed 80km. Even in America, where distances tend to be much greater, 85 per cent of all trips remain under 100km (IEA, 2009b). These aggregate values are also a bit misleading since these large geographical markets are likely to contain various niche segments. For instance, rural drivers in America present average daily travel of 64km/day, compared to 48km/day in urban areas (Davis and Diegel, 2007). In this analysis, two scenarios are considered to better reflect this degree of uncertainty – low average travel of 30km/day and high average travel of 50km/day.

However, vehicle batteries are designed to provide sufficient range to meet the most demanding driving scenarios, not the average scenarios considered above. Given this analysis considers two distinct average travel scenarios, it is reasonable to expect two solutions which better match these specific consumer segments – low range of 75km and high range of 100km. To achieve these range capabilities, assuming typical driving conditions – highway speeds, activated climate control and hot external temperature – would require batteries of 19kWh and 25kWh, respectively.[16] Notice how these range levels far exceed most requirements in major automotive markets as presented above. Thus this level of range autonomy would comfortably meet the vast majority of travel requirements across the world.

The present analysis considers a range of oil prices (US$0.75/L to US$2/L) which corresponds to the global range of prices in late 2010 (based on a crude oil price of US$90/bbl plus local taxation). According to the IEA's *World Energy Outlook 2010*, in a business-as-usual scenario, oil prices are expected to reach the 2008 average price by 2015. However, prices rose steadily over 2010 and in January 2011 they had already reached the IEA's 2015 forecast mark of US$100/bbl.[17] Given that BEV operating cost savings are key to compensating for its high capital cost, any rise in oil prices would further benefit BEVs, thus making the present analysis particularly conservative.

Battery costs are expected to currently lie between US$750/kWh and US$1000/kWh. However, given that these are expected to drop quickly in the near term, this analysis considers battery costs ranging from US$1000/kWh to US$400/kWh. This will prove useful in demonstrating the extent to which government subsidies may actually be needed.

The total lifetime cost for each of the vehicles considered above was estimated through a net present value analysis using a 12 per cent discount rate. The results of this analysis are a function predominantly of battery capital cost and oil price. Table 6.2 presents the results for BEVs in terms of lifetime cost difference against the ICV solution, according to variable oil price (x-axis) and battery capital cost (y-axis) conditions. Negative valuations indicate uncompetitive conditions for the BEV requiring financial incentives to make them viable propositions.

Table 6.2 *Relative lifetime costs (US$)*

(a) High Average Travel/Long Range

Scenario	US$/kWh						
Today	1000	−10,452	−8304	−6156	−4008	−1859	289
	850	−6702	−4554	−2406	−258	1891	4039
2011 (X%)	700	−2952	−804	1344	3492	5641	7789
	550	798	2946	5094	7242	9391	11,539
	400	4548	6696	8844	10,992	13,141	15,289
	US$/litre	0.75	1	1.25	1.50	1.75	2

(b) Low Average Travel/Short Range

US$/kWh	1000	−5882	−4594	−3305	−2016	−727	562
US$/kWh	850	−3070	−1781	−492	797	2086	3375
US$/kWh	700	−257	1031	2320	3609	4898	6187
US$/kWh	550	2555	3844	5133	6422	7711	9000
US$/kWh	400	5368	6656	7945	9234	10,523	11,812
	US$/litre	0.75	1	1.25	1.50	1.75	2

It is clear from the results in Table 6.2 that BEV competitiveness depends heavily on range expectations. Even though the High Average Travel/Long Range scenario presents a higher utilization factor of the vehicle's range (the average travel uses 50 per cent of range capacity compared to 40 per cent), the higher initial capital cost cannot be fully justified by the inflated operating cost savings.

Aside from the sensitivity to range requirements, these results demonstrate that below US$850/kWh, BEV solutions begin to look decidedly economic. Of course, in situations with very low oil prices, such as in the US, some subsidies would still be required until around US$700/kWh.[18] This is particularly encouraging since battery costs are expected to drop below these levels in the very short run (2011/2012).

Long-term social costs

These results also suggest that, despite costing more for the early adopter, EVs will soon ensure increasing savings across all vehicle types and geographical regions. The question, then, is whether, on an aggregate level, future savings can provide a decent return on the initial aggregate investment. To demonstrate this, consider Nissan Leaf sales over the next 10 years.

Based on the vehicle's initial sticker price, without tax incentives, the battery is expected to cost US$625–830/kWh. Thus, in a worst-case scenario perspective, it is assumed that all Leafs are sold in the American market, with a battery cost of US$830/kWh and that, conservatively, oil prices hold at the current US$100/bbl, or US$0.88/L at the pump. That would mean that a Leaf sold during the first year would cost consumers US$5085 more over its life relative to a comparable ICV.

This calculation can then be repeated for vehicles sold every year until 2020, assuming, again conservatively, a 6 per cent reduction in battery capital cost per year.[19] Based on initial production estimates, it is possible to estimate the

Table 6.3 *Aggregated relative lifetime cost of Nissan Leafs in America*

	2011	2013	2015	2017	2019	2021
Vehicles sold	50	250	350	450	500	500
Battery cost (US$/kWh)	830	733	648	573	506	476
Relative lifetime cost per vehicle (US$)	−5085	−2660	−535	1340	3015	3765
Annual relative cost of leafs (million US$)	−254	−665	−187	603	1508	1883
Net present value (US$)	−254	−1298	−1695	−1302	−242	1043

annual cost of Leafs for each year between 2011 and 2020. These results, along with a net present value of these costs, based on a 12 per cent discount rate, are presented in Table 6.3.

This means that, while EVs would cost more in the short term (until 2015), they would soon provide increasing savings for both consumers and society as a whole. Furthermore, as shown by the far right column in this table, if this evaluation continued just one more year, assuming no further reduction in battery

Table 6.4 *Aggregated relative lifetime cost of Nissan Leafs in Europe*

	2011	2013	2015	2017	2019	2021
Vehicles sold	50	250	350	450	500	500
Battery cost (US$/kWh)	830	733	648	573	506	476
Relative lifetime cost per vehicle (US$)	−3447	−1022	1103	2978	4653	5403
Annual relative cost of leafs (million US$)	−172	−256	386	1340	2327	2702
Net present value (US$)	−172	−670	−411	681	2405	4249

costs nor increase in sales volumes, the financial benefits of the switch to the EV would only accentuate.

This analysis is repeated for the European market (Table 6.4), based on UK petrol prices at the pump and assuming an average driving distance of only 25km. Notice how, despite the significantly reduced utilization of vehicle range, European markets prove more attractive as a result of the petrol price (which is more than double that in America).

This analysis clearly shows that early EV adoption, even given its uneconomic position today, will provide significant savings in a short/medium-run scenario. It is important to recognize, however, that early adopters would not benefit from any of these theoretical societal savings, so potential early adopters have no economic motivation to commit themselves.

Financial incentives

These results, along with the concern that some consumers, at least in the short run, will not be able to weigh initial sticker price against operating cost savings, demonstrates the importance of financial incentives in promoting the deployment of EV technologies. It can now be seen that concern over energy security and climate change is indeed motivating governments to commit to reducing EV costs to consumers, as a means of ensuring long-run sustainable transport. As this book is written, a variety of financial incentives have emerged to support EV markets.

In the UK, for example, the government has eliminated annual road taxes over the next five years for both individual and commercial EVs. This amounts to a US$800 discounted cost reduction over the vehicle's lifetime. Furthermore, sales-based financial incentives of up to US$12,000 (Table 6.5) are becoming common in many countries.

Table 6.5 *Sales rebates*

Country	Discount
Belgium	Personal income tax deduction of 30 per cent of vehicle sticker price, up to €9000 (US$12,000).
China	Automakers receive ¥50,000 (US$7320) for PHEV and ¥60,000 (US$8800) for BEV sales, which are expected to be passed on to the consumer.
Denmark	Electric vehicles are exempt from new vehicle registration tax. New vehicle registration tax is 105 per cent of vehicle price up to DKK79,000 and 180 per cent above.
Germany	Annual road tax exemption for first five years of vehicle life (no sales-based incentives).
Japan	Electric vehicles receive a 50 to 75 per cent reduction in acquisition tax, which is 5 per cent of the vehicle sticker price, and receive a direct subsidy. Subsidies range from ¥50,000 (US$550) to ¥250,000 (US$2700).
UK	Electric vehicles receive a discount 25 per cent rebate base on sticker price, up to £5000 (US$8220).
US	Federal tax rebates up to US$3400 for HEVs and up to US$7500 for PHEVs and BEVs.

Indeed, in the European context, this may very well be enough to make BEVs competitive today. While direct government subsidies may be indispensable at this early stage, it is encouraging to see rebates and other market-based incentives (MBIs) emerging in parallel.

Carbon policy is no longer a political black sheep. Rather, over the last half-decade, it has gained traction as one of the core items in any government's agenda. It is probably safe to say that society has reached a point of no return in the journey to more sustainable living. However, long-term quantitative evaluation of the costs and benefits of this journey remains blurry (Box 6.3). Consequently, analysts can only do their best to incorporate continuously evolving carbon policy into a long-term forecast. Meanwhile, short-term policies are being implemented.

One MBI to be better explored would be the use of carbon markets to obtain a revenue stream from the effective carbon reduction achieved by the shift away from ICVs. On the back of the Kyoto Protocol, carbon markets have developed into an effective mechanism for businesses in several fields to offset the cost of carbon emissions reductions. Alas, a methodology for assessing and monitoring emissions reductions from the private transportation sector has yet to emerge and be accepted by the Clean Development Mechanism (CDM) Executive Board, thus preventing the mitigation of one of the greatest sources of greenhouse gases. However, the direction of BEV development offers a potential solution to the emissions-reduction monitoring problem, thus opening the sector to carbon trading.

As discussed, the actual carbon reductions realized depend on the cleanliness of the electricity and the conventional vehicle fleet in use in the given market. Everything from the charging process to the driving history can be monitored by the BEV's computer systems. Indeed, it would not be difficult to store some of these details for monitoring and reporting purposes, thus allowing the driver to receive an energy discount according to specific market conditions.

Assuming a pessimistic carbon price of US\$20/tCO_2,[20] annual revenues from carbon credits could reach US\$100/year per vehicle. If 2020 carbon price projections (US\$75/tCO_2) are considered, this revenue would surge to US\$375/year per vehicle. While that may not be a very enticing income, carbon revenues could accumulate between US\$676 and US\$2366 over the vehicle's lifetime, which based on the results in Table 6.2 could very well prove to be the difference between a BEV being competitive or not.

In addition to carbon revenues or discounts, grid-enabled EVs, such as battery EVs and plug-in HEVs, could generate an income by providing V2G energy services (as discussed in Chapter 5). Through provision of ancillary services, the vehicle owner has the potential to earn up to US\$1835/year. However, this income is highly dependent on the overall level of market saturation. Remuneration of V2G energy would peak early in the market penetration cycle, coinciding nicely with the initial period of high battery costs. But it is unlikely to prevail in the long run. Rather, the V2G market is expected to reach

---

BOX 6.3 *THE ECONOMICS OF CLIMATE CHANGE*

There appears to be a growing consensus over the threat posed by climate change, but there is still considerable uncertainty over the economics of climate change, particularly the cost of mitigating versus adapting to climate change. Much of the debate revolves around the treatment of discount rates, more specifically the application of pure time preference rates, based on individuals' preference of consuming today rather than tomorrow.

The 2006 *Stern Review on the Economics of Climate Change*, the most thorough study regarding the economics of climate change, argues in favour of strong and immediate action to mitigate the effects of climate change based on a 1.4 per cent discount rate. Sir Nicholas Stern, Chair of the Grantham Research Institute on Climate Change and the Environment at the London School of Economics and former Vice President of the World Bank, defends the use of such a low discount rate on the basis that it is ethically inappropriate to apply considerable pure time preference rates in the case of social policy decisions. At the other extreme of the debate is William Nordhaus, Sterling Professor of Economics at Yale University, who challenges the Stern Review's conclusions based on the inadequacy of using such low discount rates.

In response to the discount rates challenges from Nordhaus and other economists, Stern has pointed out that 'we are in pretty good company here in that [the distinguished economists] Solow, Sen, Keynes, Ramsey and all kinds of people have adopted the approach to pure time discounting that we have adopted. It is not particularly unusual.' (House of Commons, 2008). Indeed, notable economists have officially spoken out endorsing the Stern Review, including Robert Solow, Amartya Sen, Joseph Stiglitz, Jeffrey Sachs and Kenneth Arrow.

While the details behind this debate are beyond the scope of this book, it is clear that climate change should be a real concern for the present generation, and the longer we stand still the faster and harder it will impact society in the future. Policymakers who remain sceptical about the magnitude and importance of action should take note of the 15th principle of the Rio Declaration on Environment and Development, which states:

> *In order to protect the environment, the precautionary approach shall be widely applied by States according to their capabilities. Where there are threats of serious or irreversible damage, lack of full scientific certainty shall not be used as a reason for postponing cost-effective measures to prevent environmental degradation.*

---

saturation with just over 10 per cent of total fleet conversion, with revenues decaying very quickly thereafter. Crucially, this is unlikely to harm EV market penetration since, by then, economies of scale in battery production are likely to have taken effect.

A Convenient Truth

It should now be clear that the EV is a fundamentally superior transportation solution compared to the ICV. Beyond the improved driving experience, the EV has the potential to be cheaper for the consumer, society and governments alike. Hopefully, this chapter has demonstrated how the EV is cost-effective when all costs are adequately taken into consideration. Before identifying the path ahead, it is worth reviewing three key elements which will be exploited a bit further in the final two chapters of the book.

First, experts are confident that the EV sticker price premium will deteriorate with increased scale. Unfortunately, this presents the industry with a 'catch-

22'. To reach the goal of reduced battery costs, producers must first achieve scale. However, it will be difficult to achieve scale unless the EV is cost-effective compared to the ICV. Fortunately, as already discussed, vehicle cost-effectiveness is determined as much by operating costs as it is by its sticker price. The challenge to be faced in order to reap the benefits of increased production is to either make the consumer clearly aware of the lifetime costs he or she incurs in alternative solutions or push the market in the socially desirable direction through financial incentives.

Second, society is finally realizing that ICVs and oil markets are both massively inefficient. Indeed, the ICV wastes the vast majority of the energy content it processes, making it incredibly expensive to operate, while oil markets are repeatedly thrown off balance by geopolitical tensions which cause spikes in already strained operating expenditures. Meanwhile, EVs enjoy high levels of system-wide efficiency and comparatively stable electricity prices. Indeed, these two cost variables combined provide EVs with critical market opportunities as well as a rationale for public policy in its support.

Finally, the ICV system's inefficiencies do not affect solely its owner. Quite the contrary, its impact reaches all levels of society. For oil-importing countries, the oil addiction means an inflated foreign trade deficit and less money invested domestically. Notice that this is not a question of environmental ethics, but rather one of national welfare. Having said that, the ICV's environmental impact is not negligible. Indeed, while these impacts are not factored into the cost of operating an ICV, they are incurred indirectly through higher healthcare and clean-up bills. As discussed, BEVs eliminate virtually all of these externalities. However, as yet, they have received no compensation for the public service they provide. Eliminating this imbalance will be crucial to make sustainable transport a reality.

Hopefully this has adequately convinced the reader of the EV's sustainability credentials. The technology not only provides energy and environmental security, it also provides noteworthy economic savings for society as a whole. This chapter has shown that given comprehensive analysis the EV is clearly a cost-effective alternative to the ICV. The two final chapters of the book aim to translate the cost-effectiveness analysis developed here into a potential path towards sustainable transport.

Notes

1   Updated costs and economic evaluations can be obtained from the Electrification Coalition website, www.electrificationcoalition.org.
2   The coalition includes John Chambers (CEO of Cisco Systems, Inc), Ray Lane (Managing Partner of Kleiner Perkins Caufield & Byers), Carlos Ghosn (CEO of Renault/Nissan), David Vieau (CEO of A123 Systems, Inc) and Richard Lowenthal (CEO of Coulomb Technologies, Inc).
3   Notice that there is no international standard for fuel economy and/or fuel consumption. Thus this text presents fuel economy in both mpg and km/L, which are the most widely presented metrics.

4   It is important to highlight that fuel economy estimates vary significantly depend-
    ing on the methodology used. Comparing EU and US fuel economy estimates, it is
    clear that the EU methodology provides more optimistic results – EU methodologies
    estimate lower fuel consumption per kilometre than US methodologies for the same
    vehicle. It is thus essential that fuel economy evaluations be based on equivalent
    methodologies. Here, the US EPA data has been chosen to match the data used by
    the Credit Suisse study.

5   Combined fuel economy is a combined measure of highway and urban fuel econo-
    mies.

6   The Honda Civic Hybrid and Honda Insight Hybrid offer 42mpg and 41mpg
    respectively.

7   Notice that as PHEVs and other hybrids are launched throughout the coming years,
    this number will expand. Nevertheless, pure ICVs are unlikely to ever reach this
    mark in significant numbers.

8   Notice that this figure is inflated by the fact that the database counts minor varia-
    tions in features such as gearbox types, engine sizes and fuel type as distinct vehicles.
    Thus, what the reader thinks of as being one vehicle model, for instance the Corolla
    sedan, can at first stage be disaggregated into the Corolla, Corolla LE, Corolla
    XLE, Corolla S and Corolla XRS, which can further be broken down into manual
    and automatic gearboxes and/or into diesel, gasoline, ethanol and fuel flex models
    (depending on regional availability). Thus, when the US EPA speaks of 143 vehicle
    models, this can easily translate to about 10–20 vehicles models for the layperson.

9   Strictly speaking, these values are not W2W efficiencies and are not directly compa-
    rable to the efficiencies presented in the previous analysis. Indeed, this analysis
    has ignored the efficiency of producing the electricity itself. This is only valid since
    electricity production is identical for both FCEV and BEV supply chains.

10 Notice that the author is not claiming coal energy to be clean.

11 Note that this proportion will vary not only across countries, depending on their
    resource base, but over time, as different energy sources are switched on and off to
    meet real-time demand.

12 Based on a coal heating value of 9.03kWh/kg coal and a supply chain – material
    processing, power generation, transmission and distribution – efficiency of 30 per cent.

13 Combustion fuels for transport are typically treated in volumetric terms – be it US
    gallons or litres – because of convenience. However, to facilitate the comparison
    between combustion fuels and electric energy, the analysis uses the following termi-
    nology: MJ for energy content and km for range. This is readily done by assuming a
    gasoline energy density of 34.2MJ/L.

14 E10 and E25 stand for ethanol/gasoline fuel mixtures containing 10 per cent and 25
    per cent ethanol by volume, respectively.

15 EU target emissions standard for new vehicles in 2012 is 130gCO_2/km, which would
    require a fuel economy of around 21.25km/L or 50mpg

16 This also accounts for a 20 per cent capacity reserve which is not expected to be used.

17 Notice that most of the market studies presented in Chapter 7 assume a weaker oil
    price inflation over the next decade, which dramatically impacts the anticipated
    competitiveness of BEVs.

18 Notice that based on the IEA's 2010 oil price forecast, corrected according to
    January 2011 prices, US pump prices should reach US$1/L (US$3.79/gal) by the
    middle of the decade.

19 This is at the lower end of McKinsey's (Hensley et al, 2009) cost reduction forecasts (6–8 per cent per year). In fact, while McKinsey projects that battery capital costs could reach US\$420/kWh by as early as 2015, this analysis assumes a significantly more conservative US\$476/kWh by 2020. If McKinsey's figures were used in the present analysis, it would only accentuate the benefits of EV adoption.

20 According to UK Committee on Climate Change's Progress report to the British Parliament (2009), the carbon price within the EU Emissions Trading System averaged €24/tCO_2 (US\$32/tCO_2) and €22/tCO_2 (US\$29/tCO_2) in the first and second halves of 2008, respectively. While prices fell to €13/tCO_2 (US\$17/tCO_2) during the first half of 2009, due largely to the slowdown in the global economy, the committee projects a rise to €56/tCO_2 (US\$75/tCO_2) by 2020.

References

Bossel, U. (2006) 'Does a hydrogen economy make sense?', *Proceedings of the IEEE*, vol 94, no 10, October

Boston Consulting Group (2009) 'The comeback of the electric car? How real, how soon, and what must happen next', Boston Consulting Group, Boston, MA, January

Credit Suisse (2009) 'Electric vehicles', *Credit Suisse Equity Research*, 1 October

Davis, S. C. and Diegel, S. W. (2007) *Transportation Energy Data Book: Edition 26*, Oak Ridge National Laboratory, Oak Ridge, TN

Electrification Coalition (2009) *Electrification Roadmap: Revolutionizing Transportation and Achieving Energy Security*, Electrification Coalition, Washington, DC

Frost & Sullivan (2009) '360 degree analysis of the global electric vehicles market', white paper, Frost & Sullivan, www.frost.com/prod/servlet/segment-toc.pag?segid=9832-00-0D-00-00

Hensley, R., Knupfer, S. and Pinner, D. (2009) *Electrifying Cars: How Three Industries Will Evolve*, McKinsey & Co., http://ww1.mckinsey.com/clientservice/sustainability/pdf/electrifying_cars.pdf

House of Commons (2008) 'Climate change and the Stern Review: The implications for Treasury policy', House of Commons Treasury Committee, London, UK

IEA (2008) *Energy Technology Perspectives 2008*, International Energy Agency, Paris

IEA (2009a) *World Energy Outlook 2009*, International Energy Agency, Paris

IEA (2009b) *Technology Roadmap: Electric and Plug-In Hybrid Electric Vehicles*, International Energy Agency, Paris

IEA (2010) *World Energy Outlook 2010*, International Energy Agency, Paris

Lovins, A., Kyle Datta, E., Bustnes, O.-E. and Koomey, J. G. (2004) *Winning the Oil Endgame: Innovation for Profit, Jobs and Security*, Earthscan, London

Stern, N. (2006) *Stern Review on the Economics of Climate Change*, UK Office of Climate Change (www.occ.gov.uk), available at www.sternreview.org.uk

UK Committee on Climate Change (2009) 'Meeting carbon budgets – The need for a step change', progress report to Parliament Committee on Climate Change, 12 October

7

Electric Vehicle Adoption Trajectory

You can get it if you really want
But you must try,
Try and try,
Try and try ...
You'll succeed at last.

Jimmy Cliff

Up to now, the discussion has focused on whether EVs are ready to penetrate the automotive market. Hopefully the discussion has demonstrated that the technology is sound and on the brink of commercial maturity, that there is currently support from consumers and governments alike, and that businesses are positioning themselves to offer a 'whole-product' solution, with complementary goods and services such as battery financing and recharging infrastructure. Indeed, it is no longer front-page news that EVs will be playing an important role in future transportation markets.

Although it is easy enough to say that supply and demand conditions look promising, however, it would be short-sighted to claim that this will automatically result in steady growth starting now. As stated in the Introduction, technological transformations are neither linear nor continuous. Rather, historical evidence suggests that they occur in sudden bursts. So when can consumers expect EVs to burst into their lives? When will consumers start to see more of them out on the streets? And when are they likely to become the commonplace vehicle of choice?

Of course, the answer is not simple. When new technologies emerge, they do not make their predecessor obsolete overnight. Just consider how it took a decade for CD sales to surpass those of cassettes – and audio equipment costs a fraction of the cost of an automobile. Indeed, in the early stage of commercialization, nascent technologies will still have limitations unacceptable by mass-market standards – high retail costs, technical restrictions, uncertainties over service reliability and so on. Thus innovations must typically face a long market approval process during which their imperfections, limitations and risks are addressed.

With a technology so ingrained and central to our lifestyle as the petroleum-based automobile, such a transition is far from trivial. Even if EVs were technically superior to ICVs in every way, shape and form, risk-averse consumers would still require a robust proof of concept. Society will not be able to teleport from ICVs to EVs without a transitional stage. In fact, it is impossible to say where we will ultimately end up – how prevalent will BEVs, fuel-cell EVs, plug-in HEVs or maybe some yet unknown technology be? Granted, this book advocates the BEV as the most suitable solution to the future private transportation requirements. However, BEVs alone cannot penetrate the mass market in this early stage, as they are still unlikely to prove appealing to most consumers. Thus, successfully reducing oil dependence and CO_2 emissions will require a transition to electric propulsion based on a portfolio of well-thought-out, prioritized solutions – and, as will be argued in Chapter 8, appropriate policy design.

This chapter looks ahead and explores what the EV adoption trajectory might look like. It begins with a literature review of market forecasts as support to the subsequent analysis. It then develops a view of market penetration in the short term based on the development of niche markets and, subsequently, evaluates what is needed for EV technology to overcome the barriers to mass-market penetration in the longer term.

Market Forecast Review

If one were to draw any conclusion from market studies available currently, it would be that the EV market will grow rapidly along an S-shaped penetration curve, typical of technological innovation trajectories. Despite a general sense of optimism, analysts have diverging expectations when it comes to making concrete estimates on how steep the curve is likely to be and where it might plateau. Indeed, it seems that much uncertainty remains regarding underlying market and political conditions such that it is difficult to identify a dominant vision.

This section begins by presenting a review of the key findings from six market projection studies. It then considers the premises behind two of these studies to better understand the reasons for diverging views on market penetration. It concludes by laying out the premise for an alternative view of EV market projections.

Diverse and diverging views

If there is a group of analysts that appears to have a consensus on EV market penetration, it is management consultants and financial institutions – Frost & Sullivan (F&S) (2009), McKinsey & Co. (Hensley et al, 2009), Boston Consulting Group (2009) and Credit Suisse (2009). In the words of Credit Suisse, 'electric vehicles offer one of the fastest growth stories over the next 20 years'. Despite this unqualified enthusiasm, their quantitative analysis is conservative and borders on contradicting their excitement.

According to Frost & Sullivan (2009) and Credit Suisse (2009), grid-enabled EV sales will represent a mere 7 per cent of total global LDV sales by 2020. Credit Suisse forecasts further indicate that GEV sales fail to significantly expand market share, reaching 8 per cent by 2030 (Figure 7.1). As a result, the global ICV fleet would continue to soar, with 2030 ICV sales nearly doubling to 136 million units.

The most optimistic among these studies seems to be Boston Consulting Group. While their results for GEVs are no better than those of Credit Suisse (hereafter CS), they invariably show an intense expansion of HEVs (Figure 7.2). Still, these results remain highly conservative in terms of the bigger picture.

Meanwhile, at the International Energy Agency (IEA) the expectations could not be more different. According to the IEA's 2009 EV technology roadmap (IEA, 2009), initial GEV growth, up to 2020, is less than inspiring and follows nearly the same path as that postulated by the conservative estimates above. However, post-2020, where the consultants' conservative forecasts either end or plateau, the IEA's projections begin to surge (Figure 7.3). Crucially, the agency also puts emphasis on the continued growth of HEVs, such that ICV absolute sales volumes deteriorate from 2020.

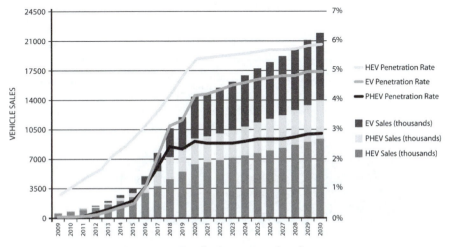

Figure 7.1 *Credit Suisse market forecast*

Source: Credit Suisse (2009)

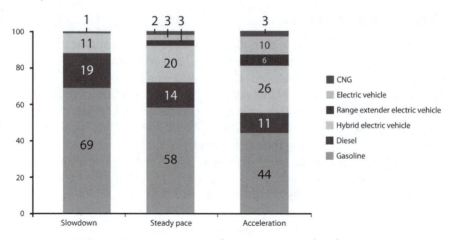

Figure 7.2 *Boston Consulting Group market forecast*

Source: Boston Consulting Group (2009)

Of course, the deeper into the industry that one explores, the more optimism one finds. The Electrification Coalition (2009) present an aggressive development plan (Figure 7.4) for the electrification of the American LDV fleet. In their eyes, by 2030, GEV sales in America alone will exceed the uninspiring 12.5 million global units forecast by CS. GEVs would make up 25 per cent of LDV sales by 2020 and 90 per cent by 2030. What is more, battery-powered EVs are expected to dominate 90 per cent of the overall GEV market by then.

It is important to highlight that the Electrification Coalition (EC) is not alone in this view. According to Frank Klegon, Chrysler's Executive Vice President for Product Development, BEVs and extended-range EVs will make up at least 50 per cent of the market by 2020 (Eisenstein, 2008). Meanwhile, Warren Buffett has claimed that all vehicles on the road by 2030 will be electric.

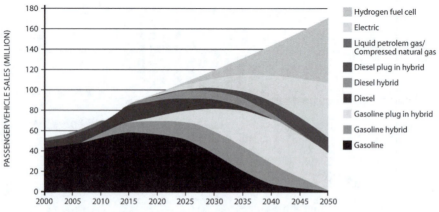

Figure 7.3 *IEA market forecast*

Source: IEA (2009)

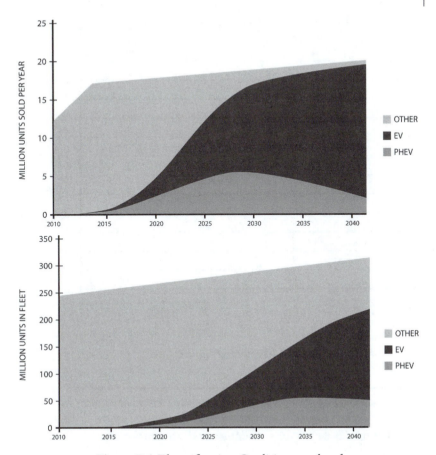

Figure 7.4 *Electrification Coalition market forecast*

Source: Electrification Coalition (2009)

Indeed, it becomes difficult to weed out blind optimism and cautious conservatism when the results are so varied. Before making any further judgement, it is important to examine these reports in greater detail. By doing this, one actually finds that each study brings both diverse criteria and valuable information to the table.

A closer look at penetration rates

Market penetration is a function of a complex relationship between various model parameters – costs, infrastructure dissemination, consumer acceptance and others. Far too often, however, analysts fail to present the audience with an explicit justification for how they evaluate and weigh these key parameters. Two of the studies reviewed – CS and EC – do, however, provide important insights through distinct approaches.

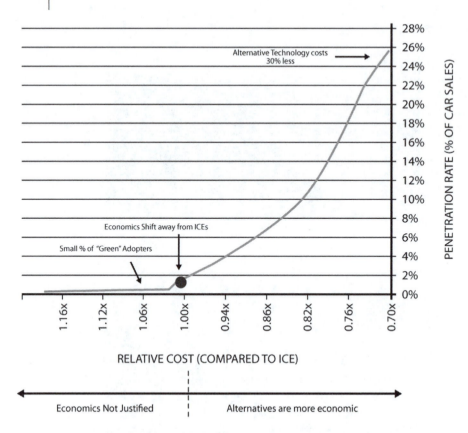

Figure 7.5 *Credit Suisse relative-cost penetration model*

Source: Credit Suisse

Credit Suisse's relative-cost model

The CS study estimates EV penetration rates based on the relative cost between EVs and ICVs plus a 'green factor' (Figure 7.5). The model resembles a classic demand curve – the less costly the product, the more customers it will attract. While the fundamental framework behind this model is very solid, its application and the interpretation of its results must be carefully considered.

CS appears to have performed multiple relative-cost evaluations for distinct market locations, varying over time. The relative cost of GEVs drops as battery prices drop, oil prices rise and taxes rise to encourage green technologies. While these factors affect the relative-cost results, they appear not to have an impact on the *shape* of the relative-cost penetration curve (Figure 7.5) over time. Two defining characteristics of this model merit special attention.

First, the model assumes what appears to be an excessive degree of inertia in shifting away from the ICV even after the break-even point. Of course some inertia is to be expected since consumers might still prefer the technology they are familiar with and for which they know the infrastructure is reliable. After all, what is the point of buying a cheap soviet-era car if you are not going to be able to find parts when it breaks down?

However, since the model presents consumers as an aggregate, underlying assumptions regarding specific market segments are not clear. As will be seen below, specific bulk consumers, such as fleet operators, are likely to reach the relative break-even point before private consumers. In their case, technological inertia is highly unlikely if the economic component makes sense. This, in turn, creates better conditions for infrastructure deployment, thus reducing much of the potential mass-market inertia.

Indeed, by 2020, EV infrastructure may have been demonstrated and in many locations could be widespread. As a result, one would expect the inertia acting against the EV to weaken over time. The concrete analytical consequence of this observation is that the slope of the penetration curve will steepen over time, such that consumers respond more directly to the relative cost/benefit. It might also be more appropriate to use distinct curves according to market locations. After all, as discussed, European markets are expected to be less influenced by range anxiety due to their elevated population densities and relatively short daily travel distances.

Second, the CS model recognizes that demand is rarely ever explained entirely by a 'rational decision'. Since consumers may be influenced by such things as the automobile's environmental impact, a 'green factor' is included in the model. This suggests that there are always a few irrational members of society who will purchase the 'green' product regardless of what a rational evaluation might suggest (just as there are the irrational consumers who fail to do their lifetime analysis and end up buying the ICV, as discussed in Chapter 6).

Notice, however, that as with the penetration inertia, the 'green factor' is taken to be homogeneous across all global markets and over time. But do Middle Eastern sheiks or Texan ranchers really have the same attraction towards green technologies as Nordics or Californians? Indeed, it seems inappropriate and an excessive simplification to use the same 'green factor' for distinct geographic market segments. Furthermore, climate change is expected to have a direct impact on Generation Y – often referred to as the MTV Generation or Internet Generation – which consists of babies born as early as the mid-1970s and as late as the turn of the millennium and thus represents the incoming group of economic and political leaders. For these consumers, it is reasonable to stipulate that the 'green factor' will escalate rapidly over time.

Notice, contrary to what the CS study might suggest, that even after relative costs plateau, EV market penetration should continue to climb. To more accurately represent the variables discussed, one would need to shift the penetration curve upwards to represent a stronger 'green factor' and make the curve steeper to take into account reduced inertia. On that note, while the CS model may underestimate the actual penetration rate of EVs, its key premises are commendable and will prove useful in our own analysis.

Electrification Coalition's target seeking

The EC study does not actually forecast penetration rates based on technological and market assumptions. Rather, it works backwards by predefining targets, based on which they outline a detailed implementation programme. As such, it is not so much a market forecast as a plan.

In contrast to other studies that expect EVs to indiscriminately penetrate the automotive mass market, the EC proposal targets niche market segments based on political and demographic criteria (Figure 7.6). The underlying principle is that, by targeting scarce resources in concentrated systems, the achievement of the programme's main goals – proof of concept, economies of scale and implementation know-how – can be accelerated.

The EC makes a valid argument here. Consumers are not likely to be encouraged by one million charging spots dispersed across the US. However, if the same million charging spots were deployed in a single urban area like San Francisco or along a densely populated urban corridor like Rio de Janeiro–São Paulo, they would ensure consumers proximity to a vast and reliable infrastructure. Crucially, the success of a demonstration project would provide the precedent to encourage a 'copy-cat' or ripple effect of infrastructure projects at a far faster rate than if resources trickled into dispersed communities.

Many readers might still question whether that would be enough to justify the unprecedented growth rate forecasts assumed by EC. But is it really unprecedented? Have we not seen similar booms over the last two decades – in personal computing, the internet and mobile phones? Indeed, what the EC proposes is nothing out of the ordinary when compared, for example, to the mobile phone boom at the turn of the century (Box 7.1).

In retrospect, the market data in Figure 7.7 suggest that once a radical technological innovation, such as mobile phones and BEVs, picks up momentum, the shift is irreversible. Indeed, from businessmen to ten-year-olds, rich and poor, North and South, mobile phones have taken over the world. Granted,

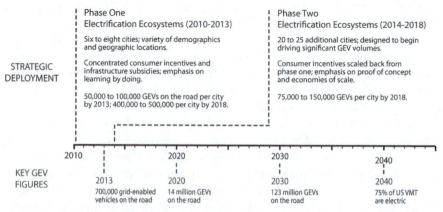

Figure 7.6 *Electrification ecosystems*

Note: VMT = vehicle miles travelled.
Source: Electrification Coalition (2009)

Box 7.1 MOBILE PHONE PENETRATION OR THE RAPID EXTINCTION OF DINOSAURS

My attention was drawn to the mobile phone analogy by my ten-year-old nephew, who recently said he was going to convince his grandfather to buy him an iPhone 3GS. While his hopes were short-lived, it got me thinking how, at his age, I did not even know what a mobile phone was … and perhaps by the time he is my age, EVs will be as common as mobile phones are today. Obviously, I then spent the night finding out how fast mobile phones actually took over the market.

The first commercial mobile network dates back to 1979 in Japan. Throughout the 1980s, the technology found its way around the world, achieving particular success in the Scandinavian countries. However, these first generation mobile phones have as much in common with today's SmartPhones as pocket calculators do with high-tech mainframe computer servers – virtually nothing.

The first 'modern' mobile phone system was introduced in 1991 in the form of the digital second generation (2G) networks. This is really where mobile phones took off (Figure 7.7). Most adults today can probably remember – or perhaps still own and use – a digital 2G phone. Over the course of the decade, coverage went global, penetrating even remote villages, while handsets went from being luxury items for the corporate executive to becoming a standard (in fact indispensable) accessory of the 21st century teenybopper, who simply can't leave home without it. And more importantly from a social standpoint, it has given millions of low-income families around the world access to a phone line.

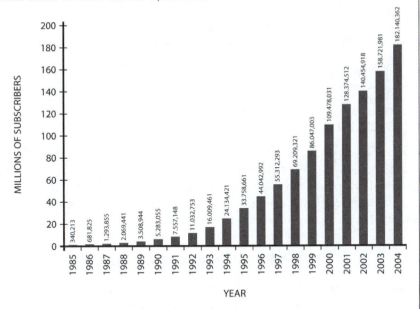

Figure 7.7 *Mobile phone subscribers*

Source: CTIA Wireless Association

Indeed, market penetration soared as soon as a truly 'mobile' phone solution was developed – in other words one that did not involve lugging around an elephant-sized device. No longer were mobile phones only suitable as (non-mobile) car phones and other niche applications. Now just about everyone can use the device with just one hand and carry them around in pockets, purses, backpacks and briefcases.

Box 7.1 CONTINUED

The technological adoption trajectory observed in the mobile phone industry is not unique in any way. Adoption can be thought of as a three-stage process. In phase 1, the technology has yet to be fine-tuned for the rigours of the mass market, but its potential advantages against the status quo solution are enough to attract some adventurous niche consumers. In phase 2, having proven the concept, amortized early development costs and established a reputation for quality, the technology is rapidly accepted by more conservative consumer groups, ultimately reaching the mass market. Finally, in phase 3, growth begins to dim as the market reaches saturation.

Both the historical account of mobile phone network development and the market penetration data presented suggest that the introduction of 2G networks was critical to the shift between first and second phases of the mobile phone adoption trajectory. While the number of subscribers grew at an astounding 73 per cent compound annual growth rate between 1985 and 1990, the fundamental consumer base remained a minority of the population. But in the subsequent 14 years, mobile phone ownership soared from 21 phones to 622 phones per thousand people.

Would any analyst in 1991 have been able to predict that the American mobile phone market would have more than 100 million consumers by 2000, or that the majority of Americans would own a mobile phone by 2003? After all, a handset cost several thousand dollars in the late 1980s and early 1990s (Table 7.1). How could such an expensive technology be marketed to the mass market? It was rather expected that mobile phones would become a must-have accessory for business executives and the social elite.

Table 7.1 *Motorola retail prices*

	Year Introduced	Nominal US$	2010 Real US$
DynaTAC series	1983	3995	8746
MicroTAC series	1989	2495–3495	4387–6146
International 3200 series	1992	£1400	3550
StarTAC series	1996	1000	1390

cars are more expensive than mobile phones or computers, plus it is unlikely that children will ever drive. But, perhaps, with some allowance made for the potential client base and its cost, it is not science fiction that BEVs could have an equivalently dramatic penetration trajectory. The following section speculates about what the penetration trajectory might look like.

The Nascent Market (2010–2020)

Which must come first – EVs or their charging infrastructure? No rational consumers would ever buy a product unless there was adequate infrastructure to support it. Yet no sane business will invest the billions required to establish such an infrastructure for a market that has yet to materialize!

While most drivers may demand long range and widespread recharging infrastructure, there are subsets of consumers whose activities are such that range is not a real issue. These consumers will be the ones providing the initial push to the market that ultimately justifies the expansion of infrastructure required by the more demanding, risk-averse subset of consumers.

Identifying niche markets

Technological innovations have a better chance of succeeding when they are shaped to meet the unique requirements of a niche consumer while offering a platform for their broader applicability. Indeed, knowing the consumer's explicit requirements helps to avoid over-engineering costs and ensure a greater level of satisfaction. Six niche market segments should prove to be crucial drivers of EV sales in the early years.

The fast and the furious (now)

As seen in Chapter 3, BEVs can significantly outshine their ICV rivals in terms of driving experience. At the end of the day, the would-be Formula 1 driver, or simply the rich and glamorous, are unlikely to care if their speed demon costs them US$100,000 or US$200,000. Hence, it is no surprise that many EV start-ups have decided to target this segment of the market.

Some might think that this will not have an impact on mass-market adoption of BEVs, since supercar consumers are not price-conscious and less concerned with getting across the state for a camping trip. Indeed, at US$100,000-plus and a rate of 1200 sales per year for the Tesla, for instance, high-performance EVs may not contribute significantly to building scale, but they should provide a much-needed platform for proving technological maturity and perhaps for spreading the word to the broader public. Over the years, Formula 1 has been at the forefront of key automotive innovations, such as electronic traction control systems, carbon fibre structural elements, ceramic components and, more recently, regenerative braking.

Early start-up carmakers that established themselves initially with a view to offering high-performance EVs are now expanding their focus towards the mass market. Tesla, for example, promises to launch a large family sedan with 480km range for US$49,000 by 2012. While this is far from a budget vehicle, it does promise to rival other mass-market executive/luxury sedans such as the BMW 5 series and the Mercedes E-Class.

The fleet vehicle (2010–2015)

The best-suited niche consumers for early BEV adoption are fleet vehicles – from mail delivery and cable TV repair fleets to bus networks and chauffeur services. In each of these cases, vehicles typically operate within limited geographical boundaries. Daily travel distances are highly predictable and infrastructural requirements can be planned with a high degree of certainty.

Chapter 6 presented the lifetime cost of various EVs and confirmed that battery capital cost was a key burden. In that scenario, the average daily travel distance was assumed to be 50km, but in order to accommodate for atypical days and the requirements of the American market, the BEV would need to ensure a 100km range. Compare this to a US Postal Service study (USPS, 2009) that shows that average daily travel distance for their delivery vehicles is only about 30km and that 96 per cent of daily travel distances remain under 65km (Figure 7.8).

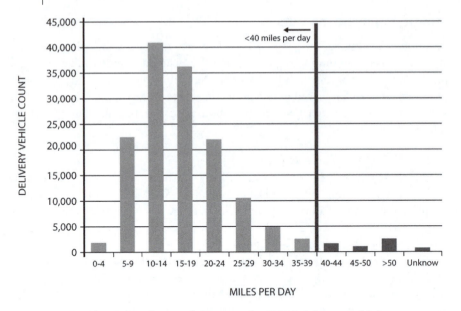

Figure 7.8 *Daily travel distance for USPS delivery vehicles*

Source: data from USPS (2009)

Assuming a maximum range of 65km and a discount rate of 15 per cent, USPS BEVs would become profitable in every oil/battery price scenario presented in Chapter 6. In fact, taking into account the US$7500 tax incentive already in place in the US, these vehicles become profitable with current battery prices and with US$0.75/L (US$2.84/gal) in less than 10 years, or under half of the vehicle's 20-year life cycle.

Based on fleet renewal data from the aforementioned USPS study and assuming a 50 per cent electrification rate, the USPS fleet would generate an order of 3400 BEVs in 2011 and about 8500 BEVs every year thereafter. Assuming now that UPS and FedEx global fleets[1] can also convert at the same rate, this would generate a further 7000 vehicles per year.

Rio de Janeiro's power distribution company, Light SA, provides similar fleet operating characteristics (Pecorelli et al, 2009). While the overall fleet does present a longer average daily driving pattern (75 per cent remain under 70km), most segments of the fleet present equivalent patterns and range requirements to the USPS case. Given the distinct nature of the USPS delivery fleet and Light's maintenance service fleet, it is reasonable to imagine that other business and government fleets would be equally suited for BEV adoption.

Indeed, businesses such as Sainsbury's (UK grocers),[2] Florida Power and Light Company and Duke Energy have already committed to EV adoption. While this is by no means an exhaustive list of EV fleet candidates, it does illustrate the potential scale of this 'niche' market.

Stepping back for a 'big picture' perspective, fleet operations, in general and worldwide, are likely to be the ideal operating environment for EV implementation. In 2005, American government agencies purchased approximately 630,000 fleet vehicles (Davis and Diegel, 2007, Section 7). According to my life-cycle cost analysis in the previous chapter, relative costs for government fleets have already reached parity, based on US$900/kWh battery cost. Based on 2005 sales volumes and the market penetration model provided by Credit Suisse (Figure 7.5), one can justify EVs snatching at least 1.5 per cent of total US government fleet sales or approximately 10,000 vehicles. A similar analysis applies for business fleets, which summed 920,000 units sold in 2005.

It is not hard to see that, even at very low penetration rates of 1.5 per cent, American EV fleet vehicle demand could easily reach 25,000 per year in the very short run. Given that the American market represents 23 per cent of global automotive sales volume, and extrapolating the data, one can conclude that global EV fleet vehicle demand could reach 100,000 per year very soon.

But is it reasonable to assume that all fleets benefit from the conditions presented by the USPS scenario or that other countries have the same purchasing power as the Americans? Well, if American market conditions are compared with those of other major vehicle markets, the above extrapolation may actually look understated.

First and foremost, American oil prices are notoriously low compared to the norm in other countries. Second, driving range requirements are comparatively high in the US, particularly compared to EU markets, which inflates the weight of battery capital costs in the lifetime analysis. Third, emissions reductions commitments and carbon markets in the US are years behind those of the EU. And finally, American automobile retail prices are well below foreign markets, making consumers more sensitive to price hikes. Indeed, these factors imply that global penetration potential is likely to exceed the crude estimate above.

In contrast, what would be the effects of purchasing power differentials? In the short term, they probably would not be significant, since the high-income US and EU and fast-growing China alone account for well over half of global fleet sales. Furthermore, the remainder of the global market includes numerous mature and prospering markets – including Australia, Brazil (and much of Latin America), Japan, Russia (and much of the former Soviet Bloc), South Africa, South Korea (and other Asian Tigers) – that jointly present equally compelling adoption opportunities.

This conclusion appears consistent, for instance, with the French government's plan to purchase up to 100,000 EVs in conjunction with private fleet operators nationwide by 2015 (Salton, 2009). Meanwhile, many fleet owners in London have initiated an aggressive switch to electric[3] and are now joining forces with City Hall to share experiences and facilitate further adoption of the technology (Greencarcongress.com, 2009).

Note that the purpose of this evaluation is not to forecast exact sales volumes, but rather to get a glimpse of the scale of the potential fleet market. Early penetration of the EV in the fleet market would have a crucial impact on other segments.

The retrofit (2010–2015)

Innovation theory explains how the very first consumers to seek out a new technology, the so-called 'technology enthusiasts', derive pleasure from discovering nascent technologies in their purest form. It is no coincidence that a large portion of the EV hype has come from YouTube videos about vehicle conversions in messy household garages. Traditionally, this market segment thrives very early in the adoption life cycle and swiftly loses its significance as the technology begins to catch the eyes of investors and big businesses.

ICV to EV conversion is uniquely positioned to play an important role in the dissemination of EVs to the mass market. First and foremost, it provides a short cut to decarbonizing the existing ICV fleet. Second, it maximizes the utility of a vehicle by prolonging its lifespan by many years. And finally, it provides a strategic entry point to the rapidly expanding low-cost markets of developing economies, which otherwise may be widely dominated by ICVs.

Eight hundred and fifty million. That is the number of ICVs currently chugging along the streets of Planet Earth. Electric conversion can offer older vehicles a new – energy-efficient and carbon-free – lease of life. It is important to acknowledge here that one-quarter of a vehicle's lifetime CO_2 emissions results from the manufacturing process, in other words before it is even driven off the showroom floor. In contrast, conversion to BEV results in negligible emissions and can more than double a vehicle's lifespan. Not good for automakers but good for the environment.

Once again vehicle fleets emerge as potential candidates for conversion across many different locations or countries. These vehicles do not come with the latest gadgets and luxuries. In fact, fleet operators tend to only renew their fleets if the alternative offers an advantage in face of increasing maintenance costs of the older vehicles. Furthermore, vehicle fleets are typically very homogeneous, which would ensure critical economies of scale during preliminary conversion projects where engineering design work would be needed.

A potentially important market segment is that of taxi fleets. As with other fleet markets, taxis present very consistent daily driving habits. However, in contrast with the typical fleets discussed above, taxis tend to run substantially longer daily shifts.[4] While this requires lots of battery capacity, it also means that taxi drivers spend particularly large sums on fuel.

While BEV conversion is likely to remain a limited market in industrialized nations, their role in the emerging markets could be significant.[5] To these consumers, surround-sound stereos are far from being a standardized commodity and heated seats are dispensable – the car itself is a luxury. Indeed, the booming emerging markets are dominated by old cars that are ready to be sent to the cemetery – or to be retrofitted. In Brazil, for instance, 40 per cent of the vehicle fleet is older than 10 years and 5 per cent is older than 21 years (Valor Econômico, 2007). Assuming these figures to be indicative of the retrofit potential in Brazil, this suggests a market pool for conversions of over 11 million vehicles. Even at a low penetration rate of 0.5 per cent, Brazil alone would generate demand for 56,000 vehicle conversions.

Given that the primary selling pitch for BEV conversion is its potential savings with respect to purchase of a new ICV, it becomes clear that target consumers are those emerging from the lower classes – for whom 'cash is king'. And for this very reason, perhaps the most important obstacle to capturing this market segment will be establishing adequate financing.

The hybrids (2010–2020)

The battery-powered EV does not 'complement' the existing ICV solution. Hybrids will continue to play a critical role in the transition from an ICV to an EV world. Indeed, hybrids, in their various forms, are likely to continue to dominate overall EV sales in early years – a fact which should be nurtured.

First, hybrids will contribute to the reduction of oil-dependence and CO_2 emissions. They may not have the same impact as BEVs would, but while the latter is not fully competitive, HEVs provide an encouraging first step.

Second, they contribute to the overall technological advancement of BEV technology. Be it through fine-tuning electric motors and control units or generating economies of scale in Li-ion battery markets, hybridization helps to improve the electric platform and reduce production costs.

Finally, they have the potential to spark consumer confidence in the electric platform. More than conventional HEVs, plug-in HEVs will allow consumers to sample the benefits and limitations of driving in pure electric mode, without experiencing range anxiety. This should help them come to terms with the pros and cons of a BEV world.

As far as the economics are concerned, the various hybrids present distinct results, as seen in Chapter 6. While higher degrees of hybridization suffer from increased battery capital cost, lower degrees fail to provide the same level of fuel economy. Simply put, in the absence of deliberate policy or marketing incentives, if oil prices are low and battery costs high, then less hybridization is more attractive, and vice versa.

For the purposes of forecasting market penetration of hybrid vehicles, it is crucial that these are not put in the same box as battery-powered EVs, as is done far too often. For example, while consumers may have questions regarding the economic rationale of hybrids, range anxiety does not apply. As such, the decision to buy a hybrid is more comparable to the decision to buy a conventional ICV: *Is it cost-effective?* This makes the launch of a hybrid akin to that of the first six-cylinder engine – an incremental innovation over the four-cylinder, the two-cylinder and even the one-cylinder engine used by Karl Benz in the Patent-Motorwagen. Demand will grow steadily so long as the price is right and the styling is pleasing.

The last decade has helped to prove that conventional HEVs have become economically viable products. Now plug-in HEVs will be put to the same test and their capacity to deliver results will have a profound impact on public opinion towards battery-powered EVs. Again, the higher the level of hybridization, the more the car will cost upfront. So demonstrating cost-effectiveness to consumers will require proactive salesmanship. While California-based start-up Fisker Automotive's luxury sports sedan, the Karma, may be the most eye-catching plug-in HEV on the market, it is the more affordable GM Volt and BYD F3DM which are likely to make the greatest impact.

The rickshaws and motorcycles (2015–2020)

One of the most prominent transportation pollution problems faced by Asian countries is that caused by the region's powered rickshaw[6] fleet. While rickshaws enjoy extremely high fuel economy due to their lightweight designs, they typically employ the least advanced VP technologies available – two-stroke engines – playing a central role in the local air pollution problems in densely populated cities in Asia.

Although governments are pushing towards the use of four-stroke and cleaner CNG fuel solutions, this has hardly reduced the population of older-generation rickshaws in the region. As 'clean' rickshaws come to market, the old polluters are merely sold off to the lower echelons of society – notably, they are exported to neighbouring countries that inherit the local pollution problem.

As with any EV, electric rickshaws would benefit from the reduced operating cost but would suffer from the upfront capital cost. This might initially seem an insurmountable obstacle given that 'pullers' (rickshaw drivers) can hardly afford to pay several thousand dollars for a battery. However, most 'pullers' do not own their vehicle outright. Rather, they rent it based on a daily tariff. This takes us straight back to the cost-analysis board.

Consider the Bangladeshi market, where a puller travels 120km per day on average, thus generating Tk240 net income.[7] An electric rickshaw alternative would reduce daily operating costs by around Tk250. If the rickshaw proprietor offered this alternative at a Tk220 rental premium, the payback period would be four to six years, while the puller would enjoy a 10 per cent increase in net income.

The preceding argument can be equally applied to the huge two-wheeler motorcycle and scooter fleet which is rampant in emerging markets. In the case of many Southeast Asian cities, such as Hanoi, Ho Chi Minh City and Phnom Penh, the motorcycle is the dominant means of personal mobility. Here, electric scooters and motorcycles would be able to provide identical mobility at a reduced cost for individuals and improved environmental impact.

With a thousand or more vehicles operating in the major cities of India and Bangladeshi, rickshaws represent a major market for electric-based transportation. Furthermore, given they do not have conventional luxuries such as air-conditioning and stereos, rickshaws provide a key market segment for conversions.

The second vehicle (2015–2020)

If retrofitting is a likely niche market in developing countries, consider now the average American family. Studies show that 57 per cent of American households have at least one additional car (Davis and Diegel, 2007, Section 8). Assume that drivers' fears regarding insufficient range are mostly based on the ability to go on family trips during holidays. Now, unless the family is very large and does not all fit into one car, it would make sense to use their ICV for the long haul while driving the EV on a daily basis. Under such a scenario, range constraints will not affect the decision to own an EV.

It is probably safe to say that the vast majority of households who can afford to own multiple vehicles are not facing a severe budget constraint. After all, when someone owns a US$25,000 minivan to transport the kids and a US$30,000 sedan to get to work, it is unlikely that the additional US$5000 dollars they might pay for an EV over 10 years would make a noticeable impact on their financial well-being. However, their popularity with their peers would probably increase.

Indeed, we are already seeing celebrities, like Tom Hanks and Jay Leno, using their EVs to tout their environmental consciousness. Politicians, executives and other sections of the global elite are likely to follow suit. It would not come as a surprise if EV ownership became a sort of prerequisite for executives in the power industry.

Even if the status symbol or political correctness argument does not sway the consumer, they can rest assured that EVs offer a more economical urban transportation solution. Here we are talking about driving to work or school and back, going to the shops, the restaurant, picking up laundry, or any other form of routine daily travel. Again, in this scenario engineers can design an EV with a range that accommodates average daily driving distances as opposed to infrequent longer journeys. The optimized battery size can probably ensure a 50 per cent reduction in initial battery costs, which in turn makes these vehicles economically viable now even in the US from the lifetime cost perspective. In fact, based on the CS model, without financial incentives, demand could exceed 4 per cent in the US and 12 per cent in the EU with existing technology.

Using American vehicle ownership data (Davis and Diegel, 2007, Section 8), one can estimate that, of the 17 million LDVs sold in 2005, approximately 9.7 million – over 50 per cent! – qualified as a household's second vehicle. In other words, this would suggest a market for 400,000 BEVs. Restricting the market to small-sized cars and urban areas, approximately 1.5 million vehicles overall, there would still be space for 60,000 BEVs using CS penetration rates. In the EU, given lower average driving distances and higher petrol prices, the market for small-sized urban cars is likely to be vast.

Production capacity (2010–2020)

In 2002, GM effectively killed the 1990s BEV market when it repossessed the 1117 EV1s on lease. Despite consumer interest, GM did not permit drivers to purchase the vehicle at the end of their lease, opting, rather, to literally crush the majority of the vehicles (Figure 7.9) and to donate a select few to museums and academic institutions. Recall how this event became the inspiration for the 2006 documentary *Who Killed the Electric Car?*

Figure 7.9 *EV1 crush*

Source: Plug In America (Wikimedia Commons)

This episode made it clear that it is not enough that there is demand for a product – someone must be willing to supply it.[8] Consequently, the fact that FedEx and Sainsbury's want to convert their respective fleets to EV is only the first ingredient in the electrification paradigm shift. Fortunately, non-traditional manufacturers – such as English electric delivery van manufacturers Smith Electric Vehicles, California-based start-up Tesla Motors Corp and Chinese industrial conglomerate BYD Group – have promised to fill the gap by supplying EVs.

Production of a vehicle from scratch is far from a trivial matter. Taking a car from a design sketch, through detailed engineering, complete homologation and so on to the showroom consumes years of work and billions of dollars. Consequently, while several manufacturers have recently launched or are planning to launch EVs, it will be a few years time before production capacity can be scaled up.

While most major manufacturers (in other words Big Auto) have confirmed their intentions to launch EVs in the coming years, few have actually announced any concrete plans for production facilities. Only Nissan and GM have launched budget EV products and confirmed mass-market production over the coming years. The rate of capacity expansion during the early years will depend on two key factors: consumer appetite for EVs and supply chain bottlenecks.

Based on the above niche market analysis, one might expect EV supply and demand conditions to remain tight over the initial years of commercialization. In fact, EV market penetration is likely to be a function solely of production constraints as opposed to insufficient demand. This is particularly relevant in the case of battery EVs. With respect to supply chain bottlenecks, manufacturers will benefit from ensuring close cooperation and even integration with battery producers – as already done by Renault/Nissan with NEC Corp and by the BYD Group and Tesla Motor Corp, both of whom develop batteries in-house.

As capacity expands – and given the automotive industry's inclination to develop excess capacity, this is likely to happen faster than many might anticipate – what factors will step in to determine the medium- or long-term penetration of EVs?

Crossing the Chasm (2015–2025)

The purpose of the niche market evaluations above was to identify the most permeable consumer groups, allowing manufacturers to tackle one segment at a time. As manufacturers aim to expand into new segments, consumers begin to expect the ultimate 'whole-product' solution.

As might be expected, designing and fine-tuning a comprehensive energy system infrastructure, one which provides widespread availability, convenience and speed at an accessible price, does not occur overnight. On the contrary, businesses must anticipate and address future concerns today – which, to their credit, is being done. Crucial to the success of this development is the forecast of a timeframe to work towards, such as the EC proposes. For instance, at what point will new consumers expect extended range to soothe their anxiety? For this we turn, yet again, to innovation theory.

Figure 7.10 shows an adaptation of the traditional technology adoption life cycle as proposed by Geoffrey Moore in *Crossing the Chasm* (1999). Moore's model stipulates that the adoption of a disruptive or discontinuous technology, such as the BEV, invariably encounters a chasm between the early adopters and the early majority. Acknowledging the fundamental differences between early adopters and mass consumers helps businesses define how to approach the mass market.

Notice how the interface between early adopter and early majority occurs at around 16 per cent market penetration. Of course, this is not a rigid measure of where the chasm occurs. Variations across different technology case studies have often placed the chasm within the early adopters consumer segment. To be conservative, one might expect that, at around the 10 per cent penetration level, consumer requirements begin to intensify. Thus, based on recent global LDV sales volumes (70 million/year), by the time annual EV sales reach 7 million, we might expect to feel growing resistance to further adoption of the BEV in the absence of clear evidence that a 'whole-product' solution is in sight. The discussion now examines the two key obstacles to crossing the chasm in the order in which they are likely to be resolved.

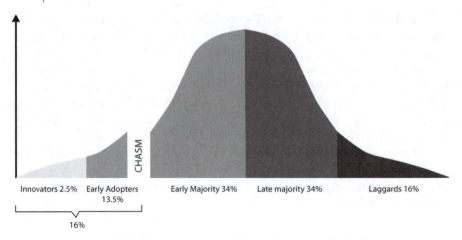

Figure 7.10 *Moore's technology adoption life cycle*

The haunted battery

The EV will become viable for different market segments as battery prices decrease. As discussed above, government and business fleets in general will find the EV attractive at US$900/kWh. At US$750/kWh, a typical consumer vehicle will prove competitive over its lifetime. However, battery manufacturers will have to reduce costs to around US$500/kWh if they expect to lure mass-market consumers. This will be the first make-or-break obstacle in the EV's path into the mass market.

In Chapter 4, it was seen that there is considerable room for reducing such costs. Up to 25 per cent of the total pack cost has been estimated to result from excessive scrap rates. Manufacturers could virtually eliminate these costs by implementing manufacturing best practices and improving the level of labour training. This should come naturally with experience gained from increased production volumes in the short run. Furthermore, the costs related to early-stage R&D and premature supply chain systems will both be largely diluted with increased production volumes.

The niche market EV sales volume estimates developed earlier suggest that battery production will easily reach the level where economies of scale will start to slash final vehicle prices. Most forecasts (McKinsey, F&S, EC and IEA) indicate Li-ion battery costs will have dropped to or below US$500/kWh by 2015 (Figure 7.11). Indeed, it is reasonable to assume that batteries can meet the necessary cost reduction requirements naturally before 'budget' consumers even take notice of their existence.

It is worth highlighting that the battery cost thresholds considered in these assessments may not be representative of many market scenarios. Most of these evaluations have been done by American organizations or are focused on the American market. As indicated earlier, higher oil prices at the pumps, reduced range requirements and stronger environmental incentives in other parts of the

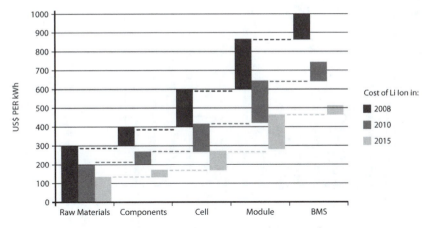

Figure 7.11 *Lithium-ion pack cost reduction*

Source: Frost & Sullivan (2009)

world could favour EVs today, assuming battery costs of US$900/kWh.

However, note also that the expansion of the EV battery market could be exposed to supply-side risks other than small production scale. According to CS, lithium demand in 2009 dropped to 68,000tLCE (tonnes of lithium carbonate equivalent units), having peaked at 85,000tLCE the year before. None of this consumption came from automotive Li-ion battery markets (Figure 7.12). CS forecasts 2020 lithium demand to surge to 200,000tLCE – or a 135 per cent increase relative to the 2008 peak. By this time, lithium demand from the automotive battery market will nearly match the combined volume of all other lithium consumption markets and will have accounted for 70 per cent of the rise in demand.

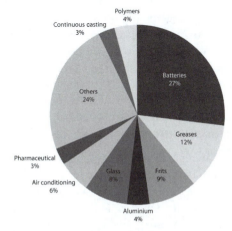

Figure 7.12 *Lithium (LCE) demand by end market*

Source: Credit Suisse (2009)

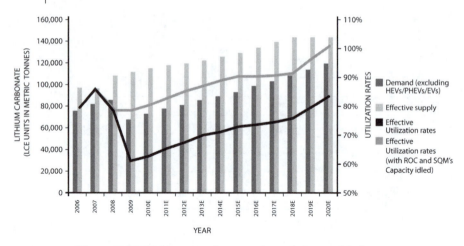

Figure 7.13 *Lithium market supply and demand balance*

Note: SQM = Sociedad Quimica y Minera de Chile (31% lithium market share); ROC = Rockwood Holdings (19% lithium market share).
Source: Credit Suisse (2009)

Is this worrying? Not really. Quite simply, lithium reserves are plentiful. Current supply and demand conditions are loose, with the capacity utilization rate expected to reach as low as 60 per cent in 2010 as a result of the 2008 financial crisis. Producers not only have excess capacity based on weak demand, but they also claim to have the ability to quickly escalate capacity levels. According to CS data, the major suppliers plan to expand capacity in anticipation of the increase in automotive battery demand. Figure 7.13 shows that, far from running the risks of undersupply, were the automotive battery market not to expand as anticipated, lithium suppliers would be exposed to prolonged low utilization rates.

While price volatility of other Li-ion battery raw materials has also been a source of concern, these are generally avoidable. Notably, the lithium-nickel-cobalt-aluminium composition, which offers the highest energy and power densities and has been widely proven, suffers from the cobalt and nickel content. However, as presented in Chapter 4, the tendency has been towards lithium-iron-phosphate chemistries for EVs, so raw material cost woes virtually disappear.

The infamous infrastructure gap

We may never know the answer to the age-old chicken-and-egg dilemma. But in the BEV market, perhaps things need not be so black-or-white. Indeed, the odd charge spot can already be found in many parts of the world, as can EVs. Furthermore, widespread infrastructure is unlikely to be a key deciding factor for the early niche market consumers. So when will infrastructure begin to influence market penetration rates and how critical will this prove?

Box 7.2 The economics of recharging

Infrastructure systems based on battery leasing – such as the Better Place proposition (www.betterplace.com) – have the advantage of providing certainty to battery service providers with regard to their likely revenue stream, making it easier to assess viability of investments. However, upfront costs are extremely high and, if shouldered by a single organization, limit the rate of network proliferation. As a result, battery leasing alone – without government incentives – is unlikely to provide a widespread solution for infrastructure scale-up.

Meanwhile, pay-as-you-go (PAYG) systems can spread investment risks among multiple agents. However, the absence of a contract will increase the initial uncertainty with regard to the utilization rate of the infrastructure and the overall investment risks, thus deterring potential investors.

A conventional charger will cost around US$2500 to buy and install and will provide a maximum power rating of 6kW, thus delivering up to 6kWh of energy per hour. Optimistically, assuming the charger is active 50 per cent of the time (4380hrs/year), it would deliver a total of 26,280kWh per year. If the station operator were permitted to charge 11¢/kWh (in other words with a 10 per cent premium on 10¢/kWh grid electricity) for the electricity, the operator would generate a net revenue of US$262.80/year (after paying for the electricity). Even with this elevated utilization rate, it would take the operator more than 10 years to recuperate the original investment.

Given that the PAYG proposition does not provide consumers with battery financing, it is likely that drivers will seek out the lowest possible electricity tariff to recuperate their initial investment. As a result, charge station operators would not have the luxury of being able to charge a substantial premium over the electricity tariff. Clearly, this is not an attractive proposition for early investors, although it could be feasible as the market matures.

As discussed in Chapter 5, power utilities could operate charging stations as a load-levelling strategy. Recall how EVs would be far more cost-effective than small-scale power generators at matching load variations inherent in the grid. However, most utilities remain sceptical about investing in a still-unpopulated market with the risk of it becoming a sunk cost.

At this point one would be hard-pressed to speculate about the adequate level of infrastructural development needed to attract mass-market consumers. There is still considerable uncertainty over the optimal infrastructural solution, as well as over how the market will be regulated. However, a key challenge is inevitably the question of how to finance infrastructure deployment (Box 7.2).

In the medium term, proof of adequate infrastructure will be a fundamental determinant of consumer acceptance. Consumers will want to see charge spots in every parking space of every garage, spread along street parking across the city and at every shopping complex. Indeed, if this were to materialize, it would eliminate drivers' range anxiety about the EV. However, it would also bankrupt every single charge station investor. Thus, investors would aim to install as few chargers as possible to maximize the utilization rate of each device. Notice, then, how consumer expectation and investment conditions in the development of EV recharge infrastructure are incompatible and that an outside force is needed to reconcile them.

The Tokyo Electric Power Company (TEPCO) provides an interesting example that should help put consumer and business aspirations into perspective. In 2006, TEPCO launched a BEV demonstration programme by

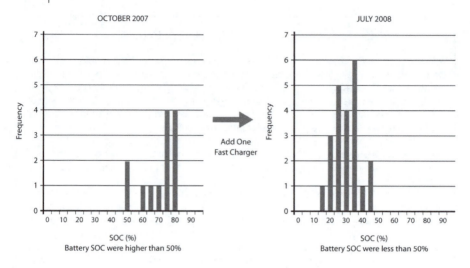

Figure 7.14 *TEPCO fleet SOC*

Source: TEPCO

introducing 10 BEVs into their regular fleet. After some time, TEPCO analysts observed that drivers regularly returned BEVs to the garage with still high SOC. A survey of the situation suggested that the drivers' behaviour was the result of range anxiety. In 2008, TEPCO responded to the problem by installing a single fast-charge station in the middle of its service area so that drivers would not feel the need to return to the office to recharge. Figure 7.14 clearly shows how the introduction of the fast-charge unit successfully eliminated drivers' range anxiety, allowing them to stay on the road longer and thus increasing the utilization of the battery's energy content.

It is important to highlight that the additional charging station expanded driving range by merely soothing drivers' concerns, rather than supplying more energy. While this has resolved TEPCO's initial problem and effectively expanded their fleet's usable energy capacity, it has come at the cost of a high-power charge station. While this may be acceptable on a small scale, it would become prohibitively expensive if replicated on a citywide scale, at least in early stages of EV adoption.

Thus one of the infrastructure developer's main objectives, invariably with the support of government, is to install the optimal level of infrastructure, one that satisfies consumer needs at an acceptable cost. This will be as much a task of marketing as one of engineering, and the first 16 per cent or so of consumers – innovators and early adopters – will act as the guinea pigs for solutions that will later be fine-tuned. Community demonstration projects such as the one proposed by the EC study (see Figure 7.6), which works with the local community to build an 'electrification ecosystem', would provide businesses with vital information about real driver requirements.

Two potentially decisive factors in infrastructure deployment need to be highlighted. First, successful deployment of infrastructure will depend largely on the dissemination of information. Again this will be as much a task of marketing as one of engineering. And second, no matter what infrastructural solution is chosen, government initiative is likely to be the single most influential factor to BEV infrastructural success.

A Silver Bullet?

The EV has been discussed and evaluated from multiple angles and invariably generated the same conclusion – moving away from petroleum-based vehicles and towards electrification of road transportation is good for the consumer, for the environment and for society at large, and it lies closer than most probably imagine. As with any other revolutionary technological innovations, it is impossible to predict when the point of no return, or boom moment, will actually occur. The intention of this chapter has not been to provide a definitive answer as to what EV solution will prevail, where and when, but rather to provide an understanding of *how* the market is likely to develop and what factors are likely to affect it. Three underlying lessons can be derived from this discussion.

First, there is great strategic value in focusing initially on niche markets. From the perspective of the individual investor, focusing on specific market segments can save significant vehicle development costs in the expensive and risky early stage. Furthermore, the value of working with an identifiable consumer base provides greater certainty for developing infrastructure based on clear needs. Indeed, the companies who take on this approach will invariably come out the winners.

Second, EV penetration will not simply grow steadily and plateau to share the market with ICVs. Quite the opposite, these are, broadly speaking, highly different 'whole products', and once BEV adoption picks up momentum, as with all radical innovation cases, the ICV will tend to become obsolete – except in some specific niches. Notice that, while market researchers may recognize and agree with this perspective, they must tend to be conservative with their quantitative forecasts: if you predict a dramatic boom and then nothing happens or, worse, markets collapse, chances are your clients will ask for your head, but if you forecast strong – but conventional – growth and miss the boom, then you can still claim triumph for predicting the upward shift. After all, who could have possibly predicted such 'unprecedented' growth in BEVs? Well, Warren Buffett did.

Finally, this market will not flourish on its own. Despite prospects that battery prices may drop more quickly than many market research studies predict, development of an effective recharging infrastructure remains a challenge. Indeed, efficient, well-targeted government policy will be absolutely crucial to promote EV development. The final chapter, then, will examine the role of governments in the development and commercialization of this technology.

Notes

1 UPS and FedEx combined operate a fleet of 143,000 ground vehicles. At a median lifetime of 10 years, one expects them to purchase 14,300 each year.
2 'Sainsbury's to launch the world's largest fleet of electric vans', from Company News section of J. Sainsbury's Corporate Website (3 December 2009).
3 The following London businesses have begun switching their fleets to electric: DHL Supply Chain, TNT Express, Go-Ahead London, UPS, Marks and Spencer, Sainsbury's and Speedy.
4 Based on anecdotal evidence, taxi drivers in Rio de Janeiro tend to run approximately 250km per 8-hour shift.
5 Informal vehicle modification on a commercial scale is already common practice in some countries. In the mid-1990s, low natural gas prices inspired Brazilian taxi drivers to install unauthorized natural gas equipment in their vehicles. Government and industry promptly responded, establishing equipment standards and safety norms for natural gas equipment, such that installing the equipment is now not only legal but as easy as installing a car radio, if not more so.
6 Rickshaws are known by different names across Asia, including three-wheeler, tuk-tuk, Bajaj and rick.
7 This result assumes daily revenues of Tk1000 for fares, daily rental expenditure of Tk500 for the rickshaw and an operating cost of Tk260 (based on Tk0.74/L fuel price and 2.9L/km fuel economy).
8 Market apologists have ample food for thought here.

References

Boston Consulting Group (2009) *The Comeback of the Electric Car? How Real, How Soon, and What Must Happen Next*, Boston Consulting Group, Boston, MA, January, www.bcg.com/documents/file15404.pdf
Credit Suisse (2009) 'Electric vehicles', *Credit Suisse Equity Research*, 1 October
Davis, S. C. and Diegel, S. W. (2007) *Transportation Energy Data Book: Edition 26*, Oak Ridge National Laboratory, Oak Ridge, TN
Eisenstein, P. (2008) 'Chrysler shocks electric car timeline with new plug-ins for 2010: Live first look (with Dodge EV test drive!)', www.popularmechanics.com/blogs/automotive_news/4284293.html, accessed 11 January 2011
Electrification Coalition (2009) *Electrification Roadmap: Revolutionizing Transportation and Achieving Energy Security*, Electrification Coalition, Washington, DC
Frost & Sullivan (2009) '360 degree analysis of the global electric vehicles market', white paper, Frost & Sullivan, www.frost.com/prod/servlet/segment-toc.pag?segid=9832-00-0D-00-00
Greencarcongress.com, (2009) 'Sainsbury orders another 50 electric vans as companies work with Mayor of London to encourage adoption of commercial EVs', www.greencarcongress.com/2009/06/sainsbury-20090609.html, 9 June, accessed April 2010
Hensley, R., Knupfer, S. and Pinner, D. (2009) *Electrifying Cars: How Three Industries Will Evolve*, McKinsey & Co., http://ww1.mckinsey.com/clientservice/sustainability/pdf/electrifying_cars.pdf

IEA (International Energy Agency) (2009) *Technology Roadmap: Electric and Plug-In Hybrid Electric Vehicles*, International Energy Agency, Paris

Moore, G. A. (1999) *Crossing the Chasm: Marketing and Selling High-Tech Products to Mainstream Customers*, HarperCollins Publishers, London, UK

Salton, J. (2009) 'France to spend US$2.2 billion on network of electric car charging stations', *Gizmag*, www.gizmag.com/france-two-billion-electric-car-charging-stations/13041/, accessed 12 October 2009

USPS (2009) *Electrification of Delivery Vehicles*, US Postal Service Office of Inspector General, Washington, DC

Valor Econômico (2007) 'Idade média da frota caiu de 9,4 para 9 anos', www.brasilcaminhoneiro.com.br/idade-media-da-frota-caiu-de-94-para-9-anos

Electric Vehicle Policy Support

We have a responsibility in our time, as others have had in theirs, not to be prisoners of history but to shape history.

Madeleine Korbel Albright

Hopefully, by now, the reader is convinced that EVs are on the brink of becoming an everyday part of their life. Nevertheless, as with any new technology that requires a large upfront capital investment and entails potential externalities, some sort of initial push is required from the public sector to overcome the market's inertia, avoiding what would ultimately become a 'free-rider' problem that the first would-be private investors would have to shoulder.[1] In the case of the automotive industry this is particularly true because of the forces working against technological innovation, as illustrated by the case of GM's aborted EV1 programme.

This chapter begins by identifying why it is in the interest of governments to act *now*. Subsequently, it outlines and discusses a menu of policy options that should help give the EV market a good kick-start.

Rationale for Government Action

Regardless of the behaviour of their counterparts, there are many reasons for individual governments, at both the national and local levels, to support the development of EV markets. Three arguments for government action are presented below. While the extent to which these are valid varies with context, each independently is sufficient to warrant public action.

Energy security

The recurring motivation behind EV development has been the concern that society is depleting scarce petroleum reserves at an unsustainable rate, exposing itself increasingly to the risks of geopolitical instability associated with the resource. Over the years, oil exploration has become more costly and political tension between producing and consuming nations has escalated. This has become a major concern for many countries.

Critics argue that, in the medium term, tighter supply conditions will push global oil prices higher and improved extraction technology will push unconventional oil-extraction costs down, combining to make currently uneconomic resources available. This, in turn, would provide more time to improve the efficiency of energy-using processes, to increase the competitiveness of sustainable fuels, to develop advanced energy storage technologies, and so on. Notice, however, that as was the case with the Stone Age, the Petroleum Age will not come to an end because we run out of the resource, but rather because the Electric Age will simply provide an all-round better solution. We are there already – it just is not sufficiently clear to the general public yet.

There is no question that EVs offer improved energy security given their association with electrical energy supplies, which can be produced using any primary energy source. This also reduces the indirect costs associated with geopolitical tensions. It has already been demonstrated that all EVs offer substantial energy-efficiency gains on a well-to-wheel basis (Chapter 6). Indeed, if the entire American fleet switched to BEVs and we used oil to supply the additional electricity, the American oil import bill could be reduced by at least US$93 billion per year.[2]

Logic suggests that the reason BEVs have not been commercialized is that automotive and oil companies are opposed to breaking from safe and sound businesses which are largely protected by long-standing government policy.

Curbing pollution

As seen in Chapter 2, local air pollution has been a concern for major urban areas since the 1950s and has been addressed through emission-control regulations. While these have been effective in reducing toxic emissions, particularly in developed countries, they have simultaneously resulted in an increase in CO_2 emissions. Given ICV technological constraints, future reductions in emissions – both CO_2 and toxic pollutants – will ultimately require a shift towards electrification, doing away with exhaust at the tailpipe.

Coupled with growing concern over climate change, the environmental claim has now become one of the most widely used, yet controversial, arguments in support of EV development. Critics, particularly those in the political and business arenas, have questioned everything from the validity of the IPCC's climate change scenarios to the cost-effectiveness of clean technology solutions – including the BEV.

Despite some dissonant voices, scientists have long come to a broad consensus on the impacts that are likely to be brought about by climate change and thus have warned of the importance of preventing further increases in global temperatures by acting now. Economists too have addressed the question, quantified the potential costs of addressing global warming, and debated the implications of early versus delayed action.

While scientific and economic assessments both hold a degree of uncertainty, given the potential magnitude, irreversibility and distributional implications of the impacts involved, it would seem advisable for society to adopt a precautionary approach. The cost of preventing climate change can be kept to a minimum, while doing nothing risks exposing society to potentially catastrophic adaptation costs. It has been highlighted that the cost of failing to prevent climate change could surpass the cost of both world wars and the Great Depression combined (Brown, 2007). It is also significant that the World Bank and other international development agencies are developing programmes and financial instruments based on a precautionary approach.[3]

EVs are one of the key solutions that should be prioritized to address climate change. First, it has been shown that BEVs will reduce both emissions per kilometre travelled and overall energy consumption (Chapter 6).[4] In fact, the high supply-chain efficiency of electrical power means that in most cases, 'even energy from a coal-fired station is less polluting than the serial explosions that drive an internal-combustion engine' (*The Economist*, 2008). Second, unlike power plants, which have a 20- to 50-year life cycle, vehicles have a fast turnover rate and thus offer the potential for critical short-term emissions reductions.

Note that the policy recommendations in this chapter are developed around the gCO_2/km indicator, which, as discussed in Chapter 2, is also a useful proxy metric for local air pollution mitigation policy. Thus, despite the climate change-oriented *nomenclature*, these policies are considered to be addressing local air pollution equally.

Economic growth opportunities

Perhaps the audience does not care that their children or grandchildren will not have Manhattan, Rio de Janeiro, Venice and Ho Chi Minh City, or Holland, much of Bangladesh, and several of the Caribbean and Pacific Islands. Perhaps the audience also believes that technological advances will, no matter how, always provide a solution to the petroleum scarcity problem – at least during their lifetime.

As always, historical facts and figures provide some insight into the discussion. The American economy ascended to the status of global superpower during the second quarter of the 20th century – in parallel with its flourishing automotive industry. On the opposite side of the Pacific, the Japanese economy faced a decadent post-war era, only re-establishing itself as an industrial power in the 1970s – around the time when its automotive industry began to prosper and expand into foreign markets. By 1980, the American automotive industry had fallen behind the emerging Japanese rivals – and the American economy fell into a recession. Even if the causal relationship is oversimplified and would require hardcore analysis to be firmly established, the correlation is striking and suggestive.

Consider the US$2 trillion annual revenues that will be 'redistributed' globally once emerging manufacturers begin to mass-produce EVs? Did some eyes twinkle? That, as seen in Chapter 1, is the combined revenue of Big Auto production today and, unless they too enter the EV market with gusto, that value will inevitably migrate to new locations across the globe. According to Better Place analysts, this is only the tip of the iceberg. The US$1.5 trillion fuel station business is likely to be hit the hardest if they do not find a way to profit from GEV adoption. Further, GEV penetration could result in a US$500 billion per annum automotive battery industry and generate up to US$300 billion per annum in carbon reduction credits. Finally, the investments that would be required to upgrade the power grid and to build additional capacity are likely to reach US$650 billion per annum. Overall, the emergence of the EV industry is estimated to impact, through the creation of new business or the replacement of existing ones, a combined US$6 trillion a year (Agassi, 2008).

Of course, this revenue will not shift or be generated immediately, but the forecasts of growth in EV-related businesses are encouraging. Credit Suisse (2009), for example, expect global EV and battery combined sales to exceed US$500 billion by 2030, while McKinsey & Co (2008) believe the Chinese market alone will be worth US$220 billion by that time. Meanwhile, Warren Buffett (2009), the American multi-billionaire investor and BYD stakeholder, recently voiced his belief that all road vehicles will be electric by 2030.

As discussed in Chapter 7, predicting the rate of technological change is notoriously difficult. However, what is apparent is that, when it comes, it is typically with a vengeance. Rather than a smooth incremental shift towards dominance of a new technology, the shift tends to come all of a sudden, in an apparently instantaneous adoption of the technology. Just consider how it took a mere 12 years for automobiles to go from representing 10 per cent of the total American vehicle fleet to capturing 90 per cent of the market share. In an equivalent period of time, the automobile industry also introduced and disseminated catalytic converters. Indeed, the likelihood that BEVs experience a similar burst in market penetration is high, such that the above forecasts could prove conservative.

Referring to the energy-related boom envisaged in *The Economist*, Geoffrey Carr (2008) wrote:

> *The innovation lull of the past few decades also provides opportunities for technological leapfrogging. Indeed, it may be that the field of energy gives the not-quite-booms in biotechnology and nanotechnology the industrial applications they need to grow really big, and that the three aspiring booms will thus merge into one.*[5]

The automotive industry may not be as glamorous as it once was, with the spotlight stolen by electronics, nanotech, biotech and other such high-tech markets. But while Big Auto's flashy gas-guzzling 4×4s may be unfashionable for being more of a liability than an asset, Green Auto's understated eco-friendly city cars are set to flourish. Assuming consumers drive sales, then Detroit may be History, though we have yet to find the automotive Silicon Valley – or rather Lithium Valley.

Examining recent facts and figures, one also begins to notice some new trends. In 2009, we witnessed two of America's Big Three manufacturers, GM[6] and Chrysler,[7] getting dissected and pawned off to foreign investors. Not long before that, Ford disposed of its luxury brands (Jaguar and Land Rover) to Indian Tata Motors. Reva, another Indian automotive manufacturer, has bet its product line entirely on EVs. Meanwhile, the Malaysian government-owned Proton is taking advantage of one of the world's most prestigious EV engineering groups, Group Lotus, which has been Proton's subsidiary since 1994. In China, BYD is leading the way to budget GEV production using its proprietary battery systems. And Geely Automotive is in negotiations with LTI, manufacturers of the London Black Cab, to produce an electric black cab in China. Thus two distinct trends can be noticed: the automotive power balance is shifting East into the hands of the emerging markets and EVs have secured a place within the product portfolios of these emerging manufacturers.

EV industry prospects have never been more promising. The US$6 trillion a year estimate of potential business revenues cited above equates to the creation of thousands of manufacturing and engineering jobs, which will come largely at the expense of jobs lost in the ageing automotive industry. Governments cannot afford to lose, nor forgo the opportunity to create, so many jobs, particularly during a time of global economic recovery. Given the balance of economic opportunities versus losses, it would seem to make sense for governments to support the shift to the future automotive industry.

The role of government

The energy security, environmental and economic arguments lined up above suggest that governments have strong reasons to focus on promoting an energy-efficient and low-carbon transportation future based on electric propulsion. Economic theory[8] tells us that governments should intervene in the operation of markets only if and when markets fail to operate efficiently due to the presence of imperfect competition (for example natural monopolies), externalities, and/or an environment of imperfect information and risk. The correction of these market failures leads either to the direct provision of so-called 'social' goods by government (for example through budgetary policy) or assumes that, once the failures are corrected (for example through regulation), the forces of supply and demand can be left to work themselves out through the market, to the general benefit of all, with suitable levels of 'social' goods being provided by the private sector.

The discussion has already referred to monopolies when reviewing GEV recharging and market architecture options. It also referred to externalities when it discussed the environmental impacts of the ICV and the BEV and of the primary energy on which they ultimately depend. Impacts on the power grid (Chapter 5) entail both indirect impacts (for example harmonic distortion) and potential benefits (for example V2G-based increases in system capacity utilization). Imperfect information is a special case of 'social' goods, where government corrects for distortions in the prevailing exercise of consumer choice, often as a result of (temporary) imperfect information.[9] Thus certain goods, such as GEVs and associated energy-supply infrastructure, that are or could be privately provided, are desirable from a social standpoint but are under-provided, at least in its initial stages, due to the high levels of uncertainty, as perceived by market agents, regarding future market penetration.

Although heavily discredited since the Thatcher era, government intervention seems to be experiencing a mild revival and reinstatement since the financial crisis of 2008. A key challenge is reaching agreement on policy objectives and assessing the cost-effectiveness of different alternatives.

Assume here that an energy-efficient and low-carbon transportation system is a desirable social good and that electric propulsion is an important means to that end. Thus there is overall a strong case for government intervention. The purpose of government policy should be fundamentally to guide the private sector to the socially optimal level of investment – through a range of instruments, combining both 'command and control' (for example emissions controls, aggregate carbon reduction commitments and mandatory inclusion of charge spots in buildings) and market-based instruments (for example tax incentives, licensing discounts and carbon credits).

Policy instruments, in theory, will need to be designed at various levels according to purpose and target – for example incentives for the individual consumer, making the shift to the GEV more attractive; policies targeting business, stimulating innovations and greater levels of production; awareness-raising for businesses such as shopping centres, supermarkets, theatres and others on the opportunities to tap into additional revenues; agreements with power utilities to facilitate smart grid implementation; and support for R&D.

As with other social goods, government should preferably provide but not produce, in other words it should not directly develop technology or infrastructure itself, but should preferably strategize, plan, regulate and in some cases provide fiscal incentives, for example through research grants and tax breaks for pilot initiatives meant to prove proposed concepts. Policy should be based on a vision of the future, assessments of what solution sets make most sense in given contexts, and staged mid- to long-term implementations plans. Investment in such upfront strategizing is an important role for the public sector and a means to encourage businesses to develop their own investment decisions in line with the overall public sector vision – presumably one that, as discussed above, expresses longer-term societal interests and has considered a range of trade-offs regarding the efficiency and equity of the alternatives, rather than the preferences of elite groups. Within a longer-term strategy and plan, policy instruments can be fitted to context.

The Road Ahead

A number of basic policy options that can be taken by governments are outlined below. The first set are policies which refer to transportation in the longer term, while the latter are policies aimed at facilitating the early stages of implementation of the GEV solution. Given policy coordinates and signals, market forces can be left to work out the ultimate solutions – for example swappable Li-ion batteries or fuel cells or hybrid ultracapacitor/battery or some as-yet-unthought-of 'cool' technology.

Promoting a low-carbon private transportation future

The discussion will consider several entry points for public policy, focusing on the vehicle, the recharge infrastructure and the power sector. In some cases, more than one policy measure is suggested, but all follow the well-established 'polluter pays' principle, variously applied, ensuring that while individuals are free to choose how they ensure their mobility, they also receive appropriate signals of what their choices imply in terms of environmental impacts. And, accordingly, they pay for the CO_2 (and other polluting substances) they emit into the atmosphere in the process.

Policies focused on the vehicle

While this book has advocated a shift towards electrification of the global private vehicle fleet as a solution to sustainable transportation, it is worth recognizing the importance of non-technological solutions. Indeed, a modal shift in transportation, for instance towards public transportation, is as important as the technological shift away from the ICV discussed in this book. Government policy has an unquestionably critical role in this case. However, since personal mobility is strongly embedded in modern society, the focus of the policy discussion is on policies that assume that the automobile will remain in use and aim to improve its performance.

- *Stricter emissions standards.* Due to enormous resistance encountered from the automotive industry regarding proposals for emissions controls, the EU has only managed to pass a voluntary commitment of $140gCO_2/km$ and $130gCO_2/km$ (on average for the industry) for new passenger vehicles emissions by 2008 and 2015 respectively. By 2008, only two European automotive groups (Fiat and Peugeot) were in compliance with the commitment, while the industry average had reached a mere $153.7gCO_2/km$.

  Despite the widespread cries from the automotive industry about potential costs and risks of endangering European manufacturing competitive advantage, Smart has managed to produce a vehicle which beat the 2015 emissions standard by 32 per cent ($88gCO_2/km$) – without so much as implementing hybrid technology. Of course, the Smart is a micro-car unsuited for most consumers. However, the 2009 Toyota Prius achieves $89gCO_2/km$ at a competitive price for a vehicle in its class. Indeed, there is no reason not to impose a mandatory emissions standard for new passenger vehicles based on what Big Auto has already achieved – $90gCO_2$/km.

Notice that if all new cars in Europe were to meet the emissions levels achieved by today's lowest emitters, the region would reach just over 40 per cent average annual emissions reductions by 2020[10] (still 10 per cent shy of the IPCC recommended target). Politicians should take this as a sign that the technology is available and competitive, and perhaps toughen up next time Big Auto starts throwing their toys out of the pram or threatens to run away from home.

- CO_2 *tax*. If a tax were levied on petroleum at the pump, consumers would pay directly for their contribution to CO_2 emissions. The value of this tax should ultimately reflect the costs of emissions incurred by society. Given that the impact of CO_2 varies depending on how much has already accumulated in the atmosphere, this could be periodically evaluated and reset, in light of aggregate commitments to emissions reduction over time. A less laborious alternative would be to use the price of CO_2 certificates traded on the open market – based, say, on the EU Emissions Trading System.

  In theory, these mechanisms would arrive at the same result, since carbon markets have been designed to internalize the costs of CO_2 emissions. In either case, drivers would be encouraged to pursue more sustainable transportation means, based on their personal requirements and without having an inadequate solution imposed on them. In signalling the actual social cost of CO_2 emissions, governments would also be levelling the playing field for BEVs and other clean technologies by effectively eliminating petroleum subsidies that have been around in the US and several other countries.

- *Congestion charges.* Beyond spending hours commuting through traffic jams daily, urban populations, especially in major metropolitan areas, are forced to breathe the concentrated toxins emitted by their own vehicles. In addition, stop-and-go driving in congested cities results in as much as 70 per cent energy loss from frequent braking.[11]

  To reduce these externalities, large cities, such as London and São Paulo, employ policies such that drivers who enter the city limits during restricted hours and/or days must pay a congestion charge. In both cases, EVs are exempt from the charge. As with the preceding CO_2 tax policy, congestion policies do not impose undesired and inadequate solutions upon a driver. Rather, they discourage excessive and unnecessary use of ICVs.

  According to a Transport for London report (2003), which studied the impact of the congestion charge six months after its introduction, the results were noticeable in Central London. During the first six months, traffic delays within the congestion zone dropped 30 per cent and average journey times dropped 14 per cent. It was also found that the time spent idling or driving below 10km/hr dropped by 25 per cent. It is particularly interesting to see how drivers adapted to the charge. The study shows that 50 to 60 per cent of those avoiding the congestion charge substituted driving with public transportation, 20 to 30 per cent had found alternative driving routes to their destinations, and 15 to 25 per cent switched to car sharing, cycling or motorcycling or altered their schedules to avoid congestion charge times.

- *ICV ownership*. If push comes to shove, certain countries or urban areas may find themselves in a situation where they may need to discourage the ICV altogether through an annual vehicle-per-household tax. The tax would increase for every additional vehicle owned by a household and according to the vehicle's emissions ratings. This would not only encourage households to rationalize excessive vehicle ownership and promote car-pooling, but would also encourage people to switch to lower-emissions and more efficient cars, or to the use of bicycles and walking, where feasible. Notice how this would be particularly effective at promoting BEVs as a second-car solution. Indeed, consumers may choose an ICV (or a PHEV) as their first car to meet eventual long distance trips, but could opt for tax-exempt BEV solutions to fulfil urban transport requirements.

Policies focused on the power sector

While it has been shown that GEVs are cleaner than ICVs even when powered by the most dirty conventional energy, society would fail to meet its climate change prevention targets if we stopped there. Indeed, making the switch to GEV is only part of the problem. Governments must also clean up the grid that powers GEVs and the rest of the economy.

Governments should impose power generation emissions standards akin to the automotive emissions standards discussed above. There are various ways to ensure such standards, which may be more or less suited to specific situations.

- *Cap-and-trade*. A straightforward and well-established mechanism is emissions cap-and-trade. In this scheme, the government establishes a maximum acceptable average emissions level for energy generation (gCO_2/kWh). Businesses where reduction is less costly can emit below the limit and earn emissions certificates which they can then sell to other businesses where reduction is more costly than average and which thus may choose to exceed the established limit. If few businesses reduce emissions, then certificate scarcity will occur, driving their price up and making it increasingly expensive not to reduce emissions. That way, market forces guide businesses towards the least-cost solution that meets a market-wide emissions cap.
- *Direct CO_2 tax*. In theory, this has a similar effect to cap-and-trade, since it introduces a financial incentive for producers to switch towards less polluting technologies. In practice, although simpler to implement, it does not guarantee that emissions will be mitigated to the desired level, since producers will often find it profitable to pay the fine and continue producing dirty power. Of course, the extent to which this is true depends on the value of the CO_2 tax. Furthermore, this approach does not encourage the development of cleaner alternatives, as is the case with cap-and-trade, since the clean alternative does not necessarily receive any of the CO_2 revenue stream.

- *Exhaust emissions controls.* Governments might choose a more intrusive maximum pollution regulation, imposing an end-of-pipe emission standard and preventing dirty businesses from offsetting emissions by purchasing emissions certificates. Here it would require polluting power plants to either switch to a cleaner fuel mix – say mixing pure coal with biomass – or introduce carbon capture and storage technology.

  Looking further afield and ahead, governments might actively discourage the development of polluting energy technologies.

- *Curbing exploration of oil fields.* Besides the environmental mitigation programmes required by their environmental impact assessments and management plans, these activities could be taxed based on the environmental sensitivity of the resource location. In this scenario, petroleum from Canadian tar sands and Siberia would be taxed for disturbing pristine ecosystems.[12]

- *Construction of new ICE factories.* These should be discouraged by imposition of heavy taxes. And, to prevent the loss of local competitive advantage, governments should impose import taxes on products from countries that do not enforce comparable regulatory standards.

- *Support for R&D.* Funding should be directed away from polluting energy technologies and towards clean options. Governments that support EV and clean energy development will be providing local businesses with a comparative advantage in a growing market. As noted, this would result in sustainable long-term job creation and future economic growth for all those who can establish themselves in the market. In contrast, those opting to support existing ICE technology will waste resources on technology that is likely to have limited long-term benefits.

A combination of policies will be justified, depending on the government's objectives. For instance, they may choose to establish a cap-and-trade system with a complementary regulatory limit. This might be an effective way to ensure some degree of fuel mixing – say if the country has a policy to reduce dependence on an imported fuel – at an acceptable economic cost to businesses.

Promoting EV market implementation

The reader may recall the discussion about the forces impeding change in the automotive industry. Indeed, proactive government support at an early stage of GEV market penetration will also be needed to provide companies and consumers with incentives to accelerate the replacement of a surpassed and unresponsive technology with one more valuable in the current context.

Policies focused on the vehicle

- *GEV tax exemptions.* By slashing 10 to 30 per cent off their sticker price, GEVs could prove to be a competitive mass-market vehicle on a lifetime cost basis today. This could accelerate sales and help producers achieve crucial cost reductions from economies of scale. Indeed, contrary to what critics might suggest, a tax cut would cost governments virtually nothing, since they would be forgoing revenues from an industry segment that is nearly non-existent and currently makes a very small contribution to the tax base. Of course, as GEV sales pick up momentum, thus displacing ICV sales and tax revenues, governments could gradually reintroduce taxes without hampering GEV competitiveness.

- *Direct battery subsidies.* As seen in Chapter 6, it is the battery capital cost which distinguishes the ICV and GEV sticker price and which will invariably deter most private consumers. While battery costs are expected to drop sufficiently and enable GEVs to be able to hold their own in the medium term (say by 2015–2020), batteries will need to be financed or directly subsidized to attract most consumers in the short run. As has been seen, battery financing and leasing solutions are being proposed by various businesses. However, where these businesses are not in place, which remains the majority of locations, governments would need to step in and subsidize the upfront cost initially.

  An excellent early example of this was put into action by the US government in February 2009. Tax credits of US$2500–7500 were offered for GEVs according to battery capacity.[13] The key merit of such a policy approach is that it rewards higher levels of electrification without potentially subsidizing vehicle luxuries as would occur in the case of a straight sales tax exemption.

- *Cash-for-clunkers programmes.* Used by the US and many European governments, these programmes have also been a positive step in the right direction. Consumers receive a discount for replacing their polluting vehicles with lower-emissions ones. It is worth highlighting, however, that governments have failed to seize the opportunity at hand by imposing more stringent fuel economy standards in the process (Table 8.1).

Table 8.1 *US Cash-for-clunkers programme*[14]

	US$3500	US$4500
Passenger vehicle	4–10mpg	>10mpg
Category 1 truck	2–5mpg	>5mpg
Category 2 truck	1–2mpg	>2mpg

Source: Car Allowance Rebate System website (www.cars.gov)

Given the bleak economic climate which prevailed in 2009, this is understandable. However, with the worst behind us, governments could use existing programmes as a starting point for more ambitious savings. The goal should not be to replace worn-down SUVs with shiny new SUVs – after all, consumers would probably have done that soon enough. If anything, the programme has merely shortened vehicle lifespan. Rebates should only be eligible for new vehicles with fuel economy above a given benchmark (say 30mpg), thus encouraging a fundamental shift in consumer preference.

Demonstration projects

A bigger push may be required before the above policies can have a significant effect. Governments should identify specific market segments, by use and/or geographical location, and promote BEV demonstration. The aforementioned fiscal incentives could then be targeted at the end uses, locations and events chosen for demonstration.

Given the concerns revolving around range, BEVs are most likely to succeed within planned service environments in urban areas, as discussed in Chapter 7. Repair vans, delivery services, taxis – these are just some of the businesses which provide very predictable operating requirements, such that batteries can be built to specifications without incurring huge costs to soothe range anxiety. Furthermore, businesses will be more aware of and willing to rationalize lifetime costs than individual consumers. Demonstration projects would help the industry overcome the chicken-and-egg infrastructure dilemma.

- *Leading by example.* Switching their ICV fleets to GEV is perhaps the most effective way for a government to accelerate the dissemination and adoption of GEVs. It can both help to secure the gains from economies of scale and promote credibility in GEV technology and infrastructure. Rather than purchasing an entire fleet of GEVs, local governments might prefer to approach EV demonstration while simultaneously stimulating the community's entrepreneurial spirit promoting the conversion of its existing fleet.
- *BEV ecosystems.* Infrastructure demonstrations have a better chance of making an impact if carried out within clear geographical boundaries. Thus national and local governments should cooperate to promote the deployment of BEV ecosystems (Figure 7.6). Early candidates for such demonstrations are islands, university towns – such as Santa Barbara (California) or Viçosa (Brazil) – and UNESCO World Heritage Sites – for example Ouro Preto, Fernando de Noronha (Brazil) and Florence (Italy).
- *International sporting events.* The FIFA World Cup and the Olympic Games offer an especially exciting promotion opportunity. The 2012 London Olympic Games,[15] 2014 Brazilian World Cup and 2016 Rio Olympic Games all provide an exceptional stage for BEVs as the solution of choice in all official transportation-related activities, while drawing international acclaim to the events.
- *Cash-for-clunkers.* Rather than condemning clunkers to a crusher or a shredder, governments could stimulate local businesses to retrofit and re-market doomed clunkers. Indeed, a cash-for-clunkers scheme would provide the ideal foundation for conversion businesses to obtain rundown but intact vehicle platforms at a bargain price. Furthermore, governments might find it easier to give local businesses the tax breaks and subsidies required to commercialize GEVs than they would foreign businesses.[16]

Policies focused on the recharging infrastructure

Moving now to the recharging problem, recall that charge station[17] deployment is faced with a supply-and-demand incompatibility. Consumer expectations with regard to the availability of recharging spots far exceed what investors can justify on a widespread scale. As pointed out, this can only be addressed through government intervention, with two solutions to be considered.

1 *Tax rebates for developers.* In countries with high electricity tax rates,[18] initial charge station infrastructure could be financed through an electricity tax rebate for the infrastructure developer. Assuming the 25 per cent tax rebate on the electricity tariff from the example in Chapter 7, one finds that developers could generate an annual revenue of US$657 per slow-charge spot installed and a payback rate of around four to five years, depending on the discount rate used. This begins to make the investment attractive.

2 *Public provision.* An alternative means of ensuring early infrastructure development would be if charge stations became a public service provided by the government. In fact, this is likely to be one of the key early market infrastructural solutions. Charge stations could be installed in multi-storey public car parks or street parking, making them convenient and widespread.

   • *Standards.* Turning away from costs and financing, hereto the predominant focus, the GEV market will soon need to be regulated with respect to the interface between vehicle and energy system. Governments can play a pivotal role in facilitating the development of industry standards. At the national level, this can be done through the coordination of negotiations with businesses – potentially car producers, parts suppliers and utilities – and by providing a formal seal of approval. This would help to avoid adaptation costs that would be incurred by all concerned if companies were to work independently. It would also prevent businesses from muscling out rivals based on incompatible 'standards'. More ambitiously, national governments can work together to promote an international unification of these standards with the help of ISO.[19] However, for such standards to gain market credibility, businesses must engage in their development, while governments and non-governmental organizations (NGOs) act as facilitators and presumptive representatives of the public interest in the process.[20]

   • *Smart grid upgrades.* Chapter 5 discussed the potential impacts – both positive and negative – that GEVs might have on the power grid. As seen, the growing use of microelectronics and penetration of intermittent power supplies, such as wind and tidal power, has increased the need for harmonic compensation and enhanced power storage and control respectively. As a result, smart grid technology is not only seen as a valuable improvement to the entire power system, independent of the penetration of GEV technology, but increasingly as an inevitable necessity in the future. Just as in the case of vehicle technology, smart grid development is exposed to free-rider behaviour. To ensure that all utilities in the power system share the burden, governments would need to intervene, imposing mandatory investment within given timeframes.[21]

- *Clean electricity guarantee.* As with smart grid technology, much of the technology available for clean power generation is still in development or expensive. In line with proposals advanced in the context of international climate change negotiations, some governments have established a commitment to install a specific amount of clean and renewable power capacity, say 10 per cent within a given timeframe or according to GEV penetration levels. This way, GEV drivers could be reassured that their GEV was not purchased in vain.

It is worth quantifying the impact of such a commitment. Consider, for instance, the Nissan Leaf which is a BEV with a 24kWh Li-ion battery and 160km range per charge. For the sake of argument, let us assume that average consumers drive the full 160km per day and thus consume 24kWh of energy a day.[22] If 100,000 BEVs are then deployed, the government would be committed to supplying 2400MWh of clean energy content daily. Now assuming a clean energy source to have a 40 per cent utilization factor,[23] the government would need to develop a mere 250MW recharge capacity system. In reality, the government would only have to install about 80MW capacity, since average daily driving range is actually only 50km.

In Conclusion

This policy menu is merely indicative. It is important to recognize that any one of these suggestions would require a thorough analysis – considering issues of incidence, efficiency and equity and taking into account direct and indirect impacts on consumers, producers, other public policies and government budgets. While each policy option discussed is independent of the others, they are in many cases complementary. With this in mind, let me finish by highlighting the importance of targeting revenues from emissions charges to fund, at least in part, the early-stage implementation of EVs.

At the start of the chapter, it was stated that policy suggestions would stay away from specific technological solutions and that the free market would provide the answers to the pressing questions of which EV technology would prevail or to what extent different technologies might share the market. Here the author briefly breaks this promise to provide one technologically biased perspective.

Governments should double their efforts to develop battery technology. As has been repeatedly suggested throughout this book, automotive fuel cell technology is still years from mass commercialization, whereas batteries are on the brink of bursting through the floodgates. Indeed, if batteries do succeed, they may well displace the need for fuel cells in automotive applications altogether.

For this reason, the author bets on short-term battery development to provide the competitive edge in the EV industry.

In the words of Sir Winston Churchill: 'The pessimist sees difficulty in every opportunity. The optimist sees the opportunity in every difficulty.' So, when all is said and done, how does the reader now view the future of the automobile?

Notes

1   In other words initial investors paying the higher price of batteries or charging facilities during the first stage of market penetration while others wait for economies of scale to kick in, bringing prices down.

2   To be conservative, calculations were based on June 2009 fuel prices.

3   For further reading on climate change initiatives, see the World Bank's *World Development Report 2010*, which focuses on climate change, and Margulis et al's (2008) *The Economics of Adaptation to Climate Change*.

4   The extremely rare (theoretical) case where the ICV is less polluting should not be allowed to discredit the BEV's potential global role. Note this would occur if a consumer in a high-polluting power grid – such as India's or worse – were to drive a small, extremely energy-efficient vehicle (50mpg plus). Furthermore, technologies are becoming available to eliminate emissions from dirty coal-based power generation – namely carbon capture and storage – which would prove more cost-effective than any method for cleaning up ICV emissions thus far envisaged.

5   We have already seen microelectronics revolutionize EV power controllers as well as battery compositions, and we remain hopeful that nanotech will provide the breakthrough to increase the energy storage capacity of ultracapacitors.

6   GM and its subsidiaries were in such poor conditions that, as of the start of 2010, GM has only managed to pawn off the Saab brand to Spyker Automotive (Netherlands).

7   Chrysler has been handed to the Fiat Group (Italy) for administration through a conditional agreement with its major shareholder (labour unions) and the US government.

8   Welfare economics assumes that markets will promote a social optimum (in other words the most efficient use of scarce resources) under a series of stringent assumptions. In practice, these assumptions seldom prevail, thus giving rise to public policy in nearly every aspect of our daily lives. Nonetheless, adopting such a framework when discussing the rationale for public policy helps to keep us honest and avoid calling upon governments to do more than they can or should do, and especially for them to step in where the private sector is best qualified to deliver results.

9   Depending on the readers' ideological inclinations, the correction of imperfect information and risk could be seen, alternatively, as the imposition of a presumably enlightened elite and in contradiction to consumer sovereignty, or yet as the correction for distortions in the prevailing exercise of consumer choice. While recognizing that such interventions can be easily subject to imposition, the discussion assumes here that in some cases they are justified and will be applied with sound criteria by policymakers.

10 This assumes, conservatively, a maximum vehicle life expectancy of 10 years.

11 While this is unavoidable in ICVs, EVs deploy regeneration braking to minimize such losses.

12 Policymakers could use the 2010 BP Macondo disaster (Chapter 2) as a justification for strong action, noting in particular the inadequacy of the environmental risk
assessment studies prepared by BP and the difficulty in holding companies accountable for such disasters.

13 The tax credit is composed of a US$2500 base rate plus US$417 per kWh above
4kWh.

14 A Category 1 truck is a 'light duty truck' weighing up to 2.7 metric tonnes; a
Category 2 truck is a 'light duty truck' weighing between 2.7 and 4.5 metric tonnes.

15 For more details on London's plans to ensure the first fully sustainable Olympic
Games, see www.london2012.com/making-it-happen/sustainability/index.php.

16 Of course, this approach may not be realistic in some countries, depending on health
and safety regulations as well as the perpetual dilemma of retrofitted vehicles being,
well, old and thus not desirable. As with other retrofit solutions, government fleet
conversions are likely to thrive in emerging markets – though industrialized governments ought not overlook this demonstration opportunity as well.

17 Notice that lease-based battery infrastructure is developed on an entirely different
economic premise and does not present the same challenge.

18 You might want to take a good look at the breakdown of your electricity bill.
Looking at my own domestic bill, I find that the cost components include energy
cost, transmission cost, distribution cost, industry charges and tax. While this is
unlikely to be the case in most countries, in Brazil the tax component represents a
whopping 35 per cent of the total charges.

19 International Standards Organization.

20 Governments will also need to work with conversion businesses to develop standardized conversion kits. As discussed in Chapter 7, BEV conversion could become
a critical market segment for accelerating the electrification process. Standardized
kits will be crucial to ensure compatibility with the GEV infrastructure, but, even
more so, to ensure safety standards, preventing accidents that could be caused by
inadequate electrical equipment installation.

21 In the meantime, direct government investment in smart grid technology demonstration projects could prove advantageous to all parties. Smart grid solutions are still
in development. As such, demonstration projects are needed to prove the technology
proposals before private utility companies can justify their adoption through multi-
billion dollar infrastructure investments.

22 Notice that this is a gross overestimate, since we have already seen that the average
American driver does not exceed 50km and only 15 per cent of trips exceed 100km.

23 Capacity utilization factors vary dramatically between energy sources. As a benchmark, typical utilization factors for renewable power sources are 20–40 per cent for
wind farms, 15–20 per cent for solar power, 45 per cent for hydropower and up to
80 per cent for biomass.

References

Agassi, S. (2008) 'Projecting the future of energy, transportation, and the environment',
eGov monitor, 4 February, www.egovmonitor.com/node/16975

Brown, G. (2007) Speech on climate change, www.number10.gov.uk/Page13791,
19 November

Buffett, W. (2009) Speech to Rice University Business School students, www.miamiherald. com/2009/12/01/1359983/buffett-says-all-vehicles-will.html

Carr, G. (2008) 'The power and the glory', *The Economist*, The Future of Energy Special Report, June

Credit Suisse (2009) 'Electric vehicles', *Credit Suisse Equity Research*, 1 October

The Economist (2008) 'The end of the petrolhead', The Future of Energy Special Report, *The Economist*, June

Margulis, S. et al (2008) *The Economics of Adaptation to Climate Change: Methodology Report*, International Bank for Reconstruction and Development/ The World Bank, http://siteresources.worldbank.org/INTCC/Resources/ MethodologyReport0209.pdf

McKinsey & Co (2008) *China Charges Up: The Electric Vehicle Opportunity*, McKinsey & Co, October, www.mckinsey.com/locations/greaterchina/mckonchina/ pdfs/China_Charges_Up.pdf

Transport for London (2003) *Congestion Charge: Six Months On*, Transport for London, October

World Bank Institute (2010) *World Development Report 2010: Development and Climate Change*, World Bank Institute, Washington, DC

Index

ACEA (European Automobile Manufac-
    turers Association) 42, 72
AC (alternating current) induction
    motors 63, 64
AC motors 62, 63, 64
AC switched reluctance motors 63, 64
adoption trajectory 155–179
    2010-2020 (nascent market) 164–173
    2015-2025 (crossing the chasm)
        173–179
    market forecast review 156–164
Agassi, S. 112, 125
air pollution *see* local air pollution
alternating current (AC) motors 62, 63,
    64
alternative energy sources 43–47
Anderson, R. 6
Asia 170
Atkinson Cycle engines 70, 71
Audi 16
automobile industry
    Big Auto 14–17, 41–42
    emerging markets 20–23, 26, 187
    history 13–19
automobiles *see* vehicles

Baker Electric 8
batteries 81–92
    battery packs 82–85
    chemical compositions 85–87
    costs 88, 90, 133–135, 146, 174–176
    lead-acid 7, 86
    lithium (Li-ion) 83–84, 87–88
    lithium reserves 91–92

nickel metal hydride (NiMH) 86
operating principle 81–82
policy support 196
R&D costs 90
subsidies 193
supply 173
swapping 109–110, 112–113,
    115–116
waste disposal 87, 90–91
whole-product solution 105–106
see also recharging infrastructure
battery electric vehicles (BEV)
    cost-effectiveness 139–147
    definition 73
    early 6–8, 10, 11, 12, 25
    ecosystems 194
    emissions 46
    and ICVs 3, 25, 179
    lifetime cost 146–147
    propulsion 63
    pure 86
    range capabilities 12
    technological paradigm shift 46
battery service providers (BSP) 105,
    113–118
Benz, K. 11
Better Place 112–113
BEV *see* battery electric vehicles
Big Auto 14–17, 41–42
Big Three 17, 19
biofuels 43–46, 142, 144
Blanch, F. 34
Bouquet, Garcin & Schivre 8, 10
BP Macondo Prospect oil disaster 34, 35

braking, regenerative 8, 68, 79
Brazil 43, 44
  Rio de Janeiro 10
BSP (battery service providers) 105,
    113–118
Buffet, W. 22, 158, 186
BYD Company Ltd 22, 172, 187
  F3DM 70

California 42
  Los Angeles 22, 39–40
cap-and-trade schemes 191
capital costs 132–135
carbon capture and storage (CCS) 145
carbon dioxide emissions
  awareness of vii
  climate change 36
  cost-effectiveness 142–144
  curbing pollution 184–185
  regulation 41
  standards 189–192
  targets 42
  tax 190
carbon markets 150, 190
carbon monoxide 41
carbon policy 150
Carnot Cycle 58
Carr, G. 186
cars *see* vehicles
cash-for-clunkers programmes 193, 194
CCS (carbon capture and storage) 145
Cervero, R. 23
CFC (chlorofluorocarbons) 36
charge spots 110–112, 177
chasm, crossing (markets) 173–179
Chevy/Geo Prizm 16–17
China 20–21, 30
chlorofluorocarbons (CFC) 36
Chrysler 17, 71, 187
clean electricity guarantee 196
clean energy development 47
climate change 36–39, 151, 184–185
coal 31
combustion-based energy storage systems
    80–81
combustion fuels 57, 80, 104
  see also coal; fossil fuels; petroleum
community demonstration projects 178

competitive markets 115–116
complex hybrids 70–72
congestion charges 190–191
consumers 135, 161
contracts 114
Corolla (Toyota) 17
cost-effectiveness 131–152
  capital costs 132–135
  electric mobility 144–151
  operating costs 135–139
  social costs 139–144, 147–149
Credit Suisse, relative-cost model
    160–161
cycle efficiency (ICE) 58–59
cylindrical cells 83

daily travel distances 146, 165
Darracq, M. A. 8
Davenport, T. 5, 81
definitions 73–75
Delucchi, M. 40
demonstration projects 178, 194
Detroit , Michigan 17
Detroit Electric 6
developing countries 30
diesel engines 71
Drake, E. 18
driving behaviour 79
driving experience x, 151, 165
  see also performance
driving performance *see* performance

economic growth 4, 20, 30, 32, 185–187
ECU (electronic control units) 61, 62–63
efficiency 55–56, 79
  ICVs 58–59
Electric Carriage & Wagon Company 7
electric conversion 168–169
electricity 139, 196
  see also power grids
electric mobility, cost-effectiveness
    144–151
electric motors (EM) 5, 13, 61–64, 72
electric vehicles (EV)
  as better product 47, 53
  definition 73
  perception of 66
  sustainability viii, x, 152

terminology 53, 73–74
see also battery electric vehicles; hybrid
electric vehicles
electrification 46–47
Electrification Coalition 134, 158, 162,
164
Electrobat 7
electrochemical batteries *see* batteries
electrolysis richness 85
electronic control units (ECU) 61, 62–63
EM (electric motors) 5, 13, 61–64, 72
emerging markets 22–23, 26, 187
emissions *see* carbon dioxide emissions;
greenhouse gases
energy consumption 29–31
energy conversion 55
energy conversion efficiency 79
energy recovery *see* regenerative braking
energy security 183–184
energy services 104–118
battery whole-product solution
105–106
fast recharge service mechanisms
106–110
market architecture 113–118
widespread recharging 110–113
energy sources, alternatives 43–47
energy storage (ES) 77–101
combustion-based systems 80–81
fuel cell systems 92–95
performance parameters 78–79
ultracapacitor systems 95–100
see also batteries; recharging
energy supply (ES) systems 54
enthalpy 56
environment, human impact on 35–43
EREV (extended range EV) 69, 74
ES *see* energy storage; energy supply
systems
ethanol 44, 142, 144
EU (European Union) 42, 189
Europe 8, 10
European Automobile Manufacturers
Association (ACEA) 42, 72
European Union (EU) 42, 189
EV *see* electric vehicles
EV1 (GM) 171
extended range EV (EREV) 69, 74

F3DM (BYD) 70
fast-charge plug-in 107–108
fast recharge service mechanisms
106–110
FC (fuel cell) energy storage systems
92–95, 141–142
FCEV (fuel cell EV) 73, 141
Fiat 42
filling stations 18
financial incentives 43, 149–151
fleet vehicles 165–167, 168
Focus (Ford) 21
food requirements 45
Ford
Big Three 17
Focus 21
luxury brands 187
mass production 15
Model A: 15
Model T: 12, 14, 15
Ford, H. 12, 14–15
fortwo (Smart) 42, 136, 144
fossil fuels 31, 80
four-stroke engines 56–57
France 111, 167
fuel cell (FC) energy storage systems
92–95, 141–142
fuel cell EV (FCEV) 73, 141
fuel economy 56, 135, 136–137
fuel efficiency 56, 79
fuels
alternative energy sources 43–46
biofuels 43–46, 142, 144
coal 31
combustion 57, 80, 104
demand for 45
fossil fuels 31, 80
price 135, 137–139
resource depletion 31
see also petroleum
full HEV 74

gasoline *see* petrol
Geely Automotive 187
Generation Y: 161
GEV (grid-enabled EV) 74, 125–126,
150, 157, 192–193
GHG *see* greenhouse gases

global warming 36–38
  see also climate change
GM
  Big Three 17
  complex hybrids 71
  EV1: 171
  EVs 172
  foreign investors 187
  microturbines 69
  Yukon models 71
government fleets 167
governments, role of *see* policy support
  (governments)
green factor 161
greenhouse gases (GHG) 36, 37, 38
  see also carbon dioxide emissions
grid-enabled EV (GEV) 74, 125–126,
  150, 157, 192–193
grids *see* power grids

harmonic distortion, power grids 118–120
HEV *see* hybrid electric vehicles
Honda 67, 137
hybrid electric vehicles (HEV)
  adoption 169–170
  capital costs 132–133
  definitions 73–75
  and ICVs 46
  operating costs 136, 137
  vehicle architecture 66–72
hybridization, ultracapacitors 98–100
Hybrid Synergy Drive (Toyota) 70
hydrogen fuel cells *see* fuel cell energy
  storage systems
hydrogen storage 94–95

ICE (internal combustion engines)
  56–59, 192
ICV *see* internal combustion engine
  vehicles
incomplete combustion 41
India 20, 30
Integrated Motor Assist hybrid technology (Honda) 67
Intergovernmental Panel on Climate
  Change (IPCC) 36, 38
internal combustion engines (ICE)
  56–59, 192

internal combustion engine vehicles (ICV)
  and BEVs 3, 25, 179
  cost-effectiveness 139–144, 152
  as dominant technology 3
  early 11
  efficiency 58–59
  electric conversion 168–169
  emissions 41
  and HEVs 46
  local air pollution 40
  market dominance 13–14, 25
  operating costs 136, 137
  ownership tax 191
  performance 59–60, 73
  petroleum 18, 104
  propulsion 56–61, 73
  starter motors 13, 61
  see also hybrid electric vehicles
Internet Generation 161
IPCC (Intergovernmental Panel on
  Climate Change) 36, 38

Jamais Contente, La 10
Japan 18–19, 43
Jenatzy, C. 10
Johnson, B. 111
Judt, T. 23

Kettering, C. 13
Klegon, F. 158
Kyoto Protocol 39

LDV (light duty vehicles) vii, 137
lead-acid batteries 7, 86
leading by example 194
Leaf (Nissan) 134, 147–149
lean manufacturing 19
leasing, recharging 177
Lexus RX450h 70–71
LFP (lithium iron phosphate) 87
Liebreich, M. 47–48
light duty vehicles (LDV) vii, 137
Light SA 166
Li-ion batteries 83–84, 87–88
lithium 91–92, 175–176
lithium (Li-ion) batteries 83–84, 87–88
lithium-iron-phosphate chemistries
  176

lithium manganese spinel or lithium manganese polymer (LMO) 87
lithium-nickel-cobalt-aluminium (NCA) 87, 176
lithium titanate (LMO/LTO) 87
LMO (lithium manganese spinel or lithium manganese polymer) 87
LMO/LTO (lithium titanate) 87
load variation, power grids 120–125
local air pollution 36, 39–41, 44, 184–185
London, UK 111, 167, 190
London Electric Cab Company 8
Los Angeles, California 21–22, 39–40
low-carbon private transportation 189–192

market architecture, recharging 113–118
mass production 15
metals, rare-earth 64
microelectronics 77
micro HEV 67, 74
microturbines 69
mild HEV 75
mixed markets, recharging 117–118
mobile phones 162–164
mobility, personal vii, x, 23, 189
Model A (Ford) 15
Model T (Ford) 12, 14, 15
monopolistic markets, recharging 117
Moody-Stuart, M. 23, 25
Moore, G. 173
Motor City/Motown see Detroit
motorcycles 170
motor vehicles see vehicles
MTV Generation 161
Murphy, J. 40
Musk, E. 65

Nano (Tata Motors) 21
nanotechnology, ultracapacitors 97–98
nascent market (2010-2020) 164–173
NCA (lithium-nickel-cobalt-aluminium) 87, 176
niche markets 165–171, 179
nickel metal hydride (NiMH) batteries 86
Nissan 172

Leaf 134, 147–149
nitrogen oxides 41
Nordhaus, W. 151

Ohno, T. 19
oil see petroleum
Oldsmobile 8
OPEC (Organization of the Petroleum Exporting Countries) 32
operating costs 135–139
Otto Cycle 58
ozone 36

parallel hybrids 66–67, 86
PAYG (pay-as-you-go), recharging 114, 177
PEMFC (proton exchange membrane FC) 93, 94, 95
penetration rates 159–164
performance
    energy storage 78
    EVs 64–65, 73
    ICVs 59–60, 73
    parameters 78–79
permanent magnet motors 63, 64
personal mobility vii, x, 23, 189
petrol
    Brazil 44
    energy storage 80
    ICE 57
    price 149
petroleum
    consumption 137
    energy source vii
    ICVs 18, 104
    industry 41–42
    oil field exploration 192
    price 137–139, 146
    resource depletion 31
    supply security 32–35
Peugeot 42
PHEV (plug-in HEV) 69, 70, 74, 86, 169
planetary gear 70, 71
Planté, G. 7
plug-in HEV (PHEV) 69, 70, 74, 86, 169
plug-in solution, recharging 116
policy support (governments) 179, 183–197

EV market implementation 192–196
low-carbon private transportation
189–192
rationale for 183–188
role of government 187–188
pollution *see* carbon dioxide emissions;
local air pollution
population growth 32, 45
pouch cells 84
power-assist HEV 67, 74
power electronics 62–63
power grids 108, 118–125, 191–192,
195–196
power sector 125–126, 144, 191–192
precautionary approach, climate change
151, 185
prismatic cells 83–84
Prius (Toyota) 42, 70, 71, 136, 189–190
private transportation 21, 189–191
Prizm (Chevy/Geo) 16–17
production capacity 171–172
propulsion *see* vehicle propulsion
Proton 187
proton exchange membrane FC (PEMFC)
93, 94, 95
public transportation 4, 10, 23, 189
pure BEV 86

range anxiety 107, 169
rare-earth metals 64
R&D (research and development) 192
recharging infrastructure 103–126
battery whole-product solution
105–106
challenge of 101, 176–179
fast recharge service mechanisms
106–110
market architecture 113–118
policy support 195–196
power grid issues 118–25
recharge rate 79
widespread service 110–113
see also batteries
regenerative braking 8, 68, 79
relative-cost model (Credit Suisse)
160–161
research and development (R&D) 192
resource depletion 31–32

retrofits 168–169
Reva 187
rickshaws 170
Rio de Janeiro, Brazil 10
Rio de Janeiro Tramway, Light and
Power Company Ltd 10
rise of the automobile 4–13
road systems 12
road transportation 33
RX450h (Lexus) 70–71

scooters 170
second vehicles 170–171
series hybrids 67–69
series/parallel hybrids 69–70
Smart 189
fortwo 42, 136, 144
smart grids 120–125, 195–196
Smith Electric Vehicles 172
social costs 139–144, 147–149
social goods 187, 188
Sony 86
sporting events 194
sport utility vehicles (SUV) 71, 72
Sprague, F. 7
Standard Oil Co. 18
standards, recharging 195
starter motors 13, 61
steam-powered carriages 5
Stern, N. 36, 151
strong HEV 74
Studebaker 8
sulphur 41
supercar consumers 165
supply security (petroleum) 32–35
sustainable transport vii, viii, x, 131,
152, 189
SUV (sport utility vehicles) 71, 72

tank-to-wheel (T2W) efficiency 55, 56,
59, 79, 139
target seeking (Electrification Coalition)
162, 164
Tata Motors 187
Nano 21
tax rebates 195
technological transformations 155–156
technology adoption life cycle 173

TEPCO (Tokyo Electric Power Company)
177–178
Tesla, N. 62
Tesla Motors 65, 111, 165, 172
thermodynamics 55
Tokyo Electric Power Company (TEPCO)
177–178
torque, ICVs 59–60
Toyota
Corolla 17
fuel economy 137
Hybrid Synergy Drive 70
lean manufacturing 19
Prius 42, 70, 71, 136, 189–190
transportation
diversifying 23, 25
energy consumption 31, 32, 33, 137
GHGs 38
private 21, 189–191
sustainable vii, viii, x, 131, 152, 189
travel distances 146, 165
Trevithick, R. 5
trolley systems 7
two-mode hybrids 71

UC (ultracapacitor) energy storage
systems 95–100
UCEV (ultracapacitor EV) 73
UK (United Kingdom), London 111,
167, 190
ultracapacitor (UC) energy storage
systems 95–100
ultracapacitor EV (UCEV) 73
UNFCCC (United Nations Framework
Convention on Climate Change) 39
urbanization 4, 20
US (United States)
Big Three 17, 19
carbon dioxide 42
Detroit 17
early BEVs 6–8, 11
early vehicle sales 11
fleet demand 167
recharging 111
see also California
US Postal Service (USPS) 165–166

variable gearing 73
vehicle propulsion (VP) 53–73
efficiency 55–56, 73
EVs 61–66, 72–73
HEVs 66–72
ICVs 56–61, 73
system costs 132–133
vehicle components 54–55
vehicles
architecture 66
components 54–55
driving experience x
ownership 21–22
personal mobility vii, x, 23, 189
range 78, 107
rise of the automobile 4–13
sharing services 25
see also automobile industry; electric
vehicles; internal combustion engine
vehicles
vehicle-to-grid (V2G) operations
122–125, 150–151
virtual reappropriation model, recharging 116
Volkswagen (VW) 15–16
VP *see* vehicle propulsion

Wang Chuan-Fu 22
well-to-tank (W2T) efficiency 55, 139
well-to-wheel (W2W) efficiency 55,
139–142
whale oil 18

Xerox 105, 106

Yukon models (GM) 71